WAR STORY

Derek Robinson read history at Cambridge, was a fighter pilot in the RAF, spent ten years working for ad agencies in London and New York, and then came home via Portugal and the Channel Islands with his American wife Sheila.

War Story is his sixth novel. It shares with the others a certain debunking of the myths of war, and may be considered a prequel to *Goshawk Squadron*, which was short-listed for the Booker Prize in 1971 and is a kind of anti-Biggles.

Derek Robinson has also written books on rugby, squash and the underground West Country patois called 'Bristle'. He broadcasts a bit. He lives in Bristol.

Derek Robinson

WAR STORY

Pan Books
in association with Macmillan

First published in Great Britain 1987 by
Macmillan London Limited
This edition published 1988 by Pan Books Ltd,
Cavaye Place, London SW10 9PG
in association with Macmillan London Limited
9 8 7 6 5 4 3 2 1
© Derek Robinson 1987
ISBN 0 330 29966 2
Printed and bound in Great Britain by
Richard Clay Ltd, Bungay, Suffolk

for my Mother

Chapter 1

On the map it was about 160 miles from the aerodrome at Shoreham, across the English Channel and down through France to Pepriac, a scruffy little crossroads village some way south of Arras.

That was on the map. In the air, and flying a BE2c, which meant crabbing against the wind and dodging the bigger clouds, the distance would be more like 200 miles. Allowing for a stop at the St. Omer depot near Boulogne to have lunch and a pee, Second-Lieutenant Paxton had guessed that the trip should take about four hours. Five at the very most.

Now, five days after leaving Shoreham, Paxton was still in the air and still searching for Pepriac. *Honestly* (he kept saying to himself), *this simply isn't good enough.* And to make matters worse he had lost the four other BE2cs placed under his temporary command. Or they had lost him.

Either way, he was now on his own, three thousand feet above France, four days late for the war and utterly fed-up. His bottom ached and he was hungry. Also he hadn't been able to change his underwear since Shoreham and he itched in several places that he couldn't scratch without upsetting the machine so that it slewed off-course. One of the things the instructors had failed to teach him was how to fly and scratch at the same time.

Not that BE2cs were temperamental; quite the reverse. The RFC had nicknamed them 'Quirks', but Paxton took that to be typical upside-down Service slang: there was

1

nothing quirky about their performance. After training on docile Avro 504s, not to mention Longhorns and Shorthorns – more like motorised kites than aeroplanes – he found the Quirk a delight to fly. Paxton had coveted one as soon as he saw it land. It was a biplane with staggered wings, the upper ahead of the lower. Angled struts gave it a thrusting, sporty look. The wings tilted upwards too: like a hawk hanging on the wind, Paxton thought. The fuselage tapered quite daringly before it flared into a long and elegant tail. The propeller had four blades and was a work of art in itself. Ninety horsepower in the engine. Properly tuned and going flat out, with no wind to help or hinder, the Quirk would do eighty. At least that's what its owner told him when Paxton strolled over and asked. Paxton flicked the taut, smooth canvas. It vibrated like a drumskin. "Nice little bus," he said. He walked away before too much excitement showed in his eyes. He was, after all, eighteen; and at eighteen an Englishman was not a schoolboy who went about with his emotional shirt-tails hanging out. Paxton's housemaster at Sherborne had made a point of that. "Feelings are meant to be felt," he had said, "not placed on exhibition like prize dahlias. Don't you agree?"

At the time, Paxton was seized by a passion for a much younger boy at the school. "Suppose one felt especially strongly about a certain dahlia, sir," he suggested. "Mightn't one show it? A bit?"

"Now you're being tedious."

"Yes, sir," Paxton said, not really understanding.

Soon the younger boy got a series of boils on the back of his neck and lost his charm. At about the same time Paxton realised that the war was not, after all, going to end by Christmas 1915 (as some people had said when the Gallipoli show began, and later when the French attacked in Champagne, and later still when the British launched an offensive at Loos). For his eighteenth birthday, on 20th December, his father gave him a motorbike. There was a Royal Flying Corps aerodrome nearby and every day during the Christmas holidays he rode over and watched.

The more he saw, the more he knew he was not going back to Sherborne He also knew he was not going to squelch about

2

in the trenches or make deafening noises with the artillery. He grew a small moustache. In January 1916 an elderly colonel interviewed him at the War Office; he was interested in Paxton's ability at ball games, especially lawn tennis and fives. After that, the Royal Flying Corps was gratifyingly keen to get its hands on him. In April 1916 he was commissioned second-lieutenant; in May he was awarded his wings.

He had flown eighteen hours solo, two of them in Quirks, when the CO at Shoreham sent for him and told him that the squadron at Pepriac – they found the place on the map after a bit of a search – needed five new BE2cs, urgently. Paxton was the tallest of the new pilots awaiting postings, so the CO put him in charge.

"Don't let anyone go skylarking about," he warned. "Those machines came straight from the factory. They're crying out for them in France."

Paxton ducked his head out of the slipstream and, one-handed, pulled off his goggles. They were speckled with oil. He tried to wipe them on his sleeve but his gauntlet was so clumsy that it was hard to do a decent job. Putting the goggles on again one-handed turned out to be impossible. He stuffed them in a pocket. You didn't need goggles to see Amiens. Everyone said it had a tremendous great cathedral. He looked everywhere and couldn't see a cathedral, large or small. He couldn't see anything except fields and roads, fields and roads. The fields were different shades of green but all had square corners. The roads were invariably straight. Everything looked like everything else. It was all pattern and no shape. What had happened to Amiens?

Paxton gripped the joystick between his knees and took another squint at the map. Then he looked over the side again. There was nothing down there that was remotely like the pattern shown on the map. Maybe he'd flown too far. He unfolded the next section of map and noticed an area that seemed vaguely familiar, right at the top, so he opened the top section too, in case it added anything useful. Yes, definitely something familiar . . . He twisted his body to get a different view of the map. His knees and feet moved and the controls shifted. The BE2c lurched and sidled. A gale of wind rushed into the cockpit, plucked the map from Paxton's hands and blew it away. "Blast!" he shouted. That was the worst word he knew, and he felt it wasn't nearly bad enough.

No cathedral, no clean underwear, and now no map. That took the biscuit, that did. Quite suddenly, Paxton had had enough. For five days he had been ferrying this blasted Quirk from A to B, and where had it got him? Nowhere. Or, if you liked, everywhere. Or if you wanted to split hairs it had got him *somewhere*, but that somewhere could be anywhere, so it might as well be nowhere, mightn't it? Anyway, Paxton had had enough. He decided to enjoy himself. He was going to loop the loop. After that, he would find blasted Amiens. And then, with luck, blasted Pepriac.

Paxton had never looped an aeroplane but he had seen it done, once, by some sport in a Sopwith Tabloid who had made it look easy: first you put the nose down, then you put it up, and over she went like a garden swing. The Tabloid was a single-seater whereas the BE2c was built for two, but Paxton didn't think that would make much difference because his front cockpit was packed with sandbags which ought to balance the whole thing properly. He opened the throttle and put the nose down.

The engine seemed to take a deep breath and shriek. Paxton had never dived at full power before, and the noise startled him. A tremor built up until the whole machine was shuddering. The flat French landscape rose into view but everything was blurred by vibration. Paxton leaned forward to get a better look at the gauge. Eighty-five miles an hour, edging towards ninety. Was that enough? The shriek had become a scream and the aeroplane was in the grip of a fever. Ninety at last. Surely something must snap? Paxton couldn't stand the racket any longer. He pulled back the stick. France quickly drained away, blue skies filled his view, a firm but friendly force pushed him back into his seat, and the shuddering ceased. The BE2c raced up an invisible wall that grew steeper and steeper until it reached the vertical and that was where the aeroplane gave up. Paxton felt all momentum cease. The Quirk was standing on its tail and going nowhere. Then it dropped.

It fell two thousand feet before he got it under control, and

4

even then he wasn't absolutely sure how he did it, except that the engine was making such a hideous din that he throttled back almost to nothing, which seemed to help matters.

As he climbed again to three thousand he tested the controls and had a good look around. Nothing seemed broken or bent.

That proved one thing. Ninety wasn't fast enough.

The next time, he made the dive a little steeper and held it a lot longer. He was prepared for the screaming and shaking: when it got too bad he shut his eyes and clenched his jaws. Oddly enough, doing that made a difference. The vibration eased a bit. He opened his eyes. Yes, definitely easier. Ninety-five, but the needle was jumping about so much it could be a hundred. This was insane. But great fun. A hundred, a hundred and five! Paxton's ears popped. He took that as a signal, and hauled the stick into his stomach. The BE2c soared, the horizon came and went, the sky rolled past yet there was always more sky. Paxton wondered if he was completely upside-down yet. How did one tell? There really was an amazing quantity of sky, it just went on and on. At last he glimpsed the horizon, wrong-side up this time, and he knew – with a spasm of joy – that he had done it. He had looped the loop! Then the sandbags fell out.

They tumbled from the observer's cockpit in a steady brown stream that went whirling away over Paxton's head so fast that he did not recognize them.

He was mystified. Was the plane coming apart? He swivelled his head, but already they were just dots. Most extraordinary! The engine was still howling. He looked for the horizon: gone. Instead the landscape of France appeared, swinging as if on pivots. He was well over the top and starting another power-dive. He throttled back in a hurry.

The BE2c came out of the loop but she was an unhappy aeroplane: tail-heavy, nose-high, unbalanced, demanding to be flown every inch of the way. Paxton found himself climbing when he didn't want to climb. He tried to stop that, almost stalled, panicked, did something original with his hands and feet, got into an enormous sideslip, panicked again, kicked the aeroplane hard, got out of the sideslip he knew not how and in desperation whacked the throttle wide open. The machine trembled as if it had struck a storm and started climbing again. Paxton looked around in despair and saw another aeroplane watching him.

It was sixty or seventy yards to his left, about a length behind him and slightly above. He recognised the type at once. A squadron of them had assembled at Shoreham en route to France. It was an FE2b, a tough-looking two-seater biplane with the engine behind the pilot and no fuselage to speak of, just a naked framework holding the tail in position. The engine was a pusher, so the pilot and his observer sat in a pod ahead of the wings. This arrangement gave them a marvellous view. Right now they were watching Paxton staggering and stumbling about the sky. After a while he noticed that they were waving, gesturing downwards very vigorously. He was sick of being messed about by this stupid Quirk, so he took their advice.

There was only one way to overcome the machine's mindless desire to climb, and that was by falling into a series of sideslips. So Paxton descended, like a bad skier stumbling down an icy mountain. The FE2b spiralled behind him, at a safe distance. At five hundred feet it levelled out and flew east. Paxton followed, climbing hard. After five miles he saw the aerodrome. It looked shockingly small. It looked about one quarter the size of the field at Shoreham. Nevertheless the FE landed easily enough.

It took Paxton half an hour of sweaty experiment at sideslip and climb, sideslip and climb, sideslip and climb, before he entered a final sideslip that sent the Quirk low over the edge of the aerodrome. He let the slide continue. The field kept rising sideways. Now he could see the grass shimmering. This was going to be the most awful crash. He shut his eyes, counted to three, then stirred the joystick vigorously, pedalled the rudder bar, and gave the engine full power. The first bounce of the Quirk jarred his spine and opened his eyes. He snatched at the throttle. The Quirk bounced again, and again. People watching said it bounced seven times before the tailskid touched, and four times after that, until a tyre burst and the machine slewed to a halt. Paxton wasn't counting. Paxton was down, and that was memorable enough.

*

6

By the time he had unstrapped and got out, a couple of mechanics had arrived at a brisk trot and were examining the wheel. Behind them came a burly young man on a bicycle. He wore neither cap nor tunic but from his khaki tie and slacks Paxton guessed he was an officer. He rode unhurriedly, and the bicycle wandered as it hit lumps and ruts. A few yards from Paxton he let it drift almost to a halt, and then stood on the pedals, concentrating on keeping it upright, as if in a slow-bicycle race. "You damn near hit me with your damn sandbags, you know," he said, not looking. All his attention was on his front wheel.

Paxton was taken aback. He had expected a sort of welcome and this sounded like an accusation. Or was it meant as a joke? He said: "Are you sure it was me?" That sounded awfully lame.

"Of course I'm sure. You're Dexter, aren't you? I'm Goss. The old man sent me up to find you, and that was easy enough. . ." He broke off as the bicycle almost toppled and he was forced to work the pedals.

"Actually, I'm Paxton, not Dexter."

Goss wasn't listening. "You were dancing and prancing all over the sky. Didn't want to see me, though. Too busy chucking your rotten sandbags about."

Suddenly Paxton understood. He walked over to the Quirk and looked into the observer's cockpit. Empty. Oh my god. At that moment his stomach felt just as empty.

"See what you nearly did to me?" Goss demanded. Now he had abandoned the slow-bicycle race and was riding in figures-of-eight near the tail. He pointed, and Paxton went over to look. The leading edges of the tailplanes were damaged, cracked, bent downwards. No wonder the Quirk had insisted on climbing. What an idiot he'd been! What a chump! Remorse seized him, and he patted the fuselage, as if it were a big dog whose tail he had trodden on. "Don't make it any worse," Goss said. Paxton flinched and took his hand away. "Joke," Goss said sadly. "Come on. You've missed lunch but you might get a sandwich, I suppose."

They headed for a cluster of wooden sheds. Elsewhere Paxton saw a windsock, a couple of FE2bs parked outside canvas hangars, a few lorries. It didn't look much. He actually had his mouth open to ask the name of the aerodrome when he saved himself. "So this is Pepriac, then," he said.

"Well, it's not Frinton-on-Sea. Look, I'm getting cramp. I'll go ahead and stir up the cookhouse." Goss raced away, making the bicycle swing briskly from side to side. When he was halfway to the camp he looked back and shouted something. The words were blurred. Paxton called: "What?" Goss, still pedalling, still looking back, pointed. His rear wheel bucked and he went flying over the handlebars like an athlete over a vaulting-horse.

Paxton ran as fast as his flying boots allowed and reached Goss as he was getting up. "It's nothing," Goss said peevishly. "I'm perfectly all right." But Paxton could see that he was not. His right arm hung loosely, like an empty sleeve with the hand tacked on the end.

"You've done something to your arm," Paxton said.

"Thanks very much. And I thought it was gallstones."

They walked in silence, Paxton pushing the bicycle, to a shed where an ambulance stood alongside. Goss pointed to another hut, the biggest of all. "Mess," he said grimly. "Make them give you something to eat. If they argue, throw sandbags. The old man says he wants to see you in half an hour." He went inside.

The old man was twenty-four: not an unusual age for a squadron commander in the Royal Flying Corps.

Major Milne had been christened Rufus because his infant hair was bright red. Within a year it faded to a mild sandy colour, and this was the first of many disappointments for his father, a commander in the Royal Navy.

Ever since Trafalgar, all the Milne sons had gone into the Navy. When Rufus was five, his father took him dinghy-sailing on a sheltered lake. There was a soft, steady breeze, not enough to make a chop, and Rufus was sick throughout the trip. The next time they went out he began to throw up before the boat left the landing-stage. The third and fourth attempts were no better. "Nil desperandum," his father said. "The great Horatio Nelson was seasick in Portsmouth harbour, so they say." The fifth time they went to the lake, Rufus was standing on the shore, putting on his little lifejacket, when he started to vomit. His father wanted to persist, and Rufus was ready to do as he was told, but the boy had lost eight pounds in a week and his mother was alarmed by his gauntness.

"Sorry, old chap," his father said. "I'm afraid it's shore duty for you until that rumblegut of yours changes its tune." Rufus, chomping his way through a second helping of scrambled eggs on toast, nodded bravely.

The tune never changed. Rufus went from short to long trousers, his voice broke, he turned sixteen and started shaving, but whenever he stepped into a boat his stomach emptied itself with an energy his father had never seen matched, not even during storms in the China Seas. The risk was too great. Milne senior wasn't going to disgrace the family name with a naval cadet who might well throw up at the mention of the word "dreadnought". In due course he pulled strings and got his son a commission in a decent regiment, the Green Howards. That was in 1910.

In 1912 Rufus took private flying lessons from a Frenchman at Brooklands aerodrome. His father felt cheated when he learned that flying did not make Rufus sick, and his mother felt relieved when he got his certificate. She thought it was all over then. But he kept on flying and in 1914, six weeks after the war began, he transferred to the Royal Flying Corps. Rear-admiral Milne (now retired) gave up. The Green Howards weren't the real thing, they weren't the Navy, but at least they were a proper lot, a decent outfit, a *regiment*. What was the RFC? A bag of tricks, a joke, and not even a funny joke that you could tell your neighbours. So be it. The admiral had nephews in the Navy and he had a younger, non-vomiting son who would follow them soon. He tried not to think about Rufus.

Rufus Milne had long since stopped thinking about his father, who existed in his memory as a gruff and discontented figure pruning roses very hard, as if he suspected mutiny below. Rufus enjoyed flying, he was proud of his rank, and he liked commanding a squadron; but he had grown up in such an atmosphere of suppressed disapproval and disappointment that even now, after six years in the army and two years in France, he hid his feelings behind a wall of disarming habits

9

and mannerisms. He spoke in a drawl that suggested nothing was as important as it seemed; he rarely looked people in the eye, preferring to let his gaze wander past the left ear while he nodded and blinked at what they said; he slouched as he walked; and he had several chunky, short-stemmed pipes that demanded a lot of attention. He often seemed vague, and vaguely elsewhere. Sometimes, when people met him for the first time, they wondered how on earth he got to be a major, let alone a squadron commander. That was what Paxton wondered as he sat opposite him. *Fellow looks half-asleep*, he thought.

"Weren't we expecting you . . . um . . . rather earlier than this?" Milne asked, so softly that Paxton leaned forward.

"Yes, sir. Five days ago, sir."

"Five days, eh? As much as that . . ."

"I'm afraid we ran into a spot of bother on the way. Several spots, in fact."

"Ah . . ." Milne slumped in his chair and squinted at the sunlight. "Spots of *bother*, you say." He seemed to be trying, not very hard, to remember what *bother* was like. Far away, thunder rumbled. The sound rolled like a slow avalanche until it made a window shiver. Milne glanced at his wrist-watch. Paxton waited, upright and alert. The door was slightly open. A fly wandered in, as if looking for a friend, and Milne watched it until it wandered out again. "Suppose you tell me," he suggested.

"Yes, sir. The first thing that happened, sir, was the weather turned rather nasty soon after we took off from Shoreham. You see I'd planned to fly due east, that is, straight across the Channel, and reach the French coast at Boulogne but some pretty stormy squalls hit us, and what with the cloud and the wind and the rain the other chaps simply couldn't keep formation on me. I was leading, you see. So it looked too dangerous to fly straight to Boulogne – not that we could fly straight if we wanted to, the wind was chucking us about so much – but anyway I knew it was at least sixty miles to Boulogne, mostly out of sight of land, and I decided we ought to follow the coast to Dover instead and then make the short crossing to Cap Griz Nez."

Paxton paused. The CO smiled encouragingly at the empty air beside his left ear, so he went on.

"Well, as I said, it was dreadfully stormy when I changed course, sir, and although three of the other chaps saw what I was up to, unfortunately the fourth man didn't. I remember a very large black cloud. We went one side of it and he went the other, and I'm afraid I never saw him again. Lieutenant Kellaway, sir . . . Anyway, the rest of us managed to stagger along to Dover, getting thoroughly soaked in the process, and I could see that a couple of our engines weren't too jolly – you know, coughing and spluttering – so down we all went and landed at the 'drome there. I mean that was the *idea*, sir. We all did our best but one chap's engine simply conked out before he could reach the 'drome and he went slap into a tree. Awfully bad luck. Chap called Wilkins."

"Then there were three." Milne took a pipe from his desk and began scratching his head with the stem.

"That was on Friday. Wilkins broke lots of legs and things, sir, and his BE2c was smashed-up altogether. Well, on Saturday our engines were okay and I led the chaps across the water, aiming for the depot at St. Omer via Boulogne. By then I think the wind must have changed or something, sir, because what I thought was Boulogne turned out to be Calais, only I didn't know that at the time. So of course St. Omer wasn't where we thought it would be, although we flew around for hours and hours looking for it. In the end we had to land any-old-where before we ran out of fuel. And that's how we came to spend the night at a Royal Naval Air Service place called St. Rambert."

Milne nodded, or perhaps he was now scratching his head against the stem.

"The naval types were jolly friendly, sir, and they asked us to a party. Frankly, I don't think Ross-Kennedy was used to strong drink, sir. He was frightfully ill next morning. That was Sunday. I made him take a cold bath and drink lots of black coffee, which I must say didn't seem to do him a lot of good, but by the afternoon I really couldn't wait any longer. We all took off and I wanted to get to St. Omer so I could send a message here, sir, in case you were worrying. Then Ross-Kennedy started flying round and round in circles. I could see him being sick over the side of the cockpit. I made all sorts of signals to him to buck up, but I don't think he saw me. In the end he went round and round and down and down until he tried to land his machine in a field and he over-turned. Did a sort of cartwheel. Dexter and I flew on to St. Omer. We spent the rest of Sunday and all Monday morning driving around the country in a tender, but we never found the BE or Ross-Kennedy. Dexter thought it might have caught fire."

"Then there were two," Milne said.

"After lunch on Monday we took off and I honestly thought we'd be here by teatime, sir, and we would have been, definitely, if Dexter's propeller hadn't bust. It just went all to pieces. He was jolly lucky to get down at Treizennes, sir, but of course they only fly DH2s there so they had to send back to St. Omer for a spare. We got off again at six o'clock, sir, and the next thing that hit us was fog. Really awful, thick, clammy stuff, sir. My compass was worse than useless – it kept whizzing around like mad – and we flew above the fog as long as possible, but eventually we had to come down into it, and then of course we lost each other. I made a forced landing in a field and bent the undercarriage. Miles from anywhere. Slept in a barn. Next morning – that was Tuesday, yesterday – I walked for hours until I found a village. They phoned the nearest 'drome, which was Beauvois. A tender came out and collected me and together we found the BE2c. They patched up the undercarriage and put in some petrol and I managed to take off and get to Beauvois. Then they mended it properly. That's where I heard about poor old Dexter. Hit a church. Then today I set off once more, sir. They told me to keep Amiens cathedral on my right and I couldn't miss Pepriac but . . . I don't know . . . Anyway, here I am. I'm sorry about the other four, sir, and I'm really frightfully sorry I'm so late, because I know how frightfully keen you are to get your hands on these Quirks."

The fly had come back in. Milne stood up and waved his hat at it, meaning no harm.

"Let's go and take a look at what you've brought us, any-way," he said.

They strolled across the grass towards the hangars. It was mid-afternoon, and skylarks sang as if in celebration of the sunlight and the giant blue sky.

"All of 'B' Flight are away on leave this week," Milne said. "'A' Flight are up on patrol at the moment, and 'C' Flight have gone swimming. Nice to have a bit of peace and quiet, isn't it? Damned traffic never stops, of course."

Paxton saw the tops of vehicles moving on the other side of a distant fence and heard the grumble of engines. "Are we getting ready for a Push, sir?"

Milne smiled. "I expect so," he said. "We usually are."

The flat tyre had been replaced. The damaged tailplane had been restored to shape, and the canvas patches were getting a final coat of dope. Paxton was amazed by the speed of the repair, and said so. "They've probably done it before," Milne said. "That stuff should dry quickly in this weather. Tell you what: when it's ready, why don't you take off and spend a couple of hours getting to know the landmarks around here. Arras is more or less north-east of us. Pick up the main road that runs south-west from Arras and follow it to Doullens, then pick up the road south to Amiens. After Amiens go north-east towards Albert, then cut back north to Pepriac. You can't miss it."

"Yes, sir," said Paxton. He had been expecting a hot bath and a change of clothes.

"And while you're up," Milne said lazily, "after you've gone round the houses a couple of times, you might as well finish off with . . . what shall we say . . . six practice landings? And let's see you do the last one from . . . oh . . . three thousand feet with a dead engine. Suit you?"

"Yes sir," said Paxton. The day was very warm and he desperately wanted to scratch his armpits and his crotch, but he dared not. "I don't suppose there's the chance of a cup of tea before I go, sir?"

"Listen to those birds!" Milne said, and strolled away.

"Bugger the birds," said a fitter when the CO was out of earshot, "begging your pardon, sir. Let's have a listen to this engine."

They listened, and the fitter wrinkled his nose. All the plugs had to be changed. While that was being done, someone took a blowtorch and a dixie behind the hangar and made a quick brew-up. They gave Paxton a pint of sweet, milky tea. He drank it with such obvious enjoyment that they gave him

a refill. The Quirk sounded much healthier with new plugs
He flung the dregs of his tea onto the grass and clambered into
the cockpit.

'A' Flight came back as Paxton took off. Milne heard the
fading buzz of the Quirk being absorbed by the deepening
drone of four Beardmore engines. He opened his office
window, perched his backside on the sill, and watched the
tiny pattern of dots grow into a neat diamond formation. The
FEs were no more than a hundred feet up as they passed.
Milne knew the flight leader was watching him, so he raised
an arm, and got half a wave of a gloved hand in return. That
meant: quiet patrol; nothing doing. He watched the flight curl
away and lose formation. FEs in the air reminded him of
dragonflies. Not from the way they moved, which was hard-
working rather than brilliant, rather like a London taxi; but
from the way they were put together. Just like a dragonfly,
everything important was clustered at the front, the machine
was all wings and nose, with a few long bare poles reaching
back to keep the tail in place. Milne closed one eye and half
shut the other. He ignored the pusher propeller spinning
behind the wings and the tricycle wheels hanging down and
the Lewis gun poking up and the struts and the wires and the
British markings, and all he saw was a khaki blur in the sky.
But when he opened his eyes it still reminded him of a
dragonfly.

The grub is Okay specially if you like bully beef but what I wouldn't
give for a pint of mild at the Dukes Head as the froggeys got no idea
how to make beer and the vin blong gives me wind something
chronic.
   You wont never guess who I met last week Bert Dixon what a
surprise! His mob just come out the Trenches he says half got
trenchfoot and they all got lice big as your finger! Bert says to me
Ted you got a nice cushy number you stay out them trenches Ted
they are murder which I am sure is correct, Bert should know. Bert
says any time a plane comes near they all fire at it they never waits
to see is it a Hun or not they all fire nobody better tell our major!

   "Have no fear," murmured Corporal Lacey. He was a slim

14

young man in well-tailored khaki. He had an auburn moustache, full and heavy, which made half his face look bigger and stronger than it was. He dipped a small camelhair brush into a pot of india ink and painted out almost all the second half of the page, starting with the line *His mob just come out the Trenches* . . . He gave the jet black shape neat, rounded corners and straight sides, so that it formed a deep frame surrounding the only words he had not obliterated. These were: *which I am sure is correct*. "And who dares deny it?" Corporal Lacey said. He put the page in a patch of sunlight to dry.

He was alone in the orderly room. A kettle was simmering on a Primus stove, and a gramophone was playing a record of string quartets. The music had a harsh, driving urgency. Lacey's eyes widened as the quartet cut the theme into pieces and flung them together again, the same only different. "That's the stuff," he said. "Stand no nonsense." The door opened and Captain Piggott came in. Lacey stood up. "Did you have a good patrol, sir?" he asked.

"Dud. No Hun, no fun." Piggott was red-haired and restless. He noticed the gramophone and went over to it. "Is the adjutant in?" His head twisted as he tried to read the spinning label.

"Captain Appleyard is not back from Contay yet, sir."

"Contay? What the devil's he doing in Contay? That's Kite Balloons, isn't it?" Piggott abandoned the label. "What's this bloody awful music, Lacey?"

"Dvořák, sir."

"Sounds foul. What is it, German?"

"Bohemian."

"Just as bad." Piggott found a typewriter with paper in it and began poking the keys. "They're all Huns, over there. When's the adj going to be back? I want to play some cricket."

"He didn't say, sir. He went there for lunch." Lacey went over and lifted the needle from the record. "Would you like a cup of tea, sir?"

Piggott nodded, still pecking away at the keys. Lacey assembled tea, sugar and milk. Piggott dragged the paper out and looked at it.

"Your filthy machine can't spell," he said.

"I believe I hear Captain Appleyard's car, sir." Lacey put three china mugs on a tray. Piggott folded the sheet of paper into a glider and waited. As the door opened he launched it. The glider flew past Appleyard's head but the adjutant didn't notice it. "Afternoon, adj," Piggott called; but Appleyard didn't hear that either. Head down, frowning, he hurried across the room. He looked dreadful. His face was dead-white about the chin and mouth, yet blotched with colour at the cheekbones. There was sweat on his brow: sweat, after twenty miles sitting in the breeze of an open car? He moved with his shoulders hunched as if holding himself together. "Glass of water," he said to Lacey without looking, and went into his room. The door banged shut.

Piggott found his glider and smoothed out the crumpled nose. He watched Lacey pour water from a jug, and spoon white powder into the glass. Lacey looked up. "Bicarbonate of soda," he said. "Incomparable for swift relief."

Piggott followed him into the office. Appleyard was lying rather than sitting in an old, padded swivel chair. His tunic and shirt collar were open, and the top of his flies were undone. One foot was propped on a desk drawer. His eyes were shut but the eyelids trembled, and the hollows below them gleamed wetly.

Lacey placed the glass in his hand and held the fingers secure until Appleyard had swallowed most of the fizzing drink. "Mr. Piggott is here, sir," he said, and went out.

Appleyard sat up and wiped his face with a khaki handkerchief. "Come in, Tim," he said. "Take a pew, have a cigar. To what do I owe . . ." He broke off to utter a belch that seemed to begin in his boots.

"You feeling all right, adj?" Piggott asked.

"Nothing to worry about. Touch of the Zulu's Revenge." Appleyard was an old-style career officer, now in his mid-forties, a balding bachelor who had seen much service in India and Africa and who wore three rows of faded campaign ribbons to prove it. So why was he only a captain? The squadron was too well-mannered to ask, and in any case there were more interesting things going on in the world. "Ever see a Zulu, Tim? Very large gentlemen. Black as your hat and brave as a bull. Bullets can't stop 'em." He had buttoned his flies and was rearranging the paperwork that cluttered his desk. "Just look at this bally stuff! Grows like weeds . . . Now then: what's your problem?"

"Oh . . . Several things. Let's start with pay. Jimmy Duncan says his pay has never been adjusted since he got his second pip, and that was *weeks* ago. Also two of the 'A' Flight mechanics still haven't got their proficiency supplements, or something." Piggott was pacing up and down, carefully placing his feet so as to stay on the same narrow floorboard. "Then there's my fitter, Corporal Lee. His wisdom tooth's giving him absolute hell, but there's never a travel warrant for him to go to Amiens and get it taken out. I mean, that's bloody silly, isn't it?" Piggott reached a wall, pivoted on his heel, and began the return journey. "And now I'm told by stores that the men's latrines haven't got a drop of disinfectant. Not a single drop. In this weather! I mean to say, adj, just think of—"

Appleyard's cough stopped him. It was a savage spasm that gripped the adjutant's lungs and seemed to attack his throat like a chained dog. Piggott turned away. The noise was so hurtful it made him feel slightly sick. Still seized by his cough, Appleyard stumbled to an open window and eventually, painfully, managed to spit outside. The spasm ceased. He came back, mopping his face. His chest was heaving and he looked exhausted. "Better out than in," he whispered. Threads of saliva linked his lips.

"You sound pretty dreadful, adj," Piggott said. "You ought to see a doctor."

"Just seen one. Chap at Contay." Appleyard slumped into his chair. "Same old story. Nasty dose of . . ." He paused to catch his breath. ". . . dose of Delhi Lung. Just got to . . . put up with it." He thumped himself on the chest so hard that Piggott winced. Appleyard noticed this, and grinned. "You do your best for India," he said, "and this is what India does for you. Never fair, is it?"

Piggott felt acutely uncomfortable. He drifted towards the door. "I don't suppose any of that stuff really matters all that much," he said, but then he heard what he was saying. "Still, the disinfectant—"

17

"I've got some coming from Contay, old chap. Toot sweet. I was there on the scrounge. Corps HQ are absolutely useless. You might as well talk to that wall. Don't worry, I'll chase up those other things, the pay and so on. Top priority. Do it now." He pulled the telephone towards him and began searching through a heap of papers. Piggott left.

It's a damn shame, he thought; but not for long. As he drank the tea that Corporal Lacey gave him he saw people strolling across the airfield with cricket bats and stumps. It was a perfect June afternoon: just enough breeze to soften the sunshine. Piggott gulped the last mouthfuls. He wanted to get out there and clout that ball over the skylarks.

The afternoon was not perfect for Paxton. It took him nearly an hour to complete the first circuit and by then a ground haze was developing. There was also a lot of bumpy air from ground level up to fifteen hundred feet. If he flew any higher, the air was smooth but he couldn't see through the haze. If he flew low enough to be able to pick out landmarks, the Quirk hit air-bumps and Paxton's bladder didn't like that.

It had been a mistake, Paxton now realised, to drink quite so much tea before take-off. His bladder ached. It was a dull, steady ache, and he could almost ignore it as long as nothing made it worse, but a sudden jolt – or even worse a sudden drop – made the ache flare, and then he had to clench and contort every muscle in order to keep control. If only he had a bottle. When he banked and headed east from Amiens, he could feel the pint-and-a-half of tea sloshing to the side and then surging back as he levelled out. The pressure was awful and getting worse. He couldn't go on like this. Land at Pepriac: that was the answer. Just touch down, keep the engine ticking over, jump out, drain the system, jump in, take off. Yes. Of course. That was what he would do.

Now that relief was almost near he felt much better. His bladder could endure two or three minutes. What frightened it was the prospect of another hour of torment.

When the aerodrome came in sight he actually felt quite comfortable. As he lost height and got closer, he could see figures running about in the middle of the field. He saw them clearly as he passed overhead. Cricket. They were playing cricket. It was inconceivable that he would land and pass water in full view of the squadron cricket match. The shame of exposing himself, and the disgrace of revealing his weakness: even the thought of it made him shudder. The shudder was nearly disastrous. He braced his thighs and his buttocks and stiffened his stomach-muscles. *You can do it, Oliver*, he told himself as he climbed away to start the second circuit. *Not far now. Grin and bear it. Play up, School!*

"Can you imagine the Germans playing cricket, Douglas?" asked the chaplain. He was umpiring the match. Douglas Goss, his right arm in a sling, had strolled out to chat with him.

"I can't imagine the Germans playing anything," Goss said.

"Exactly. They have no sense of decency and fair play. Look what they did to Belgium. Those poor nuns."

Goss paused while the bowler ran up and bowled. The batsman swung and missed, and the ball thwacked into the wicketkeeper's gloves. "What exactly happened to the nuns?" he asked. "I never did get the full story."

The chaplain was well over six feet tall. He cocked his head and glanced down at Goss. "They were ravished," he said. "The Huns ravished them."

"Gosh. All of them?"

"The Huns spare no one, Douglas."

"No, I meant all of the Huns. There can't have been all that many nuns in Belgium and—"

"*Run, man! Run like a stag!*" the chaplain shouted at the batsman, who had just mis-hit the ball between his own legs. For a moment the batsman was too startled to move; then he stumbled as he began running; before he was halfway down the pitch the ball was flung to the other end and he was run out. "Oh, bad luck," the chaplain said. "Still, you played a jolly plucky innings, Charles. Jolly plucky."

"Don't talk rot, padre. I scored three."

"And a jolly plucky three it was. Who's in next?"

While they were finding a new batsman, Goss said: "I honestly don't see how you can umpire *and* tell the chap when to run. You got him out then."

"Of course I did. He took twenty minutes to score three.

19

That's not cricket . . . Ah, here's young O'Neill to take strike, as they say in the Antipodes. Now for some excitement."

"Aim for his head," Goss advised the bowler. "It's the only bit you can't damage."

O'Neill heard, and said nothing. He was Australian, lanky and unhurried, the tallest man in the squadron. He hit the first ball high over the bowler's head, hooked the second ball far beyond the fielders, and whacked the third ball so hard that everyone could hear it fizz through the air. But the turf was less than perfect, and when the bowler flung down his fourth delivery it struck a bump. O'Neill suddenly had to change his swing to a lunge. He clipped the ball, snicked it so that it shot up almost vertically, an easy catch for the wicket-keeper, who ran forward, eyes on the ball, gloves cupped. Using the handle of the bat, O'Neill jabbed him in the stomach. He missed the catch and collapsed, gasping. All the fielders were hooting or shouting. "He ran into me," O'Neill announced. "How can I score if silly bastards run into me?"

"You're out, old boy," the chaplain called. "It's not cricket, you know, that sort of thing."

"Obstruction," Goss added.

"Of course it was obstruction." O'Neill turned to the wicket-keeper and prodded him. "Tell them it was obstruction, Tommy. You don't want to die with a sin on your conscience, do you?" The wicketkeeper grabbed O'Neill's foot and rolled over. O'Neill fell. They began wrestling. Others joined in.

"It's disgraceful," the chaplain said.

"You know how the boys like a brawl," Goss said.

"I didn't mean that. I meant the state of this pitch. That ball was virtually unplayable." The chaplain stamped on a lumpy patch. "We need a heavy roller, Douglas."

"O'Neill seems to be doing his best," Goss said.

"We'll take the tea interval now."

Somewhere during the second circuit, Paxton's bladder stopped complaining. It wasn't happy, but it had been bullied so much that a sort of numbness had set in. Paxton's understanding of human biology was sketchy (Sherborne hadn't spent much time on that sort of thing) but he thought perhaps the continual pressure might have caused a kink in a tube down there. He did his best to help by maintaining a steady height just above the air-bumps and by banking very gently when he turned corners. And at some point, although the taste of tea kept surging into his mouth, and although his knees kept wanting to knock together, his bladder had sullenly accepted its fate.

The field at Pepriac was golden green when he came in to land. The cricketers had gone. Away to his left, a soft white cloud of dust drifted above the road: probably a battalion on the march. The CO would be watching him, Paxton thought, and he tried very hard to bring off a good landing. It wasn't bad – a bit heavy, perhaps, and not exactly three-point, the tailskid came down late. He opened the throttle at once and took off. Five more landings to go.

The second was better. The third was a mess, he almost touched a wingtip and frightened himself sick. The fourth and fifth were adequate.

As he climbed away he noticed figures sitting in deckchairs outside the officers' mess. After all the stress and tension of five landings he found it quite pleasant to relax and let the Quirk climb in a long, wide spiral. Going up seemed to lessen the pressure on his bladder. The higher he went, the easier it felt.

At three thousand feet, when he levelled out, he was utterly untroubled. He switched off the engine. The sudden silence was itself an added balm. The nose dipped, the Quirk found a happy angle and started to slide back down the spiral. Its wires fluted pleasantly, drifting up and down the scale as the plane gained or lost some speed. There were clouds about, but they were small and harmless and they showed their good manners by keeping out of his way. He sailed down, shutting his eyes as the Quirk turned to face the late-afternoon sun, then opening them to enjoy the light washing over the eastern sky.

At two thousand feet he glanced below to check his position and was shocked when he could not find the aerodrome. He searched hard as the Quirk circled. The second time around he saw it, completely in the wrong place, over in the west, half-lost in the haze. At once he stopped his spiral descent and steered for the field. How had it moved so far away? All he had done was spiral up and spiral down. What had gone wrong? He glanced up. The friendly little clouds were still scudding eastward. He saw his mistake. Because it was calm at ground level he hadn't considered the risk of wind up there. All the time he'd been climbing, the wind had been pushing him eastward.

The altimeter was lazily unwinding: he was down to twelve hundred feet, and head-on to the wind. He'd be lucky to glide home, let alone land properly. He was afraid. Fear struck at his weakest point. A spurt of urine soaked his left thigh. This weakness angered him, and he stopped the flow, but his drenched leg was still shaking so much that his boot rattled in the rudder-straps.

In the end he had forty feet to spare when he sailed over the fence. Both legs were trembling now. As he saw the grass below him, a great shudder of relief went through his body. The Quirk felt the shudder, and responded. Paxton saw the wings tremble and thought it was the start of a stall, shoved the stick forward, remembered how low he was, changed his mind, snatched the stick back and overdid it. The Quirk settled on its heels and stalled and fell out of the sky.

It was only twenty feet but Paxton heard an undercarriage strut crack as the plane bounced with a jolt that shook his head like a balloon on a stick. When the Quirk came down again the strut collapsed altogether, throwing its weight on that wing, which crumpled with much ripping and snapping. The surviving wheel-strut folded up and the Quirk slid on its belly, exhausting its momentum against the grass.

Long before then, Paxton's bladder had given up the fight. It knew its civic duty but this kind of insanity was asking too much. For fifteen seconds he gushed like an open tap.

Paxton unstrapped himself and stepped out. It felt odd to be standing on the ground yet looking over the top of the aeroplane. He wanted to weep. For five days he had been doing his damnedest to get this Quirk to Pepriac, where the RFC was crying out for them. It wasn't fair. Slightly bow-legged, he walked around the wreck. Maybe they could mend it. He was as wet as a baby. He *felt* like a baby. He felt a depth of shame and hopelessness he had not known since he was a child. Five days in the air, to end up like this. He had let everyone down: Sherborne, England, the squadron commander. His boots squelched. The noise was shamefully loud in his ears until he realised that the squelching was outside, not inside. The ground was drenched with petrol. A fuel tank must have split. Oh God.

"Dear me," said Rufus Milne.

Paxton turned slowly. He was too defeated to be startled. The squadron commander was standing at a wingtip tugging at a strip of fabric. Behind him a group of mechanics waited by a tender. Part of Paxton's mind wondered how they had arrived so silently. Another part didn't give a toss. His nostrils awoke to the stench of petrol and made him move away.

"I expect you hit a bump," Milne said. He watched Paxton approach. "Did you hurt yourself?" he asked. Paxton shook his head. "Good. I thought . . . The way you were walking . . ." Milne's tugging was rewarded: he found himself holding a strip of fabric. "What d'you think we ought to do with the remains?" he said. He gave Paxton the strip of fabric like a tailor showing a customer a sample of cloth.

"I can't tell you how awfully sorry I am, sir."

Milne found his pipe. "If we chuck the bits on a wagon and send them to the repair depot, nobody will thank us for it, you know." He stuffed tobacco into the bowl. "By the way . . . Did you leave your watch in the cockpit?" Paxton nodded. "We'd better rescue that," Milne said, "before the looters arrive."

They went over to the cockpit. Milne unclipped the pocket-watch from the instrument panel and gave it to Paxton. "You signed for that, remember. You don't want some bally Equipment Officer charging you for it when you ask him for another. I'll bring your seat-cushion. Jolly nice cushion, that."

They turned, and Paxton trudged away. After a few paces he realized that he was alone, and he looked back. Milne had stopped and was lighting his pipe. He dropped the match on the grass and hurried to catch up. "Sorry to keep you waiting," he said.

They were about ten yards from the wreck when the flames went up. They made a solid-sounding *whump*, like a giant

23

beating a giant carpet. Paxton felt the heat on the back of his neck. Milne kept walking and did not look behind him, so Paxton did the same. "You could do with a bath, couldn't you?" Milne said. "Your kit's in your room, I expect."

Chapter 2

The tender took them to the huts. On the way, Milne smoked his pipe and watched the clouds as if waiting for a particularly interesting one to go by. Paxton sat hunched and silent. He felt like a victim, and that bewildered him. He felt tricked, and that angered him. He'd strained and struggled and pushed himself to the limit, and now all his effort was wasted. The tender bumped over some ruts, and Paxton's bruised backside took more punishment. Milne, he noticed, was sitting on his cockpit cushion. For a moment, anger flared into hate.

The tender stopped. He got down. Milne tossed him the cushion and pointed his pipe at a wooden hut. "Dexter, isn't it?" he called.

"No, sir. Paxton."

"Ah, yes, of course. Too bad about Dexter."

The tender drove on. Paxton went inside. There was a table and chairs, a stove, and three beds. At the foot of one bed was his trunk, sent by boat from England. He sat on that bed and stared at the dust swirling in the sunbeams. He found himself looking through the dust at a drawing pinned to the wall. It was a poster for a Paris revue, and it showed a pretty girl, peeking coyly over her shoulder. Someone had added a black eye. That single smudge made her smile seem lewd and knowing.

After a while his batman hurried in, introduced himself as Private Fidler, and declared that there was hot water in the officers' bathhouse, next door. Paxton took his clothes off and put on a dressing gown. He gave Fidler his trousers. "These need something doing to them," he said, too defeated to explain. Fidler seemed to understand. "They'll be as good as new, sir," he said. "Don't you worry, sir." On impulse Paxton gave him half-a-crown. That was accepted with the same ease. Paxton sensed that he had found an ally at last. "Terrible bad luck, your bus catching fire like that, sir," Fidler said. "Shocking bad luck, if you ask me." Paxton was briefly tempted to give him another half-a-crown, but thought better of it and gave him a bitter smile instead. Two hundred yards away the wreck of the Quirk smoked like a garden bonfire.

When he came out of the bathhouse he felt better. There had been abundant hot water; and with some Pears soap, and a new loofah, and a shampoo bought by his mother at Harrods, it was impossible not to feel better. Fidler had laid out fresh clothes and a clean uniform. After days in flying boots it was wonderful to be able to slip on a pair of shoes. Fidler offered him the monogrammed silverbacked hairbrushes he'd been given on his fifteenth birthday, and held up a mirror. "Thank you, Fidler," Paxton said, and surprised himself by catching exactly the same casual, assured, yet slightly distant tone his housemaster had used at dinner when a servant offered a dish of vegetables. He disciplined his hair, returned the brushes, picked up his cap. "Handkerchief," he murmured absently, and patted a couple of pockets. Fidler found a handkerchief in no time. "If anyone wants me," Paxton said, "I shall be with the adjutant."

"Yes, sir."

Fidler waited until he had left, and then used Paxton's swagger-stick to pick up a soiled sock. He sniffed from a distance and grimaced. "Bleedin' officers," he said. "Stink worse than pigs."

When Corporal Lacey showed Paxton in, Captain Appleyard was sitting upright and trying to fasten his shirt collar. "Hullo, old chap," he said. "Come in, take a pew. These damn buttons . . . Always letting you down . . . Settled in, have you? Who's your batman?"

"Private Fidler, sir." Paxton had never seen such an unhealthy-looking face: flushed yet grubby. And there was sweat in the hair.

"Old Jack Fidler!" Appleyard chuckled, and coughed, and swallowed. "A real old soldier, Jack is. He'll look after you, don't worry. *And* himself, of course." He gave up fumbling with the button. "Play cricket, do you?"

"Look, sir," Paxton began.

"Not sir, old boy. Adj. Or when we're in the mess, Uncle. Sir makes me feel ever so, ever so old." He blew his nose, hard, and gazed into the handkerchief. "Dreadfully old," he said. "Horribly old."

"Very well. Adj. I think you ought to know about something rather odd that happened to my aeroplane when I landed this afternoon."

"Tell your fitter, old boy. I know absolutely damn-all about flying-machines."

"It involved the CO."

"I'm strictly non-technical." Appleyard was fussing with the mass of papers on his desk. "Don't know one end of an aeroplane from the other, especially now they've gone and put the propeller in the middle. What?" He grinned, encouragingly. Paxton caught a glimpse of his tongue, and looked away.

"The CO deliberately put a match to my plane this afternoon," he said. Appleyard was still fussing, so Paxton raised his voice a little. "It was brand new, I spent five days getting it here, and he deliberately set fire to it. Result – complete and utter destruction of a machine in perfect condition . . ." Honesty checked him. "Well, almost perfect, I mean it wasn't all that badly damaged, just the undercarriage and the—"

"Heavy landing, eh?" Appleyard dumped files in a tray.

"Yes, I admit I—"

"Don't worry, old man." Appleyard came around the desk and squeezed his shoulder. "Happens all the time. Nothing to lose any sleep over. Beg pardon," he said as a slight belch escaped him. "You're a lucky chap, you know. Wish I had your problem. I can't stay awake for two minutes on end, that's *my* problem." He chuckled again, and coughed his way back to his chair.

"But I don't understand, adj," Paxton said. "Five days I took to ferry that Quirk here. *Five*. And now it's just a heap of ashes."

Appleyard sat and looked at him. In the distance, a gentle rumble of thunder quickly ran out of strength. The noise drained into the summer silence and was gone. "You feel pretty strongly about this, don't you?" he said. "I can tell. They don't call me Uncle for nothing. *Corporal Lacey!*" he shouted. "You're entitled to feel strongly." he told Paxton. "After all, it's your neck, and if the machine's as inflammable as you say . . ." The door opened. "Ah, corporal: be so good as to arrange a meeting with Major Milne for Lieutenant Dexter."

"Paxton," said Paxton.

"Really?" Appleyard was taken aback. "Not Dexter?" He waved Lacey away, and the door closed. "Well, that's different. Damn it, I'm sure I had it here . . ." He scrabbled among his papers. "Yes, look, here it is: Second-Lieutenant D.E.M. Dexter, Sussex Yeomanry."

"I'm Paxton."

Appleyard did some more scrabbling. "Paxton. Yes. Found it. My God, you should have got here last week. You're a bit late, aren't you?"

"Not as late as Dexter, I'm afraid. He flew into a church." Paxton was amazed at his own callousness, but also pleased. He felt ready for a bit of callousness.

"Nobody told *me*." Appleyard crossed out Dexter's name, firmly, several times. "Flew into a church, you say. Extraordinary thing to do . . . What sort of church? Nothing here about it that I can see . . ."

Paxton said nothing; he knew the adjutant was talking to himself. For a while there was silence. Paxton stood up. Through a window he could see the camp's transport park: a dozen lorries, tenders, petrol bowsers. A man was trying to kick-start a motorcycle. It coughed, once, each time he tried. He went on stamping, regularly, uselessly. Paxton lost patience. He turned and went out. "Don't worry, old boy," the adjutant called, "I'll sort it out." Paxton closed the door.

"Can I help, sir?" asked Corporal Lacey.

"I don't know. Can you make my BE2c fly again?"

"Rising like a phoenix from the ashes . . . What an excellent idea. Tidy and economical. War is so messy. Or so I'm told."

Paxton put his cap on and looked hard. Normally, troops stood rigidly to attention when he spoke to them. They squared their shoulders, held their thumbs to the seams of the trousers, and stared at the knot of his tie. Corporal Lacey was quite relaxed. One leg was slightly bent at the knee, a thumb was hooked in a trouser pocket, and he looked Paxton in the eye. His moustache disguised a slight movement of the lips. He was almost, Paxton thought, smiling. Almost but not quite. What a cheek. "I didn't seem to be able to get through to the adjutant," he said.

"Mr. Appleyard is having one of his days, I'm afraid. He served a lot in the tropics, you know." Still Lacey looked straight into Paxton's eyes. His voice was silky and assured. "You've heard of Delhi Belly? Zambesi Wheeze? The Zulu's Revenge? Rangoon Rot?"

"I can't say I have."

"Mr. Appleyard suffers from them all."

"How unfortunate." Paxton did not like the way Lacey held his gaze. He felt it bordered on insolence, or mockery, or something. He cleared his throat, and waited, but neither man had anything to add, and so he went away.

Paxton decided to go back to his billet. There was a book in his trunk, *The Riddle of the Sands*, a rattling good yarn.

A man was lying on the bed next to Paxton's, on his side, facing away from the door, tucked-up in the attitude of sleep, and he did not move when Paxton came in. Nobody else was there.

The trunk was half-empty: Fidler had done some unpacking. Paxton searched through his chest-of-drawers, trying to avoid making squeaks, and then looked in the bedside cabinet. It contained only his toilet kit and a writing compendium. He went back to the trunk and searched more thoroughly. No book. Yet he had *seen* it lying there, when Fidler had got him his dressing gown. This was exasperating. He leaned out of a window, hoping to find Fidler; but all he could see, through a gap between huts, was that same uniformed fool still trying to kick-start his stupid motorcycle. Or perhaps it was another fool: nothing seemed to work properly in this camp. A page rustled.

The sound was unmistakable. Paxton followed it. The figure on the bed was not asleep; he was curled up around a book, *The Riddle of the Sands*.

"That's mine," Paxton said.

The man rolled slowly onto his back. "No, I don't think so," he said.

His voice was flat, with a twang Paxton had never heard before. Maybe it was Cockney. Paxton had met very few Cockneys, and those usually railway porters. It was inconceivable that the Corps would have Cockney officers. "I tell you, it's my book," he said. "Hand it over." Memories of schoolroom squabbles returned. He tried to dismiss them by holding out a hand and snapping his fingers.

The man stared. He had a long face with no trace of expression. His nose was broken, or at least bent, and he breathed through his mouth. He managed to look wooden without seeming stupid, so the wooden look had to be deliberate. Certainly he watched Paxton very carefully. "It can't be yours," he said. "It's got my name in it."

"Show me."

He turned the first page and held it for Paxton to see. "Michael St. John Lenihan Francis O'Neill," he said.

"You've crossed my name out. You stole that book from my trunk."

O'Neill raised himself a few inches to study the trunk. "That's Toby Chivers' trunk," he said flatly. "It's Toby's bed so it's Toby's trunk. But you can help yourself. Anything you fancy, take it." He lay back. All his limbs were slack, but his eyes were alert.

"That's *my* trunk. It's got *my* initials on it, O.A.D.P. 'P' for Paxton, *I'm* Paxton, that's *my* book you're reading."

O'Neill's mouth was gaping more than ever. "Only four initials?" he said. "I've got five. Come from a poor family, do you?" He had slipped a hand down the front of his trousers and was scratching his crotch. "Toby Chivers' family gave him eight. Take a couple of his. Toby won't—"

"No doubt." Paxton could feel a tremble of rage inside him. "I don't know Mr. Chivers and I have no wish to know him. What I wish is—"

"Toby went west. Archie got him. Direct hit. He went in all

30

directions, including west." O'Neill scratched and winced. "Archie is what we airmen call German anti-aircraft fire," he explained. "It's fearfully dangerous."

"I know about archie. Just give me my book."

O'Neill withdrew his hand and wiped his fingers on his shirt. He thumbed through the pages until he found his place, then gripped the book with both hands and ripped it down the spine. He tossed one part to Paxton. "I've read that bit," he said. "This is all I need."

Paxton flung it back at him. "Irish pig," he said.

"Australian."

"Australian swine, then."

O'Neill fitted the two parts together. "What's the difference between pigs and swine?" he said, his voice as blank and unemotional as ever.

"Swine scratch more often," Paxton said savagely, and was sure he had scored a point; until he saw O'Neill's mouth turn up at the corners. It was like watching a suit of armour smile. "One does not expect much in the way of manners from an Australian," Paxton said acidly, "and one is never disappointed." At Sherborne he had scored with that remark (suitably adjusted) many times. O'Neill seemed to absorb it like flattery. He began reading again, his mouth still open, his jaw still slack. He soaked a finger and used it to turn a page. He slipped that hand inside his trousers. Paxton felt slightly sick. He couldn't stand being in the same room with him any longer. "Dinner at seven," O'Neill called as he went out. "If this is Monday it must be mutton."

"Actually it's Tuesday," Paxton told him, and put a lot of venom into it.

"Well, it's still mutton," O'Neill said, scratching.

The mess anteroom was a wooden hut with a big stone fireplace, a bar, a few sagging armchairs and sofas, and a table with a torn ping-pong net fixed to it. When Paxton went in, five officers were playing poker at this table. They ignored him until the hand had been played out; then one asked: "Bring any new records?"

Paxton, hands in pockets, balancing on the outside edges of his shoes, was looking at a piece of tailplane with a bullet-holed German cross on it. The walls were hung with bits of aeroplane, and tattered posters from London theatres, a rugby ball dangling by its lace, a zebra skin, magazine pictures of can-can dancers, photographs of crashed aircraft already sepia with age. When nobody answered he turned and saw that the question was meant for him. "Records?" he said.

"For the gramophone, fathead."

"Oh. No. No, I'm afraid not."

A flicker of an eyebrow showed what the other man thought of *that*. Paxton went and sat in a corner and turned the pages of a magazine while he wondered how on earth he was supposed to bring gramophone records in a Quirk, and how on earth he was supposed to *know* that he ought to bring records in the first place.

More people came in. The bar got busy. Eventually someone tapped him on the knee. "Guess who's turned up," the adjutant said. He had shaved, and his face was shining with goodwill.

"Not Dexter," Paxton said. "That would be a miracle."

"No, no. The other chap. Chap you lost. *Thought* you lost. He's turned up. Not lost at all." Appleyard beamed. "Good news, isn't it? Certainly deserves a drink."

Paxton stood up. "It can't be Wilkins. Wilkins is in hospital. It must be . . ." Paxton fished out a scribbled list of pilots' names. "Must be Ross-Kennedy."

"That's the chap! He'll be flying here tomorrow. Good news, isn't it? I knew you were worried. Only natural." They had reached the bar. "What'll you have, old boy?"

"But I saw him turn over."

"Two whisky-sodas," the adjutant ordered.

"He did a cartwheel, adj." Paxton saw the light of cheerful ignorance in Appleyard's eyes. "You know: the plane somersaulted, it went . . ." He demonstrated, rolling his hands around each other. "It must have been bust. *He* must have been bust. How can he fly it here tomorrow?"

"Beats me, old boy. I know absolutely damn-all about flying-machines. Simple soldier, me." He gave Paxton his drink. "Cheers." Half the adjutant's whisky-soda disappeared. He sighed, and shut his eyes for a second. "There are

32

twenty-six tropical diseases you can catch in the Gold Coast, did you know that? Twenty-six. The little bastards are still inside me, all twenty-six of them, all fighting each other for the privilege of laying me low, and the only medicine that keeps them at bay is this. My bloodstream is a battlefield that makes Gallipoli look like a football match."

"It can't be Ross-Kennedy, adj. Impossible."

"See for yourself, old boy." Appleyard took out a signal and showed him.

"Kellaway," Paxton said. He pointed. "This says Kellaway's coming."

"So it does." Appleyard took Paxton's piece of paper and compared them. "Well, that settles it. I don't know where you got your information but it looks pretty dud to me."

Paxton took a swig of whisky-soda. It had been a strange and wearing day, and now everything felt unreal: this junkshop of an anteroom, these men who ignored him, the adjutant who made no sense. "I give up," he said. "Ross-Kennedy was the chap we lost. What I mean is, he's the chap we couldn't find."

Appleyard finished his drink. "It doesn't say anything about that here," he said, and winked confidentially. "Take it from me, old boy: the Army may not always get everything absolutely right but we rarely get anything completely wrong."

A gong boomed. There was a general buttoning-up of tunics and finishing of drinks. Paxton went with the adjutant into the mess. This was simply a larger version of the anteroom, with a T-shaped table taking up most of the space. Appleyard, happily waving and calling greetings, went to the top of the T. Paxton almost followed him, but then had the sense to select a chair halfway up the longer table, the stem of the T. He stood behind the chair, uncertain whether grace would be said. Someone poked him in the ribs. "Your place, chummy," said O'Neill, "is down there." He pointed to the bottom of the table.

Paxton refused to turn his head. "I hope you've washed your hands," he said stiffly. "You never know where they've been." He found himself looking at Goss, standing opposite. "New boys start at the bottom," Goss said. "Push off, quick."

The squadron commander was coming in, chatter was subsiding. Paxton moved. He was partly numb with embarrassment and partly twitching with rage. Someone stuck out a foot and he stumbled. Stifled laughter. When he reached his place at the foot of the table he gripped the chairback and squeezed it like a strangler while the padre said grace.

Only one man spoke to him during the meal. "See any good shows in London?"

"No," Paxton said. "Pass the cheese."

After dinner he went back to his billet. The sky was still light but he went to bed. At three o'clock he woke up. O'Neill was snoring. Paxton glared into the blackness for the best, or worst, part of an hour. He felt lonely and miserable, and he was not looking forward to tomorrow, except that it would put an end to O'Neill's snoring. He drifted into fantasies of putting an end to O'Neill, all of them brutal and bloody and hugely satisfying.

Fidler woke him at seven with a mug of tea. O'Neill's bed was empty.

"I forgot to tell you about the mess table, sir," Fidler said. "You come in at the bottom and you work your way up. That's how it's done here, sir. Don't worry, it doesn't take very long. You'll be halfway up that table before you know it, sir."

Paxton buried his nose in the mug and watched Fidler busying himself. He thought about moving up the mess table. Moving up quickly. "Why doesn't it take very long?" he asked.

"Some people get posted. Other gentlemen sort of . . . drop out, sir."

Paxton thought about that. "And how long has Mr. O'Neill been here?"

"Oh . . . two months, sir."

Paxton finished his tea and went off to shave. Now that he knew that nothing was permanent he felt better. Perhaps even O'Neill might drop out soon. Anything was possible. That was the great thing about war. The sun was bright, he had a marvellous appetite for breakfast. He felt *much* better. Soon he would go up and pot a Hun. That would show them.

Chapter 3

There were only four officers at breakfast, and O'Neill was not among them.

One man was in a dressing gown, the other three in shirt sleeves and tieless. Paxton, in tunic and tie, felt very dressed-up. They ignored him, each half-hidden behind a newspaper He hesitated, wondering where to sit; then took a chance and sat opposite them. He recognised them from the previous night. The dressing-gowned man was a captain called Frank, the others were lieutenants known as Charlie, Spud and James.

The newspapers, he saw, were all yesterday's editions. While he had taken five days to reach Pepriac, the *Daily Mirror* and *Morning Post* made the journey in one.

Frank cleared his throat. "They keep going on about this chap *Russell*," he said, sounding puzzled and aggrieved "Awful lot of fuss   What d'you think, Charlie?"

"Russell," Charlie said. None of them had so far looked up from his paper. "Do I know him?"

"Ought to. You were at Cambridge, weren't you?"

"Just one term. Then they found out I couldn't do any sums and my spelling was rotten." He reached for some toast "So I got the boot, B double-O T I can spell boot."

"Well, they've gone and done it to this chap Russell. He's got the boot too."

"Absolute bastards, they are." Charlie muttered through his toast.

"Yes, but he's a don. They don't sack dons, do they?"

"Dunno. I can't spell don. Not before lunch, anyway."

A mess servant placed a large bowl of porridge in front of Paxton. "Actually, I don't take porridge," he said; but he was talking to himself. The servant had gone. There was silence for about ten seconds while Paxton wondered how best to get rid of the stuff; and then James looked over the top of his newspaper and said: "The CO's keen on everyone having porridge. It's not an order, but . . ."

"You get the boot if you don't," Charlie said.

Paxton poured milk on the porridge and began eating. It tasted grey and slippery. "Every day?" he asked.

"D'you mean a bloke called Bertrand Russell?" Spud said. "He's in my paper too. Says he made a statement calculated to prejudice recruiting. Fined a hundred pounds."

"Awful lot of fuss," Charlie complained. His nose was broken, which gave his voice a nasal tone that emphasised his drawl. "Why don't they just shoot the bugger and be done with it?"

"No, no," James said. He looked to be the youngest of the four: fair-haired, fresh of face, with a mouth as wide as a choirboy's. "You're going too far now. You can't fine him *and* shoot him. There is such a thing as British justice, you know."

"You ought to become a barrister, James," Frank said. "You'd make a red-hot barrister. You could handle all my divorces."

"No fear." James wrinkled his nose. "Rotten uniform. I prefer the Army."

More silence, while Paxton worked his way through his gruel.

"What do these coves want, anyway?" Charlie said. "That's what I don't understand."

"They want peace, old boy," Spud said. "They want the war stopped, no more shooting, everyone goes home."

"Bloody ridiculous," Charlie grumbled. "Stop the war? We've only just got it properly organised. The man's barmy."

There was a long pause, while Paxton soldiered on.

"I once made a statement calculated to prejudice recruiting," Frank said, "but I'm damned if I can remember what it was. All I know is when I said it the colonel turned white and told me he'd have me court-martialled for treason as soon as we'd captured whatever position it was we were supposed to be capturing. Ten minutes later he got blown to bits, so that was that."

"He should have written it all down," Charlie said. "If he'd written it down and given the order to the adjutant, you'd have been shot at dawn, Frank, and you wouldn't have liked that a little bit."

"Charlie's right," Spud said. "You're not really at your best first thing in the morning."

"Well . . . it's such a bloody awful time of day. It's bad enough to shoot a chap. Why get him out of bed at dawn?"

"It's a gesture," Spud said.

"Damn rude gesture." Frank discarded his newspaper and stood up. "Good God," he said. Paxton found them all gazing at him. "You don't have to eat it *all*, you know," Frank said. "A couple of spoonfuls will do."

Paxton put down his loaded spoon. He had almost emptied the bowl, training himself to swallow each mouthful without tasting it. Now a sickly aftertaste rose in his throat like vengeance.

"It's a gesture," Spud said.

"Personally, I can't stand the muck," Frank said. "I usually give one of the servants a shilling to eat mine for me. Maybe you haven't got a shilling."

Paxton nodded to indicate that he had a shilling. He didn't trust himself to open his mouth.

Spud said: "Actually sixpence would probably be enough. Private Collins here quite likes porridge, don't you, Collins?"

"No, sir." Collins replaced Paxton's bowl with a plate of bacon and eggs.

"Too late now, Collins," Frank said. "You should have spoken up earlier. Dexter's gone and eaten it."

"Paxton," muttered Paxton.

"Look here, you chaps." Frank moved behind James's chair and put his hands on his shoulders. "If we're to do some shopping *and* have a swim before lunch . . ." He squeezed until James squirmed.

"Hey, that *hurt*," James said, still reading his paper.

"Shows what a puny weed you are."

"Are you coming, Spud?" Charlie asked.

"No, dammit, I can't, I've got to . . ." He stopped suddenly and stared at nothing in particular. "On the other hand, I don't see why not," he said, and turned and smiled at Paxton. "The CO asked me to tell you that you're Orderly Officer today. There's nothing to it, really; you just stroll around with this armband on and look intelligent . . ." He tossed Paxton the armband. "Sign here, if you don't mind." He held out a clipboard and gave Paxton a pen. "This gives you authority over the entire camp." Paxton signed, and returned the pen. "What if—" he began.

"Ask Corporal Lacey, in the Orderly Room," Spud said. "Lacey knows all."

"Come on, you two," called Frank from the door.

"You're very lucky," Charlie told Paxton. "The old man must like you. I didn't get to be orderly dog for months, but then I'm not very bright."

They left. Paxton looked at his armband and his clipboard and finally at his pair of fried eggs, until he realised that they were looking at him. He pushed the plate away.

By eight the sun had burned off all the ground mist. The fields behind the British Front Line were a brilliant green. Tim Piggott, a mile high, located the spot where he knew the British battery was firing. A tiny cluster of miniature flames came and went. Piggott said: "Bang, one elephant, two elephants, three elephants, four elephants, five elephants, crash." Exactly on *crash*, a cluster of little brown flowers bloomed behind the German lines, and slowly collapsed. "Missed again," he said. "You're hopeless."

Binns, who was Piggott's observer, banged his fist on the right of the nacelle. Piggott immediately banked the FE to the right. Then he searched where Binns was pointing and found the Pfalz, blurred in the dazzle of the sun. It had reversed direction and was trying yet again to sneak around behind the FE. "Thank you, Boy," he said. He knew Binns couldn't hear him against the rush of wind and roar of engine, but Piggott liked to talk when he was on patrol.

He straightened out when he had put the FE between the

Pfalz and a BE2c two thousand feet beneath them. It was the BE2c that the Pfalz was after. Piggott's job was to guard it and let it get on with its work of artillery observation.

The morning was almost cloudless, with just a milkskim at enormous height, and the FE gave Piggott a magnificent view, like a box at the opera. But he had been trundling around this bit of sky for ninety minutes and he was ready to go home for breakfast. The Pfalz was a monoplane with a fuselage like a long, thin coffin and a cockpit slap in the middle of the wing so the pilot had to tip the machine on its side to look below him. This pilot had done a great deal of tipping and looking but only once in an hour had he dived at the BE2c, and he had pulled out of the dive after a couple of hundred feet when he saw that the FE would meet him first. He was a cautious, thoughtful Hun, and Piggott was bored with him. "You want this Quirk on a plate, don't you?" he said. "Not today, I'm afraid. Come down and fight me for him."

BE2cs were slow and steady and they could be depended upon to stay in the air for two and a half hours or until they were shot up by enemy scouts or shot down by archie, whichever came sooner. When he joined the Corps, Piggott had flown a Quirk twice a day for a month. It was the Loos offensive, a bad, busy time when the generals demanded lots of artillery observation and photographic reconnaissance Piggott soon came to hate the first and loathe the second.

Spotting for the guns meant hanging about in the same piece of sky, making random changes in height and direction to baffle the archie, you hoped. But the changes mustn't be too violent or your Morse transmissions suffered. Taking photographs, on the other hand, meant flying absolutely dead straight and level and hoping the Hun gunners couldn't believe their luck and therefore aimed somewhere else. In his four weeks with the squadron they lost sixteen BE2cs and their crews. Piggott was saved by a sliver of anti-aircraft shell. It chopped off the little finger of his left hand. When he left hospital he was posted to Hornet Squadron.

The Pfalz turned again, and again Piggott turned with it. "No imagination!" he said. "Try something different." He searched the sky, slowly and thoroughly nothing. He looked down just as a string of dense black blots created themselves a hundred yards to the right of the BE2c and immediately began to spread and fade. "Pathetic!" he said. "This could go on all day. I'm hungry."

He considered climbing up to the Pfalz and making it fight or run away. Not a good idea. It could outclimb him, and the FE didn't get better as it went higher. Besides, his job was to guard the BE2c, which (he saw) had just made the archie look silly again. Say ten shells a minute: that was nine hundred shells the enemy had wasted, not to mention the peril to their own men from the clatter of descending shrapnel on their heads. "Yah, yah!" Piggott chanted. "Can't catch me!" And at that precise instant, seemingly in retaliation for the taunt, black shellbursts straddled the BE2c and flung its nose up as if it had walked into a punch.

Piggott stopped breathing until he saw the plane straighten out. He felt painfully ashamed. It wasn't his fault; it was luck, or clever anticipation by the German battery commander; nevertheless his throat felt sick with a surge of self-disgust.

There was no way he could help but he had to do something so he shoved the stick forward and went down. The BE2c was a mess, but at least it was right-side up and the British lines were near. Something was falling, catching the light as it spun. It couldn't be a parachute. No parachutes in the RFC, except for balloonists. It looked like half a wing. *Christ*, Piggott thought, *if they've lost half a wing, have they got any controls left?* The BE2c was tipping into a gentle sideslip. It had no power. The propeller had stopped. Something else fell off and fluttered behind it. All the time, archie was staining the sky with blots, like someone flicking a loaded pen. One blot touched the BE2c and the story was over.

Piggott looked away. There was nothing worthwhile left, and what was not worthwhile he did not wish to see hit the ground. He levelled out and turned westward. Binns banged and pointed. The Pfalz had followed them down and was now circling lazily, five hundred feet above. The German pilot waved. Piggott waved back. Why not? It was just another day's work, wasn't it? Breakfast, that was what mattered now. Breakfast. Bacon, toast, maybe even some devilled kidneys. Breakfast. You had to keep your strength up for this kind of work. Breakfast. Breakfast. Great big breakfast.

Paxton took seriously his responsibilities as Orderly Officer. He wore his Sam Browne and carried his cane and walked around the camp. All was in order. The men he met gave him orderly salutes. After half an hour Paxton had found no hint of disorder. He grew bored with the camp and went to inspect the airfield. That too was in good shape. There was a black patch where his Quirk had burned but the wreckage had been carted away; the rest of the field was blamelessly green.

He walked along the tracks his Quirk had left in the grass and re-lived in reverse his disastrous landing: here was the strip where the plane slid on its belly, and beyond that the marks where the wheel-struts collapsed and gouged out turf, and further back still the spot where the plane first fell to earth and the wheels dented the grass. Now that the machine was destroyed he felt curiously proud of his arrival. A good landing, so one of his instructors had told him, was a landing you could walk away from. He sat on his heels and fingered the wheel-marks. It hadn't been perfect but it was still a damn sight better than Wilkins had managed at Dover. Or Ross-Kennedy, doing cartwheels in a French field. Or Dexter, making a mess of that church. Damn fools. Nice chaps but rotten pilots. The hard-edged drone of an engine cut into his thoughts and he looked up. An FE2b sailed overhead, sinking softly, and touched down without a bounce. Paxton felt sick with envy. Two more planes landed during the next ten minutes. Each bounced a bit. The second bounced twice. Paxton felt better.

He went for a walk around the field, and then strolled into the mess to chat with the crews about their patrol; but the mess was empty.

"They've all gone swimming, sir," a servant said. "Just ate breakfast and went."

"Ah. They'll be back for lunch, though?"

"No, sir. I think they go to an *estaminet*, sir."

"You mean I'm the only officer on the camp?"

"Well, there's the adjutant, sir. But he doesn't usually take lunch."

Paxton went to see the adjutant. Corporal Lacey's gramophone was playing the César Franck symphonic variations, but Lacey stopped the record and received Paxton courteously. "I'm afraid Mr. Appleyard is resting in bed this morning," he said. "A recurrence of an old Nigerian malady, I believe. The CO, of course, is at Brigade HQ all day."

"Ah," Paxton said. "Yes. Of course." Nobody had told *him* the CO was at Brigade. You'd think the Orderly Officer ought to be told.

In the next room, a couple of typewriters chattered, starting and stopping as unpredictably as birdsong.

"If I may say so," Lacey said, "it was uncommonly generous of you to take over Mr. Ogilvy's duty as Orderly Officer."

Paxton looked down. He found something of interest in an in-tray. It was a memo about disinfectant for the men's latrines. "Oh well," he said. "I wasn't going anywhere."

"Neither was Mr. Ogilvy. Now he's splashing happily in the Somme."

Rafters creaked as the heat baked the roof. Lacey sharpened a pencil, taking a long time to get it to a fine point. Paxton watched the tiny flakes fall and wished he knew how to drive. Then he could take an army car and whizz around the French countryside. There had been a chap at Sherborne who'd had a car. Lucky blighter. Sherborne had been a jolly good school. You got beaten, of course. Everyone got beaten, by masters, by prefects. Eventually you became a prefect and then you beat others. Didn't do anyone any harm. On the contrary, it helped to develop the proper spirit. That was the great difference between us and the Boche. We had the proper spirit.

"Sinfully languid," Lacey said. He was standing by a window, balancing the pencil on a fingertip by its point.

"What?"

"Don't you find this weather almost sinfully languid?" The pencil wavered and he deftly caught it as it fell. "Idleness is a virtue on days like this. Unless one chooses to swim, and swimming is simply the most sensual of all indulgences. Don't you think?" He had the pencil balanced again.

"No," Paxton said firmly.

"Oh, surely," Lacey murmured. "We all dream of toppling naked into a cool calm river and letting the running current do with us what it will."

"I don't," Paxton said. "I don't like rivers." This was not true, but he wanted to put Lacey in his place.

"Actually, it's a canal." Lacey let the pencil fall, and this time did not catch it; instead he kicked it before it touched the floor, sending it flying into a corner. "The Somme canal. The river's weedy, so the officers swim in the Somme canal." Lacey was brisk now, dusting his hands. "It cleanses them of the corruption of combat, you see. It washes off the sweat of death."

"What rot."

"Yes." Lacey turned and smiled a smile of pleased surprise. "Rot sums it up nicely. What rot is war. Its stench is everywhere. Nothing can resist it. What rot."

"How long have you been with the squadron, corporal?" Paxton asked.

"Eighteen months." Lacey waited until Paxton's mouth began to open and added: "Sir."

"Eighteen months and still only a corporal, corporal. *Very* slow."

"Yes. Sinfully languid, in fact." He took a small brush from his desk and began tidying up his moustache.

Paxton had had enough. "Come and get me when the adjutant surfaces," he said, and made for the door.

"Don't lend him any money," Lacey called. Paxton turned and stared. "He'll try to borrow money," Lacey said. "Don't lend him any. It's bad for him."

"What a preposterous idea," Paxton said. "Corporal."

"He picked it up in Egypt," Lacey said. "Sir."

Driving back from Brigade headquarters, Rufus Milne had a lot to think about. To his surprise he found himself thinking about other matters. In particular, about his war and the number of times it had nearly killed him.

This was something he never discussed, never mentioned in letters. He didn't keep a diary. His response to danger was to forget it as soon as it had passed. This policy had worked very well: he suffered no nightmares, no spells of depression, none of the crippling anxiety which he knew some other pilots suffered when they were getting ready to fly. For nearly two years, Milne had done his job day by day, sometimes boring, sometimes exciting, and reckoned himself lucky to have it. Now, suddenly, as the car charged along a dead-straight road, wheels drumming, poplars flickering by, he saw himself in a plane that was cartwheeling across a turnip field like a blown-away windmill, and he felt sick.

The plane was a Maurice Farman so the crash must have happened in 1914, soon after the squadron came to France. No trenches then, just armies and battles and confusion. Nobody knew where the enemy was (or, if they claimed they knew, they turned out to be wrong) so the RFC flew from dawn to dusk, endless reconnaissance patrols. The roads were crowded but the skies were empty; anyway, in those days enemy planes couldn't hurt you. Milne was at five thousand feet, busily marking troop columns on his map and wishing he had some chocolate, when the engine stopped. No coughing or spluttering, no hesitation: sudden silence. It was a very final decision.

He glided westward for several miles. The field he picked out looked green and smooth, but over the last two hundred yards the wind turned boisterous and blew him sideways, across a turnip field. He knew, as he saw the rows of turnips rushing past, slantwise, that his wheels would never run; and when they touched he wrapped his arms around his head. He felt like a man in a barrel over a waterfall: the machine was flailing itself to bits, smashing its nose and tail and wings, the earth and sky whirling, until the fit of rage had exhausted itself and Milne found himself sprawled in a battered cockpit and not much else.

That was his fifth forced landing but his first real crash. He had seen nothing of it at the time, but now, driving this car, he could follow it all in his mind, perfectly clearly. Ten seconds of cartwheeling chaos, and he'd walked away. Limped away. The memory made him shudder.

He had to slow behind a long line of horse-drawn artillery. For a mile he ambled along in low gear, thinking that if he hadn't been a pilot he might have been a gunner. It must be fun to bang away at the enemy, catch him by surprise, make him hop. Fun for the Hun gunners, too, presumably.

The German archie had certainly had fun the day they caught Milne in a skimpy little BE2a somewhere near Festubert. He'd treated those fluffy balls of black smoke as a joke, until one of them stung him. It burst below, and flipped the plane onto its back.

Milne had panicked then. The taste of terror came back to him now, and he hated it so much that he tried to drive away from it: he pulled out and accelerated past the guns, making the horses twitch and jerk their heads as he roared by.

That shellburst had cut two control cables. The BE2a wallowed on its back for a short eternity. Milne cursed it and kicked it, and the German gunners rejoiced to find an easy target. The little patch of sky was filthy with shellbursts. Milne never discovered how he righted the plane, but he knew it was sheer luck that he flew home.

And it had been sheer luck, too, when that Aviatik had failed to kill him. Milne hadn't thought of it for months but now he could see everything: those dun, translucent wings with dense black Maltese crosses, the propeller-disc shining as it met sunlight, the tail-unit that was all curves, like a big butterfly. The Aviatik had caught him at the weary end of a long patrol, had come out of nowhere and hammered him. It hit the engine. His machine was limping and labouring as Milne screwed his head around to watch the Aviatik perform a steep and elegant bank and return for the kill. The German never fired. His gun had jammed, and no amount of thumping released it. They waved to each other before they parted, but when he landed Milne was so weak that his mechanic had to help him get out of the cockpit.

Milne was sweating now, just at the memory. He stopped the car beyond a little stone bridge and washed his face in the stream. How odd to get so upset at a lot of old memories. More than odd: silly, because the only thing that mattered was that he *hadn't* been killed. In eighteen months' flying and fighting there were bound to be a few close shaves. Like that time young Jenkins damn near collided with him over Vimy.

Milne wished he hadn't remembered that. Young Jenkins had sidled across his path and almost killed them both. A week later Jenkins had flown slap-bang into his flight commander, a man called Harry Drake. That was sheer and utter waste. Harry Drake had been a very nice man.

Minnows played cheerfully in the stream. Milne threw a small pebble and scattered them. They soon came back. He envied them. When *he* came back, he decided, he was going to be a minnow.

Paxton had drawn a revolver from the armoury. He had decided that an Orderly Officer should carry a revolver; it helped to demonstrate his authority. By late afternoon, as he walked about the aerodrome in full uniform, he was beginning to regret his decision.

The officers were playing cricket again. He couldn't help feeling that if this was war he didn't think much of it. All anyone did was swim and play cricket. He was hot, and his blasted revolver kept banging against his hip in a most annoying way. Also he had been bitten inside his puttees by some blasted French insects. He itched and could not scratch. He glanced at the cricket match. Half the players had crowded together and were arguing about something; the other half were lying down. The trouble with Hornet Squadron, he decided, was that it was slack. It lacked the Will to Win.

Private Fidler came up to him and saluted.

"Mr. O'Neill's compliments, sir, and could you come and look at something suspicious he's found lying in the grass, you being Orderly Officer and all."

Paxton distrusted anything connected with O'Neill. "What is it?" he asked.

"If we knew that, sir, it wouldn't be suspicious, would it? Personally, I kept well clear of it, myself."

Paxton hesitated, but he saw no alternative. "All right, lead on," he said, and unbuttoned his revolver holster.

They walked through the camp. "I must say I'm surprised to find an Australian in the squadron," Paxton said, allowing his distaste to show. "God knows there are still plenty of decent Englishmen left."

"Bless your heart, sir, Mr. O'Neill's not what you'd call a *real* Australian," Fidler said. "It's more of an act, with him." He chuckled at the thought.

Paxton wanted to know more but he wasn't willing to ask

and it seemed that Fidler had nothing to add. They walked in silence for a few yards. "What about Toby Chivers, then?" Paxton asked. "Was he English?"

Fidler began to speak but then stopped and cleared his throat. "Sometimes I can't believe Mr. Chivers has really gone, sir," he said. "It makes no sense. Not in his case."

They turned the corner of the cookhouse and saw O'Neill standing in a patch of knee-high grass. Paxton let his hand rest on the butt of his revolver and approached O'Neill cautiously. "All right, what is it?" he asked.

"See for yourself." O'Neill nudged something with his foot. "Come on, it won't dare bite you. You're the bloody Orderly Officer." The Australian accent made his voice slack and contemptuous.

Paxton took out the revolver and advanced. Fidler had vanished. Paxton looked at what O'Neill was looking at and saw nothing but grass. "I can't see anything," he said.

"Jesus." O'Neill sighed, and shook his head. "If you can't see it I'd better pick it up and show you. Here, hold this for a minute." He thrust something hard and heavy into Paxton's left hand. Instinctively, the fingers closed. When Paxton looked up, O'Neill was ten yards away and running. "Keep the spring in!" O'Neill shouted. Paxton squeezed until his fingers hurt. He was holding a hand grenade. His stomach clenched at nothing, as it had nothing to clench, and gripped it hard.

By the time he had worked out that the obvious solution was to fling the bloody thing as far away as possible, he knew it wasn't going to explode. That meant he was holding the spring in. He knew very little about hand grenades but he felt sure that this one was safe as long as he kept a tight grip. His stomach slowly unclenched.

He could still chuck it away, of course; there was plenty of open space. But that would be much less satisfying than finding O'Neill and giving the grenade back to him. And if O'Neill wouldn't take it, Paxton would toss it to him and leave, fast. These japes were all very jolly but enough was enough.

Paxton marched back through the camp, holding the grenade in one hand and his revolver in the other, and soon saw where O'Neill was. O'Neill was playing cricket. Splendid! There would be plenty of spectators for the show-down. He headed across the field.

Tim Piggott was batting. He was enjoying himself, the ball looked big to him, he was whacking it vigorously over or between the fielders, and so far he had scored forty-seven runs, a squadron record. O'Neill was fielding very close to Piggott. "Not now, old boy," Piggott called out as Paxton advanced. "Buzz off."

"But this is important."

"Don't talk tripe. I only need three for my fifty. Get out of the way, I can't see the bowler."

The bowler was beginning his run-up. Reluctantly, Paxton moved back. The bowler flung down a fast delivery. Piggott smacked it crisply over Paxton's head, and ran two. Paxton stared at O'Neill, who was squatting on his haunches, chewing a stem of grass. "Forty-nine," Piggott said, gasping. "Now for the love of Mike, shut up and stand back. I'm going to sock this one into the middle of next week."

Paxton had heard the whizz of the ball; he knew how hard it was, how painful it could be. He circled around behind Piggott and approached O'Neill. "I believe this is yours," he said.

"For God's sake!" Piggott complained. The bowler bowled and Piggott played a dreadful shot, a cross-batted lumber-jack's swipe, his head up, his feet all wrong. The ball squirted high off an inside edge. Piggott swore, several people shouted, somebody ran to catch the ball and collided violently with Paxton. Both men fell to the ground. "Now look what you made me do," Piggott said crossly. "You made me break the squadron bat."

"Grenade!" Paxton shouted hoarsely. He had stopped an elbow with his nose and his eyes were watering from the pain. "I dropped a grenade!"

"Practice grenade," O'Neill said. "Not real. Don't bust your truss about it." He was tossing it from hand to hand.

"What a swizz," Piggott said, examining the bat. It was thoroughly broken: the handle had come loose and the blade was split from end to end.

"You swine," Paxton tried to say, but his nose had begun to bleed and his speech was clogged.

"End of game," said Goss, the man who had collided with Paxton. "End of cricket as we know it in our time. And incidentally I seem to have cracked my elbow."

"Really?" Foster, the bowler, had joined them. "You've scarcely recovered from yesterday's dislocated shoulder, Douglas. And what was it last week? A double rupture?"

"Torn muscles, actually."

"You do keep up a giddy pace. How you manage it on those poor clubbed feet of yours I just don't know."

"It's broken, I tell you," Goss insisted, flexing his arm carefully. "I shall never play the violin again."

"Forty-nine," Piggott said. "Forty bloody nine. It's tragic."

"Anyway, you were out. I would have caught that ball easily if Dexter hadn't run into me. Wouldn't I, Frank?"

Paxton glared. He blew his nose and made it bleed. "Paxton," he mumbled.

"Don't mention it," Foster said.

"I think that chap's decided to land after all," said Goss. "He's been hovering about up there for ages, waiting for Tim to get his half-century."

It was a BE2c. The plane came drifting down, the pilot giving the engine brief drumrolls of power to keep the nose up, and landed nearby. They walked over to meet him.

"Sorry I'm late," he said. He was short, and when he shrugged off his flying coat he looked even shorter. He had the kind of face that only a mother could love: decent, cleancut, obedient, trusting and honest. "I wasn't altogether sure where I was," he said. "You were here," Goss told him. "You've been here ever since you arrived." The pilot's face was spattered with oil except where he had worn goggles, and there the skin was milk-white and freckled. He took off his helmet. His hair was a deep rich red. "Hullo, Paxton," he said.

Paxton recognised the voice before the face. "Hullo, Kellaway," he said. He had dismissed Kellaway from his mind six days ago. Kellaway had gone down in the Channel. "I thought we'd lost you."

"I thought I'd lost you."

"They thought they had lost each other." Foster explained to Piggott and Goss. Kellaway slapped his gloves against his thigh and shook his head at the wonder of it all.

"I expect you'd like a nice cup of tea," said Piggott.

"Gosh, yes!" Kellaway said.

They all trailed off towards the mess. "It's probably none of my business, old boy," Foster said to Paxton, "but were you on your way to shoot someone?"

Paxton remembered that he was holding his revolver He stuffed it in its holster. "Now that the cricket's over," he said thickly, "maybe we can *all* start shooting someone." His nose began to bleed again. He threw his head back but a scarlet trickle escaped and splashed his tunic.

"Dexter here thinks we ought to start killing people," Foster announced.

"Paxton," mumbled Paxton.

"I second that," Piggott said. "Let's all kill Paxton. quick, before he bleeds to death."

Milne knew the Amiens–Bapaume road very well from the air. It was a Roman road: fifty kilometres with scarcely a bend. It ran north-east from Amiens, and it was useful to pilots because it crossed the Front. Bapaume was held by the enemy. If you were slightly lost and you could find the Amiens–Bapaume road you were okay, provided you knew north from south.

But until now, Milne had never driven on the road. From Amiens to Albert the surface wasn't bad. The town of Albert had been thoroughly knocked about, and beyond Albert shell-holes were commonplace. The traffic thinned out, and then disappeared altogether. Milne was on his own. Nothing was happening in the cratered wastelands on either side. It didn't look like the rear of a battlefield. It looked abandoned and forgotten, like miles of exhausted open-cast mines.

A military policeman came out of a dugout and waved him down. "This is the turning-point, sir," he said.

"Jolly good," Milne said.

The man pointed to a spot where the road had been widened. "This is the last good place where you can turn the car. If you drive on, you might have to reverse all the way back, sir."

Milne turned the car, parked it on the shoulder of the road, and got out. "Thank you," he said, and began walking.

"You don't want to go up there, sir," the policeman called. "Not at four o'clock. It's coming up to the afternoon hate."

Milne acknowledged this with a wave and did not stop.

The policeman went back into the dugout, where his mate was reading a newspaper. "Royal fucking Flying Corps," the policeman said. "Too fucking daft to come in out of the fucking rain."

The day was pleasantly warm. Milne unbuttoned his collar and loosened his tie. Now that he had time to look about, he saw little touches of colour between the shell-holes: iris, wild lupin, poppy, cowslip. There were occasional wrecks beside the road, mostly lorries, although he also saw a motorcycle twisted liked a corkscrew. Far away the remains of an aeroplane made him pause; but it was smashed beyond recognition. He strolled on and realised that he was whistling. He never whistled; he hadn't whistled since he came to France. How curious that he should start now, in all this silence. There was a bit of dull mumbling and grumbling going on somewhere over the horizon but it only pointed up the absolute silence all around.

A yellow butterfly arose and he made a grab for it. It dodged easily and flew ahead, zigzagging, never more than a few feet away, as if it liked being followed. "All right, you're faster than me," he said, "but can you whistle *Alexander's Ragtime Band*?" The butterfly did some clever stunts. "That's not whistling," he said, "and you know it."

A group of men came in sight, about twenty, all running from the Front. Their boots made a dull clatter, like distant farm machinery. Milne found a broken cart at the side of the road and sat on it to watch them pass.

Each man carried a shovel. They kept up a good pace, although their faces were shining with sweat. If they saw him they ignored him: nobody saluted, nobody even glanced; only one thing mattered, and that was to keep on running. A tall, thin lieutenant came pounding along behind them, head down, fists clenched. He saw Milne at the last moment, kept running for five yards, then stopped. "Carry on, sergeant!" he shouted, but the order turned into a gasp for breath. He stood

51

with his hands linked on top of his head and his chest heaving. The squad ran on, leaving a faint haze of dust.

"Jolly warm work," Milne said.

The lieutenant turned. He was blinking hard because his eyes were stinging from sweat. "It's a warm spot," he said, "sir." He wiped his eyes and looked at Milne again. "May I ask . . ." He pressed his ribs, and winced. "Are you looking for your regiment, sir?"

"No, no."

"Green Howards, I believe."

"That's right."

"Only . . . they're not in this part of the Front, sir."

"Quite so. Actually I'm Flying Corps now. I thought I'd come and take a squint at the real war. Like some chocolate?"

"I ought to tell you, sir . . ." The lieutenant's breathing was getting better. "The Hun batteries have got this road pretty well bracketed. They give it a bloody good pasting every day. Especially the afternoon hate." He accepted a square of chocolate.

"And when does that start?"

The lieutenant looked at his watch. "A minute ago."

Milne nodded, sucking his chocolate. "Maybe the Kaiser's given them a half-day holiday."

"Maybe my watch is fast."

A faint, clean-edged whistle came out of the east. The lieutenant cocked his head. The whistle magnified fast, at first splitting the afternoon silence and then tearing it, ripping it apart and finally releasing a bang that Milne felt through his boots. Two hundred years nearer the Front, a brown fountain created itself beside the road, climbed and spread, hung poised for a long moment, and fell. "You knew it would drop short?" Milne asked.

The lieutenant nodded. "One develops an ear for that sort of thing." Another shell was on its way. "A chap can't be forever diving into a hole, just because . . ." This time the explosion was fifty yards nearer.

"What if two come over at once?" Milne asked.

"You just have to listen twice as hard."

"I see. And I suppose different types of shells make different sounds?"

The lieutenant took out a filthy handkerchief and wiped his neck. "I really ought to be pushing on," he said. Flies circled his head. He seemed not to notice them.

"Don't worry about me," Milne said. "I'll find my way back, in due course." Shells were falling over a large area now. Most fell out of sight, but the persistent, irregular *crump-crump* was like the stamping of giant cattle. He saw a pulse thumping away in the lieutenant's neck, and realised he was afraid that Milne might think he was afraid to stay. "Your troops must be wondering what's become of you," Milne said. "You've been most helpful. I think I'll stroll on a bit further. Many thanks."

They shook hands. Milne knew, from his glance, that the lieutenant thought he was wrong in the head; but then, everyone thought all RFC pilots and observers were a bit mad. It went with the job.

He walked on a few paces for the sake of form, and watched the lieutenant hurry away. The bombardment grew heavier, and seemed to wander in a random fashion. Milne ate his chocolate and watched distant eruptions of mud enliven the landscape, following the fancy of some German battery commander. The howlings in the sky were suddenly louder and nearer; he blinked at the instant ferocity of the shellburst, and once or twice he lurched when the edge of a blast-wave shoved him in the chest. Then the attack grew bored and fickle and went off to blow up other bits of harmless field. The stench of high explosive drifted on a gentle breeze and made his nostrils twitch.

Milne was not testing his bravery. Where was the bravery in standing on a bare road in deserted countryside during a barrage? It made no difference to anyone whether he stayed or went. His survival was entirely a matter of luck. It takes no bravery to trust to luck. He was there to see the show, and to discover how watching the show affected him. Absurd reasons, both.

The shellfire tailed off after half an hour. He walked back towards his car, thinking about the sound and the fury. Maybe the sound was the worst part; maybe a shell that simply exploded with no warning whistle would be less frightening. But it didn't seem right; it somehow diminished the enemy. A noise like an express locomotive startled Milne. It rushed overhead, screech mixed with roar, and this time he fell flat. The savagery of the crash made every other shell-burst seem tame. The roadway seemed to rise up and punch him. After a long time the sky rained clods of earth. When he got up he was half-deaf, and staggering, and there was a smoking crater where he would have been thirty seconds later. *So now you know*, he said to himself. *That's what it's like. Now you can go home happy, you idiot.*

When Major Milne drove into Pepriac at half-past five, the intense sense of homecoming surprised him. It was only a collection of huts and canvas hangars and tents in the corner of a field; the huts were drab, the tents had faded, the hangars leaned and sagged; but he knew every detail; this was home. He stopped to look at a patch of wallflowers and tried to remember who had planted them. Harry Wild, was it? No, not Harry. They were planted last autumn, and dear old Harry shed his wings in August. Milne could see it now, quite clearly: both sets of wings folding back like a bird settling down for the night. Goodbye Harry. If the German Air Force found anything in the wreckage to identify the pilot, they sometimes put it in a bag and dropped it over a British aerodrome. Nothing came back to commemorate Harry. Except his wallflowers. No, that's not right, Milne thought, they're *not* his wallflowers. But they looked cheery all the same. Dusty and blown-about but cheery. Harry had been a bit like that. Always needing a haircut, always making daft remarks. One day somebody had called for three cheers for something, and Harry had said, "I bid four cheers!" Dotty, mindless nonsense, just what everyone needed to keep their minds off the goings-on upstairs. Good old Harry. He kept saying he was going to retire when he was twenty-one because he didn't think it right to stand in the way of young and ambitious officers. Oh well, Milne thought, at least he wasn't a flamer. The reds and yellows of the wallflowers waved in the breeze like paper flames. He stopped looking at them and drove on.

The adjutant walked into Milne's office with a dozen pieces of paper to be signed. "How is everybody at Brigade, sir?"

"Everybody at Brigade is very happy." Milne hung up his Sam Browne. "The sun is shining, partridge galore are running through the new corn, mess bills are low, and we are to have an enormous battle which will win the war."

"Jolly good." Appleyard laid the papers on the desk and strolled off to lean on the windowsill. "I could do with some decent shooting."

Milne sat down and began signing. "You're not thinking of leaving us for the trenches, Uncle?"

"What? No, no. Good God, no. But you must admit, a few brace of partridge would brighten up the menu a bit. One does get rather fed up with mutton."

"You don't seem impressed by the battle news."

"Oh, well. It's no surprise, is it? Everyone's been beavering away around here since Christmas. New roadheads, railheads, depots, shell dumps, and everywhere you look nothing but camps and camps of infantry, all busily sticking their bayonets in bags of hay, not that a bag of hay feels the slightest bit like anybody's tummy, and I should know."

Milne stopped signing. "Should you? Why?"

Appleyard hunched his shoulders and looked away. "Oh, you know," he said. "I pronged a couple of Boers in South Africa. Not normally the work of an officer, I agree, but we were a bit shorthanded that day."

Milne waited. "Well, what was the difference?"

"You don't want to hear about all that, Rufus."

"Yes, I do, Uncle. Stomachs interest me."

"All right. Suit yourself." The adjutant turned away from the window and looked up at the rafters. "First. Getting the damn thing in. That's no problem, provided you don't hit a belt or an ammunition pouch. It goes in very easily. But whereas in training your bag of hay is suspended from a branch or tied to a stake which keeps it in place, your actual human foe tends to react violently to having half a yard of steel thrust in his guts, and unless you withdraw it quick he may commence writhing. When sufficiently vigorous, this writhing will slacken your grip on the rifle, which is contrary to King's Rules and Regulations since it hinders withdrawal and furthermore presents an unsoldierly appearance. Writhing has also been known to enlarge the aperture, thus spilling the guts. You'd be amazed what a lot of guts the average man has, old boy. I know I was. Fathoms of the bloody stuff. You think it's all out and he's only half-done. God knows how the Almighty packed it all in there in the first place. Satisfied?"

"Mmmm."

"Just make sure you don't step on any of it. Extremely slippery stuff. You might go arse over tit, do yourself an injury."

"Yes." Milne resumed signing. "That's a thing you've got to watch out for in wartime, isn't it, Uncle? Doing yourself an injury."

Appleyard wasn't sure whether Milne was mocking him, so he said nothing.

Milne signed the last sheet, and re-read it. "Kellaway turned up after all. I thought Paxton said he went down in the Channel?"

"Apparently he didn't."

Milne shuffled the papers into a pile. "Funny sort of mistake to make."

"Oh, Paxton likes to impress people. I'm told he was walking all over the 'drome this afternoon, waving a revolver. Damn lucky nobody got shot, apparently."

Milne stared. "Why didn't someone stop him? Who's Orderly Officer?"

"Paxton is. It was Spud Ogilvy's turn, but Spud says Paxton was so keen to do it that he let him. Nothing was happening here today. Place was empty."

"Too complicated for me, Uncle." Milne yawned, hugely. "Why do I feel so tired all the time? I never used to feel tired . . ." There was a knock at the door. A despatch rider came in, saluted, and gave Milne a thick envelope. Milne signed for it and the man left.

"He's early," Appleyard said.

"It's the fourth of June."

The adjutant nodded, and looked at a calendar on the wall, and nodded again. He tugged at an ear while he gave the fact more thought. "Sorry, old chap," he said, "I'm in the dark."

"Eton College. Fourth of June is their big day. Brigade HQ is lousy with Old Etonians, and they've knocked off early so

56

they can go to the Old Etonian dinner in Amiens. Half of 'C' Flight are going. Frank Foster, James Yeo, Charles, Spud, they're all Etonians. That's why I put them together."

"Well, well." The adjutant collected his papers and opened the door for Milne. "Well, well, well. I never knew that."

"Yes, you did, Uncle, I told you at the time." They walked towards the mess. "How are your terrible tubes nowadays?" Milne asked. "Is that new doctor any good?"

"He's given me different medicine. Tastes foul."

"Maybe you should see a specialist."

"Nobody specialises in what I've got," Appleyard said, "because nobody else has got it."

When the squadron had assembled in the anteroom, Rufus Milne opened the letter from Brigade HQ. It was heavily sealed in a square brown envelope of thick paper, and he used a penknife to slit the end. A few men watched him but most looked at something else: the empty fireplace, the faded pattern of the carpet, dust-motes slanting in the air. When he closed the knife, its click was loud. "Flying orders for tomorrow," he said. "Morning. One flight to provide escorts for artillery observation. That'll be 'C' Flight. Various rendezvous with various Quirks from 9 Squadron at various times — Frank will have all the details. First rendezvous is 10.00 hours. You'll be over the usual areas: Pozières, Mametz, Montauban." The names produced a few soft groans. "Evening: one flight to provide escort for a photo-reconnaissance patrol from 15 Squadron. That'll be 'A' Flight, and I shall lead it. No more details yet; they'll be telephoned through to us. But if the weather is clear and sunny, the patrol will be late in the evening, when the shadows are long. It seems that shadows can be very revealing on photographs. That's all, except to welcome Kellaway, just arrived from Blighty." Kellaway blushed and looked at his boots. "Kellaway and Paxton are in reserve until we get some more aeroplanes. That's all." Paxton did not blush. He chewed on a forefinger and watched Milne. The stillness and silence broke now that everyone knew the worst, which was not so bad after all; no worse than most days, in fact. The gramophone began playing ragtime. There was laughter, and a chair fell over. "Come and have a drink," Piggott said to Kellaway. "Tell me all the latest London scandal. You too, Paxton."

"Thank you, no," Paxton said. "I have . . ." He squared his shoulders and tightened his buttocks. "I have certain duties to attend to."

"Bollocks. At this time of day? There's nothing left to be done."

"On the contrary, I have to inspect the men's latrines."

"*Now?* What on earth for? The men's latrines will be full of the men."

"I inspected them earlier and their condition was unsatisfactory. *Mens sana in corpore sano*, and vice versa. I'm sure I have no need to translate." Paxton nodded, and left.

"Pompous prick," Piggott said. Kellaway, totally at a loss, smiled with one side of his mouth and frowned with the other, and ended up looking foolish.

Chapter 4

Zeppelins strolled about the skies at night, and sometimes small bombs fell on large towns. Thus there was a blackout in Amiens. The ballroom of the Grand Hotel du Nord had been converted to an enormous dining room and it was brilliantly lit but the windows were heavily curtained in velvet. Each set of curtains was made in different colours: red and black, chocolate and orange, fawn and blue, green and grey, and so on. These were the house colours at Eton. The windows nearest the top table were curtained in purple and white, the colours of the college itself.

About three hundred Old Etonians were present. The vast majority were in uniform, with many of the uniforms representing the Brigade of Guards. At least eight full generals could be seen. The average age was about forty. "Quite a decent turn-out," said Lord Trafford, who had travelled from England to preside. "Perhaps not so many young chaps as last year."

"No, not so many," said the general at his side, and got on with his soup.

"It would be a shame if the younger chaps lost interest."

"I'm sure that's not the case." The general knew what the case was. Fifty thousand British casualties in the autumn offensive at Loos, that's what the case was. Loos was an idiot place to pick a fight, nothing but a tangle of coalfields; and the fighting had grown more ferocious as it became more pointless. Bad for the men, worse for the officers – the young officers – because they were in front, leading. So that was where a lot of Old Etonians came to a sticky end, at Loos, and at lesser scraps called Neuve Chapelle, Festubert, Aubers Ridge, he couldn't remember them all. No ground had been gained anywhere. or none worth having; but a tremendous number of Germans had been killed and that was what mattered. The general could not tell his lordship this it was not done to talk shop on these occasions But he wished the man would use his imagination. Where the devil did he think the younger chaps had gone? To the cinema? To see Charlie Chaplin?

Trafford opened his menu. "I see we are to have Hungarian *crêpes*. Sounds rather jolly. doesn't it? Hungary . . . I'm afraid I've forgotten whose side the Hungarians are on."

"Austria," the general told him. "But that's a technicality. The Hungarians are on the side of the Hungarians. a very loyal people, they don't mind who they betray."

Trafford smiled. "Neither do I," he said. "as long as they make good *crêpes*." They gazed out at the brilliant gathering, at the snowy tablecloths, at the ranks of heavy cutlery and the parade of crystal. all buffed to a fine shine. at the Spode crockery, specially made for the occasion and bearing the college arms, at the constant flow of waiters and wine-waiters: the best of everything, either human or material, all caught in the glow of a hanging garden of chandeliers; and all enhanced by a gentle thunder of conversation. the heart-warming noise of male fellowship.

"Yes, quite a decent turn-out," Trafford said.

At a distant table, Charlie Essex fingered his soup-plate and squinted at the chandelier. gauging range and height.

"Not yet," Ogilvy said. "We can't eat without light."

"Only six courses to go," James Yeo added.

Foster studied him, and then looked away

"What's up?" Yeo asked.

"Your haircut. It's a trifle too severe. Doesn't suit you, James."

"Rubbish. It suits me fine, because I can't see it."

A bread roll passed overhead at high speed. "Hullo!" Charlie Essex said. "School's out!"

*

The T-shaped table in the mess at Pepriac was less than half-full for dinner. They were served roast pork. "I've got a complaint," said Douglas Goss. "This mutton tastes of pig."

"You must have bitten your tongue," said Jimmy Duncan, one of the gunner-observers. The remark drew some laughter, not because it was all that funny but because Duncan had said it. He was a short, thickset Scot, who usually took so long to say anything that he got interrupted before he finished.

"That reminds me," Milne said. "We're to get another medical officer."

"Last one got rabies," O'Neill told Kellaway. "That was after the adj went and bit him in the arse. Isn't that right, Uncle?"

"Absolutely true," Appleyard said.

"I've been thinking," Milne said. He spooned apple sauce onto his plate. "Now that summer's here we ought to make the most of it. Enjoy ourselves a little. We could invite another squadron to dinner. Maybe even hold a dance, if we could find some girls and some music."

"How about a horse race?" Piggott suggested. "Lots of cavalry hanging about doing nothing."

Milne nodded eagerly. "That's the stuff. I mean, just because there's a war, it doesn't mean we can't make the most of life."

"Concert party," said Appleyard. "Song and dance. Comic turns. Funny hats."

The others discussed the ideas at length, but Milne had no more to say. Paxton, bored by the conversation, glanced at Milne from time to time, and saw that he had stopped eating. One hand propped up his head while the other hand gathered breadcrumbs and made them into a tiny ball. *The fellow's a dreamer*, Paxton thought. *Look at him, he shouldn't be leading a squadron, he's past it, he ought to be pensioned off.* There was a fine tremor in Milne's fingers, a mere shimmer. *What this squadron needs—*

A bit of bread struck Paxton in the face, and made him recoil. "I just asked you," said Piggott, "in English, which is the language we use around here, whether you'd be willing to organise a boxing tournament."

"No." Too brusque; far too brusque. "Not my sport," he added.

"No boxing," Milne said. "I don't like boxing." He took his fist away from his face. Tim Piggott was surprised to see how old he looked. His eyes were pouchy and there were unhappy brackets dragging down the corners of his mouth. The old man looked thirty if he looked a day. "Tell you what I think we ought to do," Milne said. "We ought to get in a tender and drive to the nearest decent *estaminet* and celebrate something. I know: we'll celebrate my birthday." They liked that. It earned some pounding on the table.

"Your birthday's not until October," the adjutant said.

"Oh, Uncle," Milne told him. "What a bore you are."

Of the 'C' Flight pilots at the Fourth of June dinner, only the flight commander, Frank Foster, looked at all like the popular conception of an Old Etonian: tall, slim, dark-haired, handsome if you like the long nose and broad upper lip of the British aristocracy. He managed to appear aloof and languid at the same time. His title – he was the Honourable Frank Foster – was a piece of social baggage he carried around but never used. The adjutant had once suggested that it might buck up the tone of the squadron if he used it, but Foster, gently straightening the adjutant's tie, had said, in a voice as grave as a hanging judge, "Those who know me, don't care, and those who don't know me, don't matter. There now, that's better. You really must learn to look after yourself, Uncle, even if you do spring from humble peasant stock, I mean that's not your fault. Just look at poor Spud Ogilvy here. Born out of wedlock to a pair of Irish charcoal-burners, never wore shoes until he was nineteen, yet he's a credit to the squadron, isn't he? Do up your flies, Spud, there's a good chap. You're not in Connemara now."

In fact Ogilvy's father was Master of the Hunt in Galway and one of the richest barristers in London; but it was true, Spud did look a bit like a gypsy: wavy black hair that flopped forward, high cheekbones, a quick smile that seemed too big for his face. James Yeo, by contrast, had left Eton a shy, somewhat lazy schoolboy and gone through the subaltern-factory to emerge transformed into the classic young English officer, upright and alert and privately very grateful for his luck in being born at exactly the right time to fit into a big war. Soldiering was the perfect life for Yeo; it gave him everything he wanted – comradeship, excitement, purpose – and he was happy to do it for ever. He especially enjoyed the chance to do a lot of flying and win a few medals before peace came and put a damper on the glory.

Charlie Essex saw things differently. It was not true that he had been sent down from Cambridge in his first year because he was no good at sums or spelling; plenty of stupider undergraduates than Essex strolled through their nine terms (and many got a degree). The truth was that he had gone to Cambridge because he wanted to win a boxing Blue. It was Essex's bad luck that there were a lot of good boxers in his weight that year. He lost more contests than he won. Finally he got his nose very thoroughly broken, and he knew he would never be good enough to get a Blue, so he quit. He didn't much care. He'd learned that everything was a matter of luck, anyway.

"That can't be Bunny Bradley, can it?" he asked. "Over in the corner. Scratching his ear."

"Quite impossible," said Yeo, without looking. "Bunny had a stutter, if you remember."

They ate cold poached salmon. Essex considered what Yeo had said. He drank some *Blanc de Blancs* and stopped chewing while he considered it again. "I don't see how that stops him scratching his ear."

"Oh yes. Bunny was at Mons in 1914, eating a beef sandwich, when he said to his sergeant-major, 'Those chaps look like b-b-b-b-b . . .' So the sergeant-major said 'Beg pardon, sir?' and before Bunny could answer, the Boches had shot him."

Essex stared at him. Yeo shrugged. Waiters removed their plates.

"So who's that in the corner, then?" Charlie Essex wondered, frowning. Ogilvy selected a crusty bread roll and threw it, hard. They watched its fall. "D'you mean him?" he asked.

Essex shook his head. "No. Why? D'you know that chap?"

"Never hit him before in my life."

"He looks a bit annoyed. In fact he looks hopping mad."

63

"Probably just concussed. It'll wear off."

Foster stopped a waiter. "Be so kind as to bring us another bottle of this appalling filth," he said. "In fact, bring two."

A bread roll whizzed past Ogilvy, he fended off a second, but the third struck him in the face. He licked some crumbs off his lip. "Not concussed after all," he said. He collected the rolls and hurled them back. Somewhere nearby a dinner-plate shattered. No heads turned. "Bunny would have liked this," Yeo said.

"Hey," Essex said. They all looked. "Wait a minute," he said. They waited. "How do you know," he asked Yeo, "that Bunny was going to say 'Boches', if he got pipped before he could say it?"

Foster pointed with his fork and called, "Look out!" A wine glass came sailing over a chandelier and, amazingly, bounced off their table. Behind the top table, on a platform, the band of the Coldstream Guards struck up *Gilbert the Filbert, the Kernel of the Knuts*. On the far side of the room, waiters dodged as two staff officers began fighting each other with chairs. "Ripping tune, that," Foster said.

Kellaway had been billeted with Paxton and O'Neill. He was lying on his bed, bloated with pork and roast potatoes, listening to Paxton describe the way Ross-Kennedy had crashed, when O'Neill poked his head through the window and interrupted. "The tender's ready," he said. "Get your bonnets on."

"I'm awfully sorry," Kellaway said. "I didn't think I was included."

"Everybody goes on a CO's party. It's like the Sunday School's annual trip to the seaside: good clean fun and all the lemonade you can drink. I can't remember the last time anyone got raped at a CO's party. You won't need your boilerplate drawers, Dexter."

Paxton turned his back on him and said: "I happen to be Orderly Officer."

"So what?"

"The men's letters have to be censored."

O'Neill blew a long, descending raspberry. "Give Corporal Lacey five bob and he'll censor them. That's what everybody else does."

Paxton uttered a high-pitched snort of contempt. "Do they, now? Well, I was taught not to shirk my duties."

"Well, you're a fart."

"And you're a clod."

Kellaway said goodbye and went out. Watching from the corner of his eye, Paxton saw O'Neill leave. "Swine," he whispered; but that was not enough and he looked around for something to kick, saw nothing suitable and so eventually shouted "Clod!" quite loudly.

"I do most honestly and sincerely believe," said Frank Foster, "that after cricket and Salisbury cathedral, England's greatest gift to the world has been roly-poly suet pudding."

"Shut up and eat," Ogilvy said. "We're all waiting."

"My parents got married in Salisbury cathedral," James Yeo said. "Quite pretty inside, so my father said, but a bit cramped. You had to keep your elbows well tucked-in."

"Rather like the trenches," said Essex.

"Finished." Foster spooned up the last fragment. "Ready."

They all raised their plates. "One-two-three-go!" said Ogilvy. The plates were smashed against each other. "Cheese!" Ogilvy shouted to a waiter. The bits of plate they held were tossed over their shoulders, to join a layer of debris that made a constant crunching under the waiters' feet.

"I think it's significant," Foster told them, "that more men get elbowed to death in the trenches than are struck by lightning on Tuesday afternoons in Maidenhead."

"You think too much," said Essex.

"The fruits of a good education."

"I'll drink to that," said Ogilvy. "To the education of good fruits!" They all drank.

Rufus Milne drove the tender, which was unusual, and he drove it at a furious pace, which was surprising. The roads were cobbled and the wheels were shod in solid rubber; traffic was fairly heavy and Milne's right foot danced from accelerator to brake and back again.

It took them fifteen boneshaking minutes to get to a small town called Montvilliers. Milne let the tender trundle around the main square, its headlights washing over a drifting population of troops – a few French, some Australians, but mostly British. Only the occasional French soldier wore red and blue; otherwise khaki was everywhere. Khaki puttees, khaki breeches, khaki tunic, khaki cap. The world was brown. A French civilian, all white moustaches and rusty black clothes, looked wrong, looked foreign. "That's for us," Milne said, and parked outside a bar-café called *Le Trictrac*. "Are we late for something?" Appleyard asked; but Milne was already out of the cab and heading for the bar.

"What's the panic?" Tim Piggott said, rubbing his backside. "He nearly got us up to flying speed, for God's sake "

"Beats me, old boy," the adjutant said. "I've never seen him like this before."

The airmen trailed into the bar The atmosphere was a warm stew of tobacco smoke. wine fumes and noise Milne had found an empty table, and a waitress who looked about twelve years old was bringing him bottles and glasses

"You are a sweet little thing," he said, kissing her hand, "and later on I shall devour you in one bite with an apple in your mouth. Sit down, you sluggards. Have a drink. You're just in time for the cabaret."

"The way you drove, we were nearly in time for eternity," Goss said.

"If it's built to do sixty miles an hour." said Milne, "it's obviously meant to do sixty miles an hour."

Jimmy Duncan was gazing about the room. "I don't see any cabaret," he said.

"Who speaks Russian?" Milne was pouring wine by running the bottle up and down a row of glasses. Nobody answered. "All right, who speaks *any*thing? Cheers."

They all drank. "I've got a bit of Spanish," said an observer called Mayo.

"That'll do. Remember to wave your arms." Milne climbed onto the table and shouted for silence. Eventually the gentle roar of talk faded to nothing. "Gentlemen, tonight we are privileged," he announced. Derision came back like an echo. "We are indeed privileged," he cried, "because here tonight is a member of the Russian royal family, none other than His Highness Prince Boris Romanoff!" Milne led the applause. Mayo reluctantly stood, waved once, and would have sat down if Milne had not seized his shoulder. "Prince Boris would like to say a few words in his native tongue," he said. "I shall translate."

Mayo clambered onto the table. He didn't look like a Russian prince. He was short and stocky, slightly bow-legged, with very wide shoulders and a heavy black moustache. He looked more like a gamekeeper or a ghillie.

"*Buenas noches*," he mumbled. "*El menu, por favor.*"

"His highness says you are the bravest of the brave!" Milne cried. "Everyone in Russia is thrilled by your deeds of tremendous courage. People stop each other in the street to exchange tales of the glorious Gloucesters, the wonderful Warwicks, the invincible Irish Rifles, the incomparable Cameron Highlanders. . ." Men from each regiment cheered at the sound of its name until the combined din made Milne pause. "Together we shall squeeze the Huns from east and west until their eyeballs pop out," Milne told the troops. Huge cheer.

"*Guadalahara*," Mayo announced.

"Prince Boris recommends to you a traditional Russian drinking game known as the Boat Race," Milne said. "Each team has eight drinkers. Kindly pick your team! Prince Boris has generously agreed to buy the drink for everyone."

"*Caramba!*" Mayo said; but in the storm of applause his voice was lost.

The waiters had retired. The King's health had been drunk. The smoke from three hundred cigars rose and mingled and mellowed the light from the chandeliers. Decanters of port slid softly from hand to hand. A great, cathedral hush possessed the room, with only a rare and well-cushioned belch to point up the silence. Lord Trafford, swaying slightly, making an occasional irrelevant gesture but without a note to assist him, was delivering his presidential speech, as tradition required, in Latin. He was reaching the end of his second joke.

"*Omne ignotum pro magnifico*," he said, "*et certe errare est humanum.*" He paused to let that sink in, but only briefly; his main thrust was yet to come. "*Et fortasse virtus incendit vires, sed non licet in bello bis peccare.*"

Everyone saw the point. It was a show-stopper, and Trafford knew he had ample time to sip his wine, while their laughter surged and sank and surged again, until it was crowned with warm applause. Trafford smiled at the friendly blur which, without his glasses and with a mixed litre of wine inside him, was all that he could see. He knew there were three jokes still to come, each one a sure-fire crackerjack.

"Prince Boris will start the Boat Race by dropping his handkerchief," Milne announced. "Are you ready?"

"*Enchilada*," Mayo told him.

"Not you, fathead," Milne muttered. "Them."

Eight teams were lined up: four from infantry regiments, two lots of sappers, one set of gunners, and an entry from Hornet Squadron. Each team had eight men standing on a bench, and each man held a tumbler brimful of red wine. As Mayo raised his handkerchief there came a shout and a crash from the back of the team of the Warwickshire Regiment. "Sorry, sir," their leader said. "We just lost a bloke. No head for heights, see."

"Let me take this opportunity of reminding you all of the rules," Milne said. "No man starts to drink until the man in front has emptied his glass, turned it upside down and put it on his head. Anyone who cheats begins again with a full glass. Puking, or falling off the boat, disqualifies the whole team. Good, I see the Warwicks are at full strength again. . ."

Mayo dropped his handkerchief.

The leaders of each team began drinking, gulping, gasping, sometimes choking and spluttering. The tumblers were deep and the wine was raw. All around, troops roared encouragement, stamping and whistling.

"I say, old boy," the adjutant said. "D'you think this is such a good idea?"

"Piss off, Uncle."

"Half of them are fairly bottled already, you know."

"Yes, I do know. And the other half are going to be completely bottled soon, you watch."

The Warwicks lost to the Gloucesters by a couple of mouthfuls. The Irish Rifles romped home after a young sapper tried too hard and poured a flood of wine up his nose. Two Cameron Highlanders got into a fight while their team was leading the other sappers, fell off the bench and were disqualified. Hornet Squadron came from behind to beat the artillerymen.

"The draw for the semi-finals," Milne declared, "is the Gloucesters against the Irish Rifles and the sappers against the airmen."

"Look here, Rufus," Piggott said, hiccuping painfully, "why don't we call a halt now?"

"What? And let the others down?"

"Thing is, if we win again we'll have to drink again."

"Twice, at least. The finals are best of three. That's how they do it in Russia. Don't they, Boris?"

"You feeling quite all right, Rufus?" Piggott asked.

"Fine. You look bloody awful, but I feel fine."

"I don't care how many nuns got raped in Belgium," James Yeo said. "That speech was the biggest atrocity of this or any war."

"Bags me those chandeliers," Essex said.

"Better hurry," Foster advised. He was lobbing coffee-cups over the next table. Nearby, there was a violent splitting and rending as a group of staff officers began ripping a door from its hinges. A brigadier wandered by and punched Ogilvy in the head. "That's for hitting me with a bread roll," he said amiably, and punched him again. "And that's for missing. Bloody awful markšmanship." He wandered off, dodging a crossfire of crockery and crystal. "Told you he wasn't Bunny Bradley," Foster said. "Not a hint of a stutter." Ogilvy picked himself up. The first chandelier came down like a bomb.

The Gloucesters beat the Irish Rifles, and the airmen beat the sappers.

"They weren't really trying," said Douglas Goss. "Did you see their number seven? He kept spilling a bit so that he had to be topped up again."

"Ask me, they should be disqualified," said O'Neill.

"Can't do that, old boy," the adjutant pointed out. "They've already lost."

"Don't deserve to lose," Mayo said. "Wouldn't be allowed to lose in Russia."

"The Gloucesters are ready," the adjutant said.

Piggott groaned. "They must have guts like firebuckets. Come on, then. Where's Kellaway?"

"Throwing up his guts into a firebucket," O'Neill said.

"Prince Boris will take his place," Milne declared.

"I'll get another firebucket," O'Neill said.

"Russian royal family never throws up," Mayo told him. "In Russia, I have a serf who throws up for me."

The contest had attracted a lot of spectators from the square. In corners, a couple of private fights were going on: sprawling, ineffectual brawls between men too drunk to punch. The adjutant watched it all with the eye of experience. "You know, old man," he said, "at this rate the military police are bound to turn up soon."

"If they care to enter a team, Uncle," Milne said, "we shall be more than willing to entertain the challenge."

One of the gunners performed the starting ceremony. The leader of the Gloucesters' eight was so keen that he choked on his wine, and his team never recovered. Hornet Squadron won the first leg handily.

The night was warm and still. Bats hunted moths by the light of a moon that was as white and pure as a new gas mantle. A trail of translucent cloud lay beside it; otherwise the sky was clear and rich with stars. If you stared at them long enough it was possible to feel the Earth turning. Or maybe that was dizziness helped by a stiff neck. Paxton rubbed his neck, and the universe went back to behaving itself properly.

He was sitting in the pilot's cockpit of an FE2b. It had been a very boring evening for him. After he had censored the men's letters there was nothing left to fill his time. He could have sprawled in a chair in the mess and drunk whisky, but his lunchtime drinking had left him feeling that whisky was overrated, and he was too restless to sprawl for more than ten minutes, so he went for a walk.

Inevitably it led towards the aeroplanes. Some were inside canvas hangars; some were in the open, tied down at the wingtips and the tail in case the wind strengthened in the night. Paxton strolled around one, touching the nose, stroking the wings. The smell excited him: burnt engine oil, the tang of dope, a whiff of petrol, and something new to him, something harsh and peppery that might possibly be cordite.

Nobody was watching; the camp was asleep. And besides, he was Orderly Officer wasn't he? The canvas cover peeled off the cockpit easily and he climbed in. The seat fitted like a snug armchair. His feet found the rudder pedals and his hands closed on the joystick. A slight move, a tiny pressure, and he sensed an answering tension in the control cables. Paxton took a great breath through his nose. The way the plane sat forward on its tricycle undercarriage, nose-down and tail-high, he could easily imagine he was flying. There was nothing to be seen in front but the night, nothing above but the stars. He stared at them for a long time. When he looked down he saw a figure walking on the airfield.

It turned out to be Corporal Lacey. Paxton put his revolver away. "What are you doing out here, corporal?" he asked.

"Picking dandelions. They abound."

"Pretty silly thing to do, isn't it?"

"Perhaps. It depends on your yardstick of silliness. Man took millions of years to emerge from the swamp and now look at him! Armies and armies of soldiers, all squatting in the longest ditch in the world. It's really quite funny. Provided you're not in the ditch, of course." Lacey plucked another dandelion and blew its crown of seeds away.

Paxton was annoyed by Lacey's lack of patriotism but he was also taken aback by his casual reasoning. He said: "You ought to be careful. You're in danger of becoming a pacifist."

"I am a pacifist."

"Are you, indeed?" Paxton felt challenged. It took him a few seconds to remember the correct response. "And what would you do if you saw a German soldier raping your sister?"

"I'd get the brandy bottle. The poor man would need comforting after a dreadful experience like that."

Paxton scoffed. "It's clear you've never seen anyone being raped."

"It's clear you've never seen my sister. Rape is her only hope. She prays each night for a speedy German invasion of

71

Bognor Regis." Lacey smoothed his hair. "Which reminds me: how are you getting on with Mr. O'Neill?"

"The man's an absolute pig."

"Ah." Lacey demolished another dandelion. "I was afraid of that. You see, your difficulty is that you're not Toby Chivers."

"And never will be."

"True. But you're in Toby Chivers' bed and I'm afraid Mr. O'Neill can't accept that. They were terribly close, you see."

"I don't care if they were Siamese twins, he has no right to behave like an Australian pig." Paxton realised that he shouldn't be talking to a corporal like this, but it was too late now. "According to Fidler, the fellow's not even a genuine colonial. Is that right?"

"Yes and no. He was born in Australia, but his family sent him to England to be educated when he was only six. As it was scarcely worth going home for the holidays, he stayed until he was eighteen, and then joined the Army."

"So all his Australian rubbish is just . . . just rubbish."

"A natural reaction against the Anglican piety and cold baths of Lancing College. Not to mention the food, which I'm told was even worse than—"

"Hey! Who's that?" Paxton pointed to a dim, remote figure walking across the airfield. "Stop!" he shouted. The figure immediately ran. He chased it but within twenty paces it had merged into the night.

"Probably only a peasant," Lacey said. "They often do a bit of poaching. Hares and partridge and so on."

"Not while I'm Orderly Officer they don't. Where's the damn Duty NCO?"

"In the guardroom, I expect. Goodnight." Lacey waved a hand in farewell. It was not a salute, but Paxton didn't stay to argue about it.

The Fourth of June had been fully celebrated. There was nothing intact left to celebrate.

Lord Trafford was staying overnight with a cousin who was a general and who occupied a small château outside Amiens. Trafford liked talking and he knew that his cousin alone would be a poor audience, so he invited fifteen o twenty officers to join him for champagne at the château. The quartet from Hornet Squadron went along.

"He was always called 'Sally' Chandler," Trafford said. "Eton had some mighty floggers in my day but Sally Chandler stood out. He had a magnificent arm. He once flogged thirty boys before breakfast. Thirty boys! Just think of it." Trafford beamed. "That was the great thing about Eton in my day. There was none of this modern nonsense about justice, or fair play. Everyone got flogged whether he deserved it or not. And, of course, we *did* deserve it. But I understand all that's changed now."

"Not entirely," Foster began; but Trafford had paused only to refill his glass. "People complain about bullying at schools," he said. "I tell them they don't know what they're talking about. Did you ever hear tell of Miles Pratt? No? *Sic transit*. Pratt was a famous bully of my day. I bear the scars still. Pratt would strap on a pair of spurs, climb onto the back of his fag, and ride him around a room as if it were the Grand National! My thighs were like raw beef. Oh, Pratt was famous. People had far more respect for Miles Pratt than for the Headmaster, wouldn't you say, Rupert?"

"Never knew him," the general said. "He got expelled the year before I started."

"What for?" asked Ogilvy.

"The usual thing," Trafford said. "I suppose that's all changed, too."

"On the contrary," said Foster, "it's part of the entrance examination now."

"When the school captain examined my entrance," Charlie Essex said, "he gave me two lollipops and an orange."

"That's nothing," said a major in the Rifle Brigade. "I got a box of chocolates and a crate of champagne. Is there any more champagne, by the way?"

"I don't suppose there will ever be another flogger like Sally Chandler," Trafford said wistfully. "D'you know, he once flogged a pair of choristers who just happened to be passing his study?"

"Miles Pratt won a VC in the Second Afghan War," said the general. "Posthumous, thank God."

*

As the military police fought their way in through the front door, the adjutant led the airmen out through the kitchen. "Quickly but quietly," he urged. O'Neill carried Kellaway on his back like a sack of coal. "Hurry, hurry," the adjutant said. Goss stumbled and fell. "I think I've broken my ankle, Uncle," he said. "Break what you like," the adjutant told him, "but do it fast." The *patron* was holding the back door open. "*Merci mille fois*," the adjutant said, giving him a handful of money. Then they were all out in the night. The distant crash and shout of battle was cut off as the kitchen door closed. Mayo began wandering off, down the alley that backed the bar. "Not that way!" the adjutant said.

"You can't talk like that to me," Mayo said thickly. "*Moi, je suis* the next Czar of Russia but three and I'll have your bloody head chopped off if—"

Piggott grabbed him and dragged him back. There was a ladder against the alley wall and the adjutant was pushing men up it as fast as he could. Mayo, unable to escape from Piggott, surrendered to him and began to waltz. Soon this struck him as hugely funny, and he stopped waltzing to laugh. "Shut him up!" the adjutant hissed. Piggott punched Mayo in the stomach. The laughter turned to a groan, the groan to a gurgle as Mayo was sick. Spitting and wheezing, he let himself be steered up the ladder.

They were in a churchyard.

"One short," O'Neill said. "Where's the old man?"

"Vanished ten minutes ago," the adjutant told him. "No idea where he's gone."

"Gone berserk, if you ask me," Piggott said.

A deep sigh came from Kellaway. He lay stretched out on the top of a tomb, his arms crossed on his chest.

"He wants to die here," O'Neill explained. "He reckons it's handy for the pub."

"Did we win the boat race?" Jimmy Duncan asked. "I sort of lost count."

"Stand him up," the adjutant said, pointing to Kellaway. As he spoke there came a glow of light in the alley, a rush of boots and oaths and the thud of blows. O'Neill shook Kellaway by the foot. Kellaway rolled over twice and fell off the tomb, crushing something fragile, a vase perhaps. "Follow me," the adjutant muttered. He hurried them through the churchyard, down a muddy track and into a cobbled street. The street led back to the town square. "Rufus can look after himself," the adjutant said. "We're going to take the tender and get out of here, now." But the tender was not where they had left it. "Damn," said the adjutant. "Damn, damn, damn. Also bugger."

They sat on the edge of a fountain in the middle of the square and watched *Le Trictrac* being emptied by the military police. There were several bloody heads and a few men being carried by their friends. The police whacked and kicked indiscriminately to keep the crowd on the run.

"Just like Piccadilly Circus on Boat Race night," said Piggott.

"Did we win?" Jimmy Duncan asked. "I lost count."

"He must have gone somewhere," the adjutant said. "Who else would have taken it?"

O'Neill said: "Big question is, where's he gone?"

"I'll ask a policeman," Mayo said, and made off. "I say, constable!" he shouted. Piggott chased him and dragged him back. "Sit down and shut up," he said.

Mayo shook himself free. "Russian policemen finest in the world," he said loftily. "Russian police know all the answers." He found himself looking at Jimmy Duncan. "What's the question?" he asked.

"Did we win?" said Duncan. "I lost count."

For a long while, nobody spoke. Kellaway was asleep, propped up against O'Neill. Appleyard was wondering how long they should wait. Goss was rubbing the ankle he said he had broken. The others were staring at the moon, or combing their hair, or just standing with their hands in their pockets, rattling their small change. A mule trotted into the square. By now the troops had gone. *Le Trictrac* was shuttered and dark. The mule stopped and looked around. It heard the tinkle of falling water, walked to the fountain, eyed the airmen and found them unthreatening, and began to drink.

"That's a mule," Duncan said.

The animal flapped its ears. Water dripped from its nose. A clatter of hooves made it look over its shoulder. Another mule cantered into the square.

"There's another," Duncan asked.

"How many does that make?" Piggott asked.

"Two."

"You're not as stupid as you look, Jimmy."

"Wrong," O'Neill said. "It makes four." Two more mules had arrived. He pointed, and the gesture disturbed Kellaway, who toppled backwards into the fountain. The first mule tossed its head and backed away. "And six makes ten," O'Neill said. "And ten makes twenty. After that it's bloody ridiculous."

Kellaway stood up in the fountain. His eyes were open but he was seeing double. He was utterly bewildered. He had no idea where he was or how he got there. Everywhere he looked he saw moonlit mules: double images of moonlit mules, dozens and dozens of them, all running, but the more they ran the more there were of them until the square was crammed with mules. It was a nightmare. He dropped to his hands and knees and shut his eyes and crawled away from it.

"I don't like the look of this," the adjutant said to Piggott. They were standing on the fountain wall, for safety. It was not a big square and mules were still pouring in. "There's got to be a reason for this sort of nonsense."

"Here he comes," said Piggott.

Rufus Milne cantered into the square on a mule with reins and a halter but no saddle. He saw the airmen and forced his way towards them. "Hullo, you lot!" he cried. "Where on earth have you been?"

The square was dense with braying and stamping. Still more mules were arriving. Faintly, from a corner, the whistles of the military police could be heard. "What's the game, Rufus?" Piggott shouted.

"These are all mine," Milne announced. "Aren't they jolly? This one's called Alice. She's a wise old bird. Aren't you, Alice?"

"Mules are neuter," said Goss, "and yours looks stupid."

"Does she really? Trick of the light, I expect. The sergeant said she has the brains of an archbishop."

"What sergeant?" the adjutant asked.

"Chap I met in the *Trictrac*. Awfully nice fellow. I said to him, you look a bit fed-up, and he said so would you look fed-up if you had to look after five hundred bloody mules, so I said that's an awful lot of bloody mules, and he said you bet it's an awful lot of bloody mules, and to cut a long story short we went to see them and he swapped them for the tender."

"He must have been drunk."

"Soused as a herring."

"We need the tender," Piggott said, "to get home."

"Take a mule. Take any mule." Milne waved at the moonlit mass of animals. "Shop around. Find one that fits. Take two, and give the other to your mother."

"I'll go and get the tender," Piggott said to the adjutant.

"You'll have to run," Milne said. "He told me he was going to drive to Paris."

Mayo gave a little scream of pain. "That beast *bit* me!" he said.

"He's got a girlfriend in Paris, you see."

"Bugger the girlfriend," the adjutant said bleakly.

"Very unlikely," Milne said. "Not according to what he told me."

Lord Trafford fell asleep, in mid-sentence, in an armchair. His cousin Rupert, the general, played poker with the hard core of the Old Etonians, including the four from Hornet Squadron. After an hour or so they stopped to eat sandwiches of beef tongue and chicken.

"Has it ever occurred to you," said the general, "that this would be a much better war if all the Russians were in France, and we and the French were in Russia? Our men rot in trenches until they get blown to glory. Any bloody fool can do that. The Russian army is perfectly qualified for trench warfare. They've got an endless supply of bloody fools. But there's no trench warfare to speak of on the Eastern Front. It's all war-of-movement. Professional fighting. That's what we're good at. *We* should be *there*, having the time of our lives in the wide open spaces. *They* should be *here*, doing what they're good at, which is dying for Holy Mother Russia. This is a very badly arranged war."

"What about Salonika and Gallipoli?" someone asked.

"Not a funny joke," the general said. "Your deal."

*

Kellaway kept falling off his mule.

He was unused to wine. His father kept a bottle of sherry in the house and it always lasted a year. The pungent *ordinaire* of *Le Trictrac* had gone down Kellaway's throat like water. The faster he drank it, the less he noticed its coarse taste. His speed amused other people, and they kept refilling his glass. He was flattered by their attention, so he kept entertaining them. He was, inevitably, sick; but once his stomach was empty he found it easier still to pour more wine into it. He had been standing, singing, when the room lurched. He had tried to grab a table. The table had turned into two tables. He missed them both. His legs were as slack as string. The roaring noise faded like a big wave receding. He collapsed and knew nothing of it.

Now, every time he fell off his mule he banged and bruised his arms and shoulders, which made it all the harder for him to remount and cling to the animal's skimpy mane. "Grip him with your knees, for God's sake," the adjutant kept telling him. "Use your thighs, man. That's what they're for." Kellaway did his best, but from time to time his mind wandered off and left him; and then everyone had to stop again until Kellaway had been found and picked up.

Only Milne remained cheerful. "This is wonderful exercise," he said. "The night, and the countryside, and the fresh air – it brings you closer to nature. Don't you agree, Tim?"

"As long as it brings me closer to my bed I'll agree to anything," Piggott said.

Mayo said: "Keep your bloody mule away from me, Douglas. The brute keeps trying to bite me in the leg."

"I'm nowhere near you, damn it," Goss snapped.

"Well, who's *that*, then?" Mayo kicked at the mule alongside.

"You do that again and I personally will bite you in the arse," O'Neill said.

"Jesus . . ." Piggott tried to ease his aching backside. "At this rate it'll be dawn before we get home, and I'm flying after breakfast."

"Are you absolutely sure this is the right road, Rufus?" the adjutant asked.

"Well, it may not be the quickest route," Milne said, "but it's by far the prettiest." A bank of cloud slid over the moon. Now there were two sorts of blackness to look at: earth and sky. Kellaway swayed and tried to make his knees do something other than tremble. Despair filled him like a fever. He had joined the RFC quite willing to die, but not like this. This was not just rotten, it was endlessly rotten.

The cloud thickened. A wind came in from the west, ruffling the poplars that lined the road, and a light rain drifted over the plodding mules. The night and the journey seemed endless, shapeless, hopeless. Kellaway slept, and awoke feeling utterly lost. "Here we are, home again," said Milne.

The adjutant grunted. He recognised the Pepriac crossroads. Now for a hot toddy and bed, a great deal of both.

"*Halt!*" The challenge was so loud that the leading mules checked. "*Who goes there?*"

Milne peered at the figure standing in the entrance to the aerodrome, and saw the dull gleam of a bayonet. "Good heavens," he said. "Friend, of course. Several friends, in fact."

"*Advance, friend, and be recognised.*" The order was crisp.

Milne got off his mule. He could see a roll of barbed wire in front of the sentry, blocking the entrance. "I'm Major Milne, commanding officer," he said. "Who are you?"

"Corporal Lee, sir. I shall have to ask you for the password, sir."

"Password? What password?"

There was a pause. "That's for you to tell me, sir."

"Look here . . ." Milne walked forward and Lee operated the bolt of his rifle. Milne stopped. "You wouldn't actually fire that thing, would you, Lee?"

"Not unless I have to, sir."

"Sensible fellow."

Behind him, Tim Piggott lost patience and dismounted. "Look, this is bloody ridiculous," he barked, striding towards the sentry. "We're all—"

The bang made everyone jump, and the puff of flame from Lee's rifle was imprinted on their vision. He had fired high. Now they heard him re-load. "Jesus Christ," Piggott breathed.

They went back to the others. "Does anybody know anything about a password?" Milne asked. At first nobody spoke. Then Kellaway, sitting in the middle of the road, swallowed something that he should have spat out. "Shit," he muttered.

"That's not it," O'Neill said.

"I remember brigade gave out passwords," Milne said, "in case we got shot down in No-Man's-Land, or something. Trouble is, the password gets changed every day. But I think they were names of flowers."

"Geraniums," Goss called to Lee. No response. "Roses Tulips. Daisies, marigolds, daffodils, pinks, carnations, dahlias, winter-flowering jasmine." Lee was silent.

"Jasmine isn't a flower," Jimmy Duncan said.

"Yes, it is."

"No, no. Jasmine's a bush."

"Balls! It's a flower, ask anyone. Ask Lee. Corporal Lee, is jasmine a flower or a bush?"

It had begun to rain again. Lee's voice came out of the wet, black night: "I couldn't say, sir."

"Well, you're a fat lot of good."

"But I can tell you one thing, sir. It's not the password." Lee sounded as if he might possibly be enjoying himself.

"This is absurd," Milne said. "Who put you here?"

"Orderly Officer, sir. Mr. Paxton."

"Bloody Paxton," the adjutant said in a voice like rust.

"Go and get him," Milne ordered.

"Not possible, sir. Not allowed to leave my post, sir. Court-martial offence, sir. Could be shot, sir."

"Forget all that. I'm CO and I'm giving you fresh orders."

"That's as may be, sir. But you still haven't given me the password, sir, so how can I take your orders? You lot could be anyone, sir. You could be the Boches."

"All right, just suppose we *were* the Boches. What would you do about it?"

"I'd telephone Mr. Paxton, sir."

"Then for God's sake go and telephone the silly bugger before we all drown."

In fact Lee had to telephone the duty NCO, who had to go and wake Paxton. "Why tell me?" Paxton said. "I'm not

Orderly Officer any more. That was yesterday. You do as you like. Goodnight."

The duty NCO, cursing, bicycled out to the gate and took over from Corporal Lee. "Very sorry about all this, sir," he said to Milne across the wire. "Mr. Paxton said—"

"Forget Mr. Paxton," Milne said. "I'll strangle Mr. Paxton at breakfast. Just shift this wire." But the ends of the coil had become tangled in the fence and were unwilling to be released in the darkness. Goss got his hands scratched and gave up. The rain suddenly intensified. Mayo was proposing that they get some rope and use the mules to drag the wire away when headlights appeared. A large staff car arrived, turned towards the entrance and stopped.

The rear window was opened a few inches. Foster said: "Are these your mules? Awfully Biblical. Jolly wet, too."

"Was it a good dinner?" Milne asked.

"Dull. But we had some good poker afterwards. I won this car. Until tomorrow, anyway, then it goes back. How was your evening?"

"Oh . . . quite amusing, until we got home and found this wire everywhere."

"Nasty stuff, wire. Bad for the skin."

In the glare of the headlights the wire was soon unhooked and dragged clear. "Most kind," Foster said, as he was driven through. "That will be all, thank you."

Chapter 5

Dawn came too soon. Breakfast came too soon. Drymouthed brainthrobbing foultasting hangovers came too soon. Batmen with cups of hot, sweet, undrinkable tea came too soon. And of course the weather was unspeakably bad: nothing but sunshine wherever you looked. The treacherous rain belt had passed over in the night. 'C' Flight's morning escort duties would not be cancelled.

Frank Foster was 'C' Flight commander. Shuffling to the mess in carpet slippers and dressing gown he stopped when he saw Paxton in shorts and singlet and gym shoes. Paxton was running backwards. "I say!" Foster called. Paxton came to a halt but kept working his legs and arms. "What the hell are you doing?" Foster asked.

"My daily run. It tones up the system."

"Must you do it here? It's unsightly. You've got the whole damn aerodrome to run around."

"I've just done that. I like to do the last two hundred yards backwards, just for fun. It gives the muscles something extra to think about."

"I'm sure they find it hugely amusing," Foster said. "Don't let me hold up the show." They parted.

Collins had fresh black coffee ready for Foster in the mess. Nobody else had arrived yet. "I trust you had an enjoyable evening, sir," he said.

"A sombre affair, Collins. Sombre and sober. Heavy with pomp and circumstance." Foster took a cube of sugar and dropped it and missed his cup by two inches. "Keep still, damn you," he said to it.

"I thought it was going to be a proper beano, sir." Collins put the sugar in the coffee and stirred it. "Sounds more like a wake."

"George the Third's birthday. Very important date."

"German gentleman, wasn't he, sir?" Collins forked grilled bacon onto a plate. "Hanoverian, I believe. Also not too right in the head. A bit barmy."

"Are you sure that stuff's dead?" Foster touched the end of a strip of bacon with the point of his knife. "I thought I saw it move."

"Funny chap to have a party for," Collins said. "A barmy Jerry. Still, it's none of my business, sir."

Foster picked up his cup, using both hands, but did not drink. After a while his eyes closed. The cup slowly tilted and began to spill coffee in a steady stream. "God, I feel dreadful," he muttered. Collins placed a napkin to soak up the spillage. He removed the bacon and put it back in its hot dish.

Mayo wandered in. He wore slacks, and a white sweater over his pyjama top, and his hair was not brushed. "Bloody awful wine," he grumbled. "Bloody awful taste. It's given me a bloody awful head."

Foster did not open his eyes. He rested his forehead on his cup. Collins poured coffee and handed it to Mayo, who was pressing and prodding his stomach in a cautious, exploratory way. "It's not right," Mayo said to himself.

"Gus," Foster said. "Is that you bawling and shouting?"

"Bloody awful coffee," Mayo said.

"It *is* you. Can't you put a sock in it? I'm trying to die."

"Lucky you." Mayo sipped again, and winced.

"As a matter of fact I put a pair of socks in it when I made it, sir," Collins said, "but if you think it's not strong enough I could easily—"

"No." Foster opened one eye and looked at Collins through the handle of the cup. "No jokes," he added.

Mayo reversed a chair and straddled it, with his chin on the top. "Dunno how you feel, but there's only one way to describe how I feel," he said.

"Who locked everyone out last night?"

"I feel bloody awful, that's how. Paxton."

"Paxton." Foster thought about that. "He runs backwards, you know."

"Bloody well thinks backwards, too."

Five minutes later Paxton came in. He was fully dressed and his hair was wetly slicked back. "Good morning," he said. "I'll have some of everything except porridge," he told Collins.

"Why did you shut us out last night?" Foster asked.

Paxton polished a knife with his napkin. "I took what I considered to be the necessary precautions."

"Then you went to bed." Foster threw a lump of sugar at him and missed.

"It was nothing to do with me, after midnight." Paxton tapped his wristwatch, to avoid any misunderstanding. "At midnight I ceased to be Orderly Officer."

"Ceased to have any brains, too," Mayo said. "How were we supposed to get in?"

"Password." Paxton filled his mouth with bacon.

"You're a bloody fool," Foster told him.

"I second that," Mayo said. "Put to the vote, passed nem con."

Paxton kept his eyes on his plate and got on with his breakfast. He had expected criticism. He found it stimulating.

Douglas Goss came in. "I knew you were a damn fool," he said to Paxton. "What I didn't realise is what a raving idiot you were. See this?" His right hand was heavily bandaged. "Your bloody barbed wire did that. I shall probably die of lockjaw. Glass of milk," he told Collins. "I've got a head like a bass drum in a circus."

"I was guarding the aerodrome," Paxton said.

"Why? Aerodrome's no damn good without the squadron . . . Christ, this isn't really milk, is it, Collins?"

"Yes, sir."

"Tastes terrible."

"So would you, sir, if you'd passed through a cow."

Spud Ogilvy and James Yeo arrived together. "What's all this about mules, Douglas?" Yeo asked. "I say, you do look dreadful. Is it booze, or have you caught trench foot in the face?"

Foster grunted and rested his head on the table.

"What makes you two so bloody chirpy?" Mayo demanded, but Yeo was sitting at the table and was building a house out of toast.

"He's still half-cut," Ogilvy explained. "Don't squeeze him or he'll squirt champagne from both ears and his belly button. I've seen him do it."

"For God's sake shut up," Mayo snarled. "I had enough bloody silly jokes played on me last night by this clown." Without looking at Paxton he gestured at him. His hand was trembling from a mixture of anger and hangover.

"It wasn't a joke," Paxton said. "It was a measure of security. Excuse me." He reached across the table and removed a wall from Yeo's house of toast, which collapsed.

Yeo looked at the ruins. "Only a true Hun would do a thing like that," he said.

During the exchange Tim Piggott and Frank O'Neill had come in and were helping themselves to breakfast. "I have the feeling that the various bits of my body are tied together with old rubber bands," Piggott said, "so I'm going to make this very, very simple. You ordered the sentries and the barbed wire?"

Paxton said, "Yes, but—"

"And then you went to bed?"

"Yes, but you see—"

"The act of a true fart."

"And a Hun," Yeo said.

For a while there was silence apart from the sounds of breakfast, and occasionally of a stomach complaining as the wrong sort of food fell into an angry gut. Paxton had finished eating and wanted to leave but he didn't know how to do it. So he sat up straight and looked between people, or over their heads. A vicious little truth was beginning to take shape in a corner of his mind. That truth was that maybe he had got it wrong last night. He knew he wasn't a fool or a fart, but it was beginning to seem just possible that he had, for once, acted in a way that some people might quite well regard as the behaviour of a fool or a fart. Paxton pressed his knees together and chewed his upper lip. Surely to God breakfast must be over soon?

Charlie Essex strolled in, wearing flying goggles. "Will this damned heat wave never end?" he said to nobody in particular. He took off the goggles and peered about him. No one moved, no one spoke. "This must be purgatory," he said. "It's too lively for limbo." He took a seat at the table. Collins brought him coffee. He put his goggles on again and examined the coffee. Steam coated the goggles. "Just a spot of cumulus," he said. "We'll soon climb through it."

Paxton had enjoyed eating his breakfast. Now his stomach clenched the food grimly. Before he could suppress it, indigestion rumbled like a delivery of coal.

"Oh, I wouldn't go that far," Yeo said to him.

An orderly tapped on the door, looked inside, saw Collins. Collins went to him, then crossed to Paxton and murmured: "Major Milne's compliments, sir, and could he see you in his office." Everyone heard. There were grunts of satisfaction. O'Neill slid the mustard across the table. "Take it, you'll need it," he said. "The old man's going to eat you alive."

On the way to his billet to get his Sam Browne, Paxton passed Jimmy Duncan, who was walking carefully, as if the ground were icy. Even so, he stumbled. "Did we win?" he asked, and the words stumbled too. "We did win, didn't we?" When Paxton said nothing, Duncan looked up. "Oh, it's you." He snuffled wetly and unpleasantly. "What a bloody fool you are, to be sure," he said.

The sight of a mule eating the commanding officer's breakfast made up Paxton's mind for him.

He was convinced now that Hornet Squadron was a joke, and a poor joke at that. He marched up to Milne's desk and saluted. "I request an immediate transfer, sir," he said. That wasn't what he had meant to say; in fact he hadn't meant to say anything; but when the words came out they sounded exactly right. The sooner he escaped from this fifth-rate comic opera, the better.

But Milne appeared not to have heard. His desk was close to an open window, where the mule was looking in. Milne had swung his chair around and was feeding the mule from a breakfast tray. "That business last night," he said, sounding as mild as ever, and paused while the animal licked half a slice of toast from his palm. "All a jolly jape, wasn't it?"

Paxton didn't know what to say. Agreeing or disagreeing seemed equally dangerous. For a moment he was flustered. Then he counter-attacked. "If you say so, sir," he said. *That's rather clever*, he thought. *Rather adroit*. On the strength of it he stood at ease.

Milne dipped a strip of bacon into an egg yolk and offered it to the mule. Paxton could see now that Milne had a bottle in his lap. He leaned sideways to get a better view. Actually the bottle was tucked into Milne's trousers. It was full of gin. Or, if not gin, something just as clear. One hand was curled around the bottle, while the other fed the mule. *Extraordinary*, Paxton thought. *And what a shocking example to set the men. No wonder there's no esprit-de-corps here.*

"This is Alice," Milne said. He might have been running donkey rides on Margate sands. "Hasn't she got beautiful eyes?"

"No, sir."

"Shall I tell you what I think? I think you thought that nobody was taking you seriously."

"If you say so, sir." It didn't work so well the second time. For no reason, Paxton suddenly suspected that his flies were unbuttoned. He dared not look down.

"The truth is," said Milne, buttering toast for Alice, "that nobody *was* taking you seriously, and quite right too, because you're a joke, Dexter."

"Everything is a joke here, sir." He linked his hands in front of his flies. "I didn't come to France to play cricket. Or swim. I came to fight for my king and country." Under cover of looking modest he glanced down. All was well, which encouraged him to add: "And I'm Paxton. Dexter's still dead."

"You're quite right: everything *is* a joke here." Milne got bored with feeding Alice and dumped the entire breakfast tray, coffee and milk and all, out of the window. "This whole war is a joke . . . Ah, I've offended you . . . Paxton. There, you see? I got it right." Milne curled himself in his chair and cuddled his bottle.

Paxton sniffed. "You're entitled to your point of view, sir. One of my cousins died of wounds last year, which wasn't very funny."

"Tall, was he?"

"Six foot two."

"I thought so. All the tall ones go first. Their heads stick up over the tops of the trenches. If this war does nothing else it'll reduce the average height of the average man to five foot three. In fact the only visible result of this war so far has been to shrink the infantry by blowing the heads off the tall ones and standing the others in several feet of water. And that, you must admit, is a small triumph for science." Milne smiled amiably and scratched his head with the stem of a pipe.

Paxton didn't believe a word, but hearing it from his squadron commander made him feel uncomfortable, like listening to the vicar poke fun at the Church of England. "I'm prepared to take my chance," he muttered. "Just give me a chance to fight."

"Ah, yes. Fighting. What exactly did they tell you about air fighting, back in dear old England?"

Paxton cleared his throat. "Enough, sir," he lied; but since Milne wasn't serious, what difference did it make?

"Tell me some." Alice, the mule, brayed. "She gets jealous," Milne explained. "Pay no attention."

Paxton remembered the ceremony when pilots had been awarded their wings. A one-armed general with hard, unblinking eyes and deep vertical lines in his face as if split by the sun, had told them he envied them. They were the new cavalry of the clouds, and superbly well mounted too.

"War's a bit like a game of rugger," Paxton said. "It's no good hesitating because the other fellow looks bigger than you. You must rush in and tackle your man. That's the only way to get the ball." The general's voice had become quite husky when he'd got to that point.

"God Almighty!" Milne said. "What a load of suicidal bollocks!" He stood up, tossed his pipe into a bowl and banged the bottle on the desk as if he wanted to smash it. Paxton took a pace back. "Suicidal bollocks!" Milne shouted.

"What difference does it make?" Paxton shouted back. "I can't die if I never fly, and you won't let me—"

"You want to fly? Go ahead and fly." Milne was seized by impatience. "Go now. Do what you like." He kicked the desk.

"You said there are no machines."

"Take the bloody silly Quirk that whatshisname brought."
Fury was growing in Milne, twisting his face, corroding his
voice. "Go on! Do what the sodding hell you like!" He kicked
the desk again, savagely, hurting himself and making the
bottle topple and roll. Paxton grabbed it before it fell off the
edge. It was hot. The bottle was hot. He stood it upright,
stared at it, stared at Milne. "Who cares?" Milne said. Fury
had turned to defeat. Paxton got out.

Paxton ran all the way to the hangars, to tell the mechanics
to get the Quirk ready. *So the old man's potty*, he thought
as he ran. *Who cares as long as I can fly?* The sergeant on
duty was doubtful. "Don't know about *immediately*, sir," he
said.

"CO's orders," Paxton said, between gasps.

"Ah. She'll be ready for take-off in half an hour, sir."

He ran back to his billet. As he passed the mess, Tim
Piggott poked his head out of a window and shouted. Paxton
changed direction and cantered over. "Where's the fire?"
Piggott demanded. Paxton explained. "And when were you
going to tell me about all this?" Piggott asked. "Me being your
flight commander."

"Ah."

"You're a prize tit, Paxton. Who are you flying with?"

"Um . . ."

"You're a double prize tit. Last night you were a prick,
today you're a double prize tit. What next? Are you going to
whistle Tipperary while you fart Rule Britannia?"

"No, sir."

"No. And you're not going to fly alone, either. Get Kellaway. And get a Lewis gun put on that plane." Paxton's face
brightened. Piggott scowled. "And don't use it!" he barked.
"Stay within ten miles of here and keep out of trouble!" The
window slammed shut.

All over the camp, the new day was gathering pace.

In the Orderly Room, with some early Mahler on the
gramophone, Corporal Lacey was checking the morning
mail. A small, square box for Lieutenant Ogilvy: chocolates

from his fiancée. Larger package for Captain Foster: his shirts and silk underwear back from the St. James Express Laundry in London. A small but heavy packet for Lieutenant Duncan: probably more books on salmon fishing. Duncan read nothing else. A couple of cases of medical supplies. Saturday's newspapers, of course – Lacey glanced at a headline: *Great Naval Battle. British Fight Against Odds* – and the padre's *Illustrated London News*. Letters for half the squadron, and a package shaped like a cigar box for Lieutenant Paxton. Lacey sniffed it, and neatly unsealed one end. It was cigars. He put them aside, and sat back while Mahler finished the first movement. "Bravo," he said. Then he released the rest of the mail for distribution.

The adjutant's dreams made sleep intolerable and yet he resented having to wake up. It was the usual pattern, and familiarity made it no less unpleasant.

He sat on the side of his bed and tried not to swallow. He knew that if he swallowed he would regret it. The last fading impression of his dream drifted about him like mist: the more he focused on it the less he saw. It was about India, of course. Whenever he had a bad dream it was always set in India and everything was always grey and dingy and hot. He was always trying to get somewhere in a hurry and failing because there were too many people in the way, and his failure always grew worse and worse until it woke him up.

He took out his medicine bottle. He took one long swig and whacked in the cork. That killed off his dream. What a bloody day. He pulled out the cork and took another swig. *Be warned*, he told the new day. *You be bloody to me and I'll be bloody to you.*

Kellaway didn't want to wake up. When Paxton shook him, he moaned; and as Paxton shook him more and more vigorously his moaning wavered and broke, until at last his eyes opened. "Get up!" Paxton said. "We're flying in ten minutes."

Kellaway's body had been drained of strength and filled instead with a dull, wearying ache. When he tried to speak his throat hurt and he couldn't swallow. The furnace glare of sunlight became unendurable. He rolled over to escape it, and fell out of bed.

"Oh, for God's sake," Paxton said. He was disgusted, not so much at Kellaway's behaviour as at the fact that he was fully dressed. His uniform was stained with dirt and vomit. There was grass in his hair and dung on his shoes. His nose was cut, half his upper lip was swollen, and all that side of his face was scratched and bruised.

"Fidler!" Paxton shouted. "Fidler!" He kept on shouting until the batman arrived, on the run. "Get black coffee and run a bath for Mr. Kellaway," Paxton ordered

"Looks like he needs a doctor, sir."

"Have we got a doctor?"

"No, sir."

"Then don't be a prize tit."

"Yes, sir." Fidler hurried out. By the time Paxton had got Kellaway's clothes off, Fidler was back with a jug of coffee. They sat Kellaway on the bed. Fidler held a tin mug to his lips, but Kellaway seemed to have no control over his mouth, and the coffee ran down his neck and chest and dripped onto his thighs. With his shoulders slumped and his arms dangling he looked very young. A feeble belch made his head twitch. "What's that disgusting smell?" Paxton asked.

"Well, it could be *vin ordinaire*, sir," Fidler said, "or it could be mule's piss. Hard to tell the difference, sir."

"Oh, shut up. Help me get him in the bath."

They draped a dressing gown around Kellaway and walked him to the bathhouse. On the way they passed O'Neill. He said, "Constipation, it's a terrible curse."

"Kellaway's not constipated, for heaven's sake," Paxton said.

"I didn't mean him. Have you tried prunes?"

"Lout."

The bath was nearly half-full. Fidler turned off the taps. Paxton said, "Go on, get in." Kellaway blinked at him. His eyes went out of focus, and slowly the lids came down. "God in heaven!" Paxton said. He removed the dressing gown. Kellaway was trembling. A cut in his upper lip had reopened and blood was trickling down his chin. His eyes remained closed.

They picked him up and put him in the bath. "I didn't tell you to run a *cold* bath, you fool," Paxton said. "This is scarcely tepid."

"Best I could do, sir. Boiler's probably run out of coal."

Kellaway's eyes had opened. He was still trembling, making a confusion of ripples, but otherwise he did nothing. "Get on with it, man," Paxton said. "We haven't got all blasted day." But Kellaway just lay there, his small white body looking flat and continually crumpled by the ripples. Paxton lost patience. He cupped his hands and threw water into Kellaway's face and onto his head. "If that blasted Quirk is ready before you are," he said, still splashing hard, "I'll kill you." Kellaway's bottom lost its grip and his head slid below the surface. It was a big bath and his toes were nowhere near the other end. Bubbles and bits of grass and a smear of blood came floating up. "What the deuce?" Paxton said.

"He can't hear you, sir," Fidler said.

Together they hauled Kellaway, spluttering, into a sitting position, Paxton getting soaked to the elbows in the process. "Look here," he said, "I'll hold the silly ass and you wash him."

Fidler sucked his teeth and screwed up his face so that one eye was shut. "Don't know about that, sir," he said. "He's not my officer, properly speaking. Mind you, supposing . . ."

Paxton waited. "Supposing what?"

"I was just thinking, sir, any problem can be solved with a bit of what you might call . . . give-and-take."

"Take the soap," Paxton said, "and give him a scrub."

Fidler sniffed. "You realise what I'm doing is above and beyond the call of duty, sir."

Even when Kellaway had been washed and vigorously towelled, he was still more asleep than awake. "He's no blasted good like this," Paxton said bitterly as they walked him back to the billet. "He'll fall out of the cockpit. What else can we do? There must be something else we can do. How about brandy?"

"Just as likely to put him to sleep altogether, sir."

O'Neill was about to leave as they brought Kellaway in. "No luck?" he said. He strolled over, adjusting the silk scarf inside his shirt collar, and studied Kellaway's limp body.

"Well, no wonder he won't start," O'Neill said. "You forgot to pull the choke out." He gave Kellaway's shrunken penis a sharp yank, and walked away.

Kellaway gasped. His eyes bulged and his limbs jerked as if they were on strings. "I say!" he breathed. "Play the game!"

Paxton was first astonished, then encouraged. "Did you see that?" he said to Fidler.

"Yes sir, and don't ask me, because you gentlemen can get away with it but any private soldier touches an officer's private parts gets himself court-martialled."

Kellaway, meanwhile, had shuffled off to his bed and was sitting down, hands guarding himself against further attack. "Not bloody fair," he whispered.

Paxton looked at his watch, and looked at the huddled figure. Kellaway licked blood from his lip. Fidler said, as if to himself: "It might work, if . . ."

"What might work?"

Fidler was looking the other way. "Needs a bit of what you might call give-and-take, sir." He shook his head. "That's what it needs. Yes."

Paxton gave him ten francs. Fidler went out. Within two minutes he was back with a medical assistant who was carrying a bottle of *sal volatile* and a small cylinder of oxygen connected to a facemask.

The *sal volatile* put Kellaway back on his feet, coughing and cursing. Several lungfuls of oxygen restored his strength, if not his health. His eyes were red, but so were his cheeks. The medic took his pulse. "Hammering away like a machine-gun, sir," he said.

It took Kellaway ten minutes to get dressed, with occasional pauses for a whiff of oxygen. Paxton paced up and down and looked at his watch. 'C' Flight took off; he went to the window and watched them climb eastward. Kellaway brushed his hair. "Never mind that," Paxton said. "Come on, we're late. Get a move on."

But the night had changed Kellaway. It remained in his memory largely as a blur of noise and colour and misery, but he knew he had experienced astonishing heights and depths: people had been cheering him and giving him endless drinks, and other people had been cursing him and picking him out of stinking puddles in total blackness. He was nineteen, and he had survived a CO's party, which was more than Paxton could say. Kellaway wasn't afraid of Paxton any more. "I'm hungry," he said.

Paxton shouted. Kellaway put his hat on and went to the mess, where he ate a bacon-and-egg sandwich that tasted metallic, so he poured lots of Daddies Sauce on it. Paxton stood with his arms crossed, and watched. His fingers clenched and unclenched. He counted every mouthful. At length he said: "I can't tell you how unspeakably filthy you looked this morning."

"Then don't," Kellaway said. He drank a second cup of tea.

"I wouldn't drink too much of that if I were you," Paxton said.

"Then don't."

Paxton's eyes widened. His heartbeat made a sudden rush. "Don't let the war hurry you," he said harshly, and wished he hadn't.

"I won't," Kellaway said, and he didn't.

They said nothing as they went to the pilots' hut and put on their flying kit: fleecelined, thigh-length boots, sweater, scarves and double-breasted, high-collared sheepskin coat. Gently sweating, they lumbered across the field to the aeroplane. Paxton went straight over to the fitter and rigger, who were standing by the engine, and so he failed to see Piggott, sitting on the grass beyond the tailplane. "Who's driving today?" Piggott called out.

"I am, sir," Kellaway said. Paxton turned and gaped.

"Then listen to me." Piggott got up. "No stunts. No low flying. Don't bully the engine, it won't thank you for it, and don't go faster than seventy. If you can't see Pepriac, you've gone too far. Learn the landmarks. Stay out of trouble. Don't even *think* about doing anything heroic. See you at lunch. Goodbye." He walked away.

"You little swine," Paxton said. He tried to duck under the wing, and banged his head on the leading edge. "This is *my* show. The CO gave this flight to *me*." But Kellaway was already climbing into the rear cockpit. "Hard cheese," he said. "I've just taken it back. Get in, I'm ready to take off."

"It's a rotten swindle." Tears of pain and frustration blurred Paxton's eyesight. "You watch, I'll get you for this."

"Can't hear you," Kellaway announced, as he fastened the strap of his helmet.

Chapter 6

Milne dropped a pile of papers into a sack held by one of the Orderly Room clerks. "I should have done this months ago," he said. "It's all nonsense, you know." He dumped the contents of a desk drawer. "All bally nonsense, every bit of it."

"Beg pardon, sir," the clerk said. "Wasn't that your cheque book just went in?" He fished it out.

"My stars, so it was. What big eyes you've got, grandma." He stuffed the cheque book into a tunic pocket. "Time for a little rest." A young lime tree grew outside his office. As the breeze shook its leaves, a constant flicker of shadow and sunlight chased itself across Milne's desk. "What does that remind you of?" he asked, pointing.

The clerk cocked his head. "A sideboard?" he said. Milne wasn't listening. "It reminds me of the way you get a run of fast water in a river, and then it gradually smooths out," he said. "This is June, isn't it? Best month for trout on some rivers."

"Don't know, sir." The clerk gave the sack a shake.

"I always got sick in a boat, never got sick in a river," Milne said. "The ripples used to look just like that. Alive. And I'll tell you something else . . ." His telephone rang. "Can you get this bloody instrument in your bag?" he asked.

"No, sir."

"I was afraid not. Oh well. Go and burn that lot."

He picked up the phone. "Mary, Queen of Scots," he said. "You have an appointment?"

"She's dead," said a voice he knew. "Try again."

"Dead, is she? Where did she cop it?"

"Shut up, Rufus. This is serious."

"So is war. War is hell. Ask Colonel Bliss. He knows."

"This *is* Colonel Bliss. Listen—"

"What a coincidence, I was talking to him just a moment ago and—"

"Shut *up*, Rufus. I mean it, this is really serious."

Milne sighed. "Hang on, Bob." He found his hot bottle and wedged it in the top of his trousers. "You were more fun when you had a squadron. Go on, fire away."

"That was your mob that ran amok in Montvilliers last night, wasn't it?"

"Dunno. I was miles away, playing whist with the vicar's wife."

"What matters is the Corps Commander's told me to kick your arse till your balls ring like a bell-buoy in a gale. His words, not mine."

"I'm innocent," Milne said. "Nice turn of phrase, though."

"You were seen, Rufus, by dozens of people. Those bloody mules caused absolute havoc. The Assistant Provost-Marshal's raising hell. The sergeant you got the mules from went and crashed your tender right through a shop window. Killed himself."

Milne was briefly silent. Then he said: "And he swore to me he'd been a crack racing driver. The man's a fraud. Don't believe a word he says."

"I'm coming over. Now." Bliss hung up.

Milne took the telephone and stretched out on the floor. He suddenly felt utterly weary, washed-out, drained. He telephoned the cookhouse. "I'm going to have rather a large party for lunch," he said sleepily. The sergeant cook asked how many. "Hundred. Hundred and fifty." What should they prepare? "Everything. Cook everything." Milne said. Then he called the hangars and told them to warm up his aeroplane. Then he fell asleep.

The sight of a buzzard, circling a hundred feet to their left and fifty feet above them, startled Paxton out of his boredom. He shouted and pointed. The rush of air pressed his arm back as the buzzard was quickly left behind. He sat down. Excitement over.

They had been flying for fifty minutes. Kellaway had climbed to fifteen hundred feet and cruised around Pepriac at a safe sixty miles an hour. The morning had been golden and clear at the start but now clouds of all sizes were beginning to tumble out of the west, and the BE2c occasionally shook or even bounced. Each time, of course, it steadied itself without any help from him. It was very comforting.

For Paxton it was very tedious. He had forgotten to bring a map, so the landmarks meant little. Besides, the countryside was dull and he'd seen it all before. Lots of troops in lots of camps, tens of thousands of them, and all about as interesting as ants. Even the river Somme wasn't worth a second glance: not big, and in no hurry to get anywhere.

Paxton played with his Lewis gun instead.

It was longer and heavier than he'd expected. It had a cocking handle on the end shaped like a shooting-stick, a drum of .303 cartridges on top and a pistol grip below. The barrel was a good two feet long and encased in a cylinder. In the middle of the gun, at its balancing point, was a socket that fitted onto a metal prong attached to the rim of the observer's cockpit. There were several of these mountings, and Paxton practised shifting the Lewis gun from one to another, firing at an imaginary foe, then shifting again. It was cramped and awkward. He stopped for a rest and noticed that his final aim had been dangerously close to the propeller disc. He swung the gun further out. Now his aim crossed a bracing wire that ran from nose to wing. He avoided the bracing wire and found himself looking at the exhaust pipe, which rose vertically until it cleared the upper wing.

After more experimenting he came to the conclusion that it was virtually impossible to fire forwards without hitting something. Firing sideways or downwards or upwards, you had to avoid the wings or the wing struts. You could fire backwards quite safely provided you took care not to shoot off your own tail, but that involved kneeling on your seat and aiming above your pilot's head. And what if the enemy pilot failed to place himself where you could hit him? What then?

Paxton looked around, and wondered who had put the gunner inside this birdcage of struts and wires and why he had thought it was such a bright idea. That was when he noticed the buzzard. He shouted and pointed, but Kellaway didn't seem to notice. What dull company Kellaway was. On impulse, Paxton fired a short burst over the top of the tail. That made him jump!

Kellaway gestured. "We nearly got bounced by a buzzard." Paxton bawled. "Or maybe an Albatros." He grinned. Kellaway didn't hear or understand, but then, Kellaway was an idiot.

The telephone awoke Milne. He felt as if he had slept for hours but it was only ten minutes. Sergeant Widgery told him his aeroplane was warmed-up.

The mule Alice followed him as he walked to the hangars. "I wish I'd learned to swim," he told the beast. "I wish I'd done lots of things. Wish I'd taken a chorus-girl to a champagne supper. Taken lots of girls to lots of suppers. Wish I'd seen the Pyramids." He returned a salute. "You ever seen the Pyramids, Jennings?" he asked, not pausing.

"No, sir."

"Shame, isn't it? Maybe I'll learn to swim today, though."

His FE was ticking over, the wash from the propeller making the tailplane flutter. A mechanic stood by each wingtip, to help steer when he taxied out. The legs of the undercarriage stretched slightly as Widgery jumped down from the cockpit. The mule, disliking the noise, hung back. "No kit, sir?" Widgery said. "It'll be chilly up there."

"I'm only going for a stroll. Want to come? Just for balance. You won't have to shoot anyone down. You can take a pot at a pheasant, if you see one."

They took off. Milne levelled out at three hundred feet. Two miles away he found a cavalry regiment in camp and he landed in the next field. The officers' mess welcomed him. "Come to lunch, all of you," he said. "We're celebrating." Jolly decent of you, they said. What's up? "Don't know yet," he said. "I haven't decided. Who else is around here? I want cheerful chaps, like you." Well, they said, the Artists' Rifles were just up the road. A laugh a minute, they were. Widgery swung the propeller and scrambled aboard, and they took off

*

99

Kellaway had never flown through cloud, and on this morning he didn't feel brave enough to start. The stuff seemed far too crisp and dense. When he looked to the west it was like being in a small boat on a stormy sea: whitecaps everywhere. He decided to get well above it and worry about getting down later.

It worked. There was clear air above twenty-five hundred feet, a colossal amount of it in fact, reaching upwards and outwards for miles and miles to a sky that was so big and so blue it made his head swim if he tried to see it all. The sun was more than he could take: even with goggles on, his eyes watered when he looked eastward.

Which made map-reading quite hard. He ducked his head into the cockpit and blinked while he worked out where he was. Thus he was in a crouched position when the BE2c flew into a patch of turbulent air and dropped into a hole fifty feet deep.

The metallic taste of bacon and egg rushed up his throat He forced it back. The aeroplane rocked and slithered as it bounced into and out of a series of air pockets. His breakfast surged and surged again, backed now by a tide of sweet tea laced with Daddies Sauce. Kellaway got his head outside the cockpit and was horribly sick. Each new air pocket pumped a little more from his stomach until the plane flew into calm air and he was drained and spent and useless.

Paxton glimpsed some of this, and enjoyed it. A couple of minutes later he heard a fist being banged on the outside of the fuselage and turned to see Kellaway reaching forward with a scrap of paper

The message read: *Compass bust. Which way Pepriac?*

Paxton did not hesitate. He pointed towards the Trenches. Kellaway looked uneasily to left and right, and did not change course. Paxton gestured more strenuously. Kellaway turned the aeroplane and flew to the east. Paxton settled down, out of the draught, and ate some chocolate to show his stomach who was boss. He reckoned that in four or five minutes Kellaway would start getting worried again and look for holes in the cloud. By then, they should get a good view of the Front.

Kellaway's trust lasted only three minutes. It was more

than enough. Ever since they got above the cloud, a brisk wind had been shoving them eastward. When Kellaway went down to find a landmark he emerged above the German trenches.

Paxton was delighted. He leaped from side to side of his cockpit, shaking the plane with his eagerness to enjoy this magnificent view of modern war. Trenches, endless zigzag lines of trenches, a vast pattern of black lines rimmed with white chalk in green fields splattered with shell-holes, all repeating itself into the distance. *Like tapestry,* Paxton thought. *No, more like a colossal snakeskin, one of those snakes with a pattern down their backs, only this was a mile wide and hundreds of miles long. Spiffing! If only I had a camera. Or a bomb!*

Kellaway was too shocked and startled to know what to do for the best. Those must be the Lines down there. But whose Lines? He tried to work it out. If he was flying south they would be the British Lines, so he should turn right for Pepriac. But if he was flying north they had to be the German Lines and turning right would be the worst thing to do. Meanwhile he wandered northward, just below the cloud base, as clear as a fly on a ceiling. It took the German anti-aircraft batteries fifteen seconds to find him, estimate his height, fuse the shells, load, aim and fire.

Out of nothing, as cleverly as the act of a music-hall magician, a string of black woolly balls appeared to the left of the BE2c. Instantly, they started to fade and unravel. Kellaway heard the *woof-woof* and said aloud: "That's archie." But it took him a couple of seconds to realise that it was archie aimed *at him*, and then he banked smartly away from it and drove up into the cloud, shutting his eyes at the moment of impact, opening them again when nothing bad happened. Damp gloom streamed past. Abruptly he popped into dazzling sunlight. The plane was shaking; the joystick flickered in his gloved hand. Too many revs! He throttled back, but still everything shook. What was broken? Kellaway held his breath to listen for the sound of damage and heard his heart stampeding. The plane wasn't shaking. He was.

The sun, by great good luck, was behind them so he knew they were going home, more or less. And the compass seemed to have mended itself. He steered west, skimming along a hundred feet above the cloud, which didn't scare him now and which was a handy refuge in time of trouble.

Paxton was pleased with himself: he had seen the fighting, he had heard shots fired in anger. He played some more with his Lewis gun, shifting it from one candlestick mounting to another and shutting his left eye while he swung the sights onto an imagined Fokker or Albatros storming in to attack. Thus he failed to see a very real Albatros biplane steadily overhauling them in a long flat dive.

Kellaway did not feel well. His stomach suffered spasms as if it wanted to throw up some more. His legs and feet trembled, his head throbbed, and from time to time his eyes went out of focus. He thought perhaps he had caught influenza. All he wanted was to go home and go to bed for ever and ever. A large bump of cloud came towards him and he slammed straight through it. "See if I care," he said feebly, and immediately regretted it because the plane started making breaking-up noises.

Paxton heard them too: crackings and bangings. Holes appeared in the wings; then more holes, and flying splinters and strips of fabric. He stood up to get a better view, leaning into the rush of air, and from the corner of his eye saw a flicker of tiny flame and with it heard the whizz of bullets and sat down with a wallop that broke the seat. The Lewis gun, miraculously, was on the right mounting. The enemy machine was above and to the right of their tail, not much of a target, just a purple silhouette. Paxton cocked and fired. The gun made a wonderful high-speed battering sound so he kept on firing, hugging the Lewis so as to share its power. At last he paused, and looked for his victim. Not there. Nowhere. Yes: on the left now, and curling in for another attack. Paxton yanked the Lewis off its pin just as Kellaway came out of his state of shock and thrust the Quirk into as steep a dive as possible. Paxton stumbled. His finger was still on the trigger and he put a dozen rounds through the upper wing. Then he was on the floor, tangled in his straps, hearing the whipcrack of bullets all around. Then the cloud rushed up and saved them.

Kellaway loved this cloud. He wanted to live in it for the

rest of his life, or at least for an hour. As the dank greyness raced past he knew that he would soon fall out of the bottom, so he hauled back on the stick. Too much. Now he was climbing. Or was he? It felt like climbing. It might still be diving. He couldn't read the speed in this gloom. He might stall and spin. The engine sounded under strain. He might pop out of the top and get shot to blazes. *Oh God*, Kellaway prayed, *Oh God, what should I do?* No answer came. He did a little of everything: middled the stick, opened the throttle, worked the rudder pedals once each way for luck. It worked. Or maybe it made no difference, maybe he was doing the right thing in the first place; anyway the cloud was still doing its merciful job half a minute later. And when at last the BE2c slid out of the bottom, crabwise, right wing down, the Albatros was not behind it. The Albatros was half a mile in front and coming towards them, zigzagging through a field of white puffballs: British archie.

Kellaway saw none of this. He had his head down and he was trying to make sense of his restless compass. Paxton saw it, saw black Maltese crosses on the wings, guessed that the German was heading for home. He shouted: "There's our Hun! There's our blasted Hun!" The words were blown away and when Kellaway looked up, all he saw was delight on Paxton's face, and his outflung arm. It must point towards home, to Pepriac. Now Kellaway knew he was going to live, and the day seemed golden. In fact as he turned onto Paxton's course it *was* golden: sunlight had broken through the clouds! Kellaway felt saved. When Paxton pointed left, he steered left. Paxton waved downwards; he pushed the plane into a gentle dive. Paxton spiked the Lewis gun onto a forward mounting and changed the drum. Kellaway looked where the gun was pointing and shut his eyes.

The Albatros was apparently laying its own carpet of white archie, fresh puffballs always appearing ahead, old ones dying behind. Paxton, aiming out and down, fired a long burst as the paths of the two planes crossed until he lost it beneath the BE2c. By the time he had dismounted the Lewis and slung it across the cockpit the Albatros was on fire and nearly out of range. He blasted off more shots. Its tail broke off and blew away. Kellaway got a glimpse of the pilot, seemingly unhurt, throwing up his hands in rage or despair. The archie was everywhere, endlessly grunting. The Albatros fell, nose down, as if desperate to escape. A wing peeled back, clung to the side of the fuselage, snapped its roots, fluttered free. The guns stopped.

"I thought it was like driving a car," said a captain in the Gordon Highlanders. "I thought you had a sort of a steering-wheel and when you wanted to go fast you put your foot down."

"No, no," Piggott said. "Completely different."

Five officers of the Gordon Highlanders had been the first guests to arrive for Milne's party; and as Milne himself hadn't returned, Piggott was looking after them. They peered into the aeroplanes, touched them and sniffed them with a mixture of amazement and amusement. Piggott hid his feelings, but he was not amused. "You've seen an aeroplane before?" he said.

"Oh, to be sure. But not one like this."

"Perhaps if you thought of it as a boat. There is the rudder, on the tail. Here is the propeller, which drives it forward. The propeller's in the middle of the machine because that gives the observer a clear field of fire at the enemy in front."

They walked to the front and looked at the nose. "What if a Jerry sneaks up behind you?" one of them asked.

"Then he's a cad," Piggott said, "and we never speak to him again." While they were laughing he excused himself to go and welcome fresh arrivals. The Gordon Highlanders agreed that all RFC pilots were mad. "You'd need to be an imbecile to go up in that thing," the captain said. "It hasn't even got any brakes."

Milne landed at last, carrying a side of smoked salmon he had bought from a lieutenant in the Border Regiment who had just been sent two and who wasn't all that keen on salmon anyway. He gave it to the sergeant cook. "Thank you, sir," he said. "I hope I done right. I sent off two drivers to get all the food and drink they could find. I couldn't feed a hundred guests on what was in stores, sir."

"Of course you couldn't. Did they find anything?"

"Lots of stuff, sir. Cost a packet, too."

"If we get through this day alive," Milne said, tossing his hat in the air, "I'll put you up for a medal."

Somebody had strung up some bunting and the flags of the Allies. Every table and chair had been brought out. Two bars had been set up. Seventy guests had arrived and another staff car rolled in every five or ten minutes. Milne, strolling about and making small-talk, was impressed by his own achievement: all these regiments, all these different uniforms, all those cooks carving cold ham and tongue and roast chicken, and batmen opening bottles of wine – it was like a garden party. Even the sun had come out. Everyone smiled. He'd borrowed a ten-piece band from the 8th Devons (camped only a few miles away) and they were playing a selection of hits from the London shows, jolly tunes like *When you wore a tulip* and *Alexander's Ragtime Band*. Just like a garden party. No girls, of course. Pity about that. He stopped at a group of the Green Howards who were laughing at something Douglas Goss had told them. He said: "Pity we haven't got any girls. Sorry about that."

They were slightly embarrassed, and said nothing. What was there to say? Some smiled politely, some shrugged, some drank.

"I've got a girl," Goss said, "but she's in Norfolk."

"I can beat that," said a Green Howards captain. "I've got a wife in Brighton."

"You can see Brighton from here," Milne said, "on a clear day." They looked at him, doubtful, afraid of further embarrassment. "At eight or nine thousand feet, that is. And no cloud."

"Of course," said the captain. "No cloud."

"Can I get you a drink, sir?" Goss asked.

"I suppose you miss each other rather a lot," Milne said.

"Oh well. You know how it is. One gets plenty of letters, but—"

"I knew a very pretty girl once," Milne said. "Not in Brighton, though." To Goss's horror, a tear was leaking from Milne's right eye. Goss looked around for a drinks-waiter and saw the adjutant approaching instead. "This is our adj," he said. "Anything goes wrong, it's his fault, isn't it, Uncle?"

"Could I have a word, sir?" Appleyard said.

"The salmon is excellent," Milne told them. "I caught it myself." He moved away, walking backwards. "And after lunch we'll all have a great big game of cricket," he announced. "With two balls, to speed things up." To the adjutant he said: "See to it, would you?"

"Yes, of course." Appleyard scribbled *cricket* on his clipboard. "Bloody good bunfight, this. Brilliant idea, old boy. Absolutely brilliant. Caused us some problems, mind you."

"Just feel that sun." Milne tilted his head back and enjoyed the warmth on his face.

"End of the month, you see, Rufus. The mess account was pretty low. Couldn't pay for all this stuff, not even half of it."

"That's the trouble with stuff. It costs money. I tell you, Uncle, the first man to invent free stuff will make a fortune."

"I'm sure he will. The thing is, Rufus, I had to make up the difference out of my own pocket."

"How much?" Milne was watching a bird, high, balanced against the wind.

Appleyard took out a sheet of paper and studied it as he spoke. "The fact of the matter is, Rufus, I've been lending my own money to half the squadron . . . I mean, no names no pack drill but some of these young chaps just don't seem to be able to manage their affairs . . . It's all down here if you want to . . . Anyway, the point is, this little party of yours has burst the bank with rather a loud bang, and yours truly could do with a spot of—"

"Bend over, Uncle." Appleyard stooped and Milne rested his cheque book on his back, signed a cheque and gave it to him. "Now for God's sake stop waffling."

"But this is a blank cheque. I can't take this."

"Then throw it away." He left Appleyard flapping the cheque to dry the ink and looking not unhappy, and walked past the band – now playing the *Londonderry Air* – to an open-top Bentley. A colonel and a captain were sitting in the back seats.

"Hullo, Bob," Milne said. "I invited a few friends. Didn't want you to feel lonely."

Bliss looked at the crowd, now well over a hundred, at the band, the hurrying waiters. "The Corps Commander thinks you've blown a gasket," he said. "You're overdue for it, God knows. You've been flying for nearly two years, you've had this squadron for a year, it's high time you went round the bend."

"He doesn't think I'm good enough. Is that it? Time I got pensioned off." Scarlet patched Milne's face as anger rose in him. "Bastard!" He kicked the car. "Bloody bastard!"

"You can't break it," Bliss said. "It's a Bentley."

"I don't care if it's a babbling brook." Milne kicked it again, but already his anger was subsiding. "Damn, damn, damn. I'm sorry, Bob. This is . . . this is all wrong. Completely cockeyed."

Bliss took off his cap, smoothed his hair, replaced his cap. Milne licked his fingers and tried to rub out a scratch on the car. In the distance, the band was playing a polka.

"I don't understand any of that," Bliss said, "but I don't suppose it matters. The remarkably patient chap sitting in the car is Captain Dando, your new medical officer. Corps Commander's asked him to take a close look between your ears and report what, if anything, he finds."

Milne and Dando exchanged nods.

"And now," Bliss said, "I'll go and get myself a drink, because I'm sure you will want to attend to that rather wobbly aeroplane of yours."

Milne turned to see where Bliss was looking. The plane was a BE2c. It was coming in to land and its approach was very uncertain, full of swerves and dips. The playing of the band had drowned its engine, but now the band stopped and they all heard the blips and spurts and crackles. A red flare soared from the plane, creating the brief illusion that it was hanging from a string. "Hell's bloody bells," Milne said wearily. An ambulance came by and he chased it and jumped on the running-board.

Chapter 7

It was a heavy landing. Kellaway, worried about his revs, chose the wrong moment to look at the gauge and he crashed his head against the instrument panel. Left to itself, the plane ran to a halt in the middle of the field. 'C' Flight circled overhead and watched the ambulance pull up alongside it. Kellaway was unconscious. A small cut on his forehead had released enough blood to cover his face but the real problem was his right foot, which was jammed behind a rudder pedal. By the time the medics had slit open his flying boot and heaved him clear, Bliss and Dando had arrived with a crowd of guests, and Paxton was telling Milne what had happened.

"This Hun came at us from behind, sir," he said. "Hard to tell what it was. Probably a Fokker. Not an *Eindecker*, definitely a biplane." The crowd pressed closer. Paxton paid them no attention, but at the same time he made his account sound matter-of-fact, almost casual, as if this sort of thing were quite routine. The ambulance left with Kellaway. "He began potting at us. I got a few good shots at him, although Kellaway was chucking the grid all over the sky. We shook him off in the clouds and next thing I knew . . ." Paxton took off his helmet and goggles. Oil stains gave his face a grim, piratical look. ". . . he came at us again, this time from the side, which wasn't very clever of him because I gave him half a drum, and he whizzed underneath us and came out the other side on fire." Paxton demonstrated this move with his hands. "I gave him a few more, down he went and . . . well,

Bob's your uncle. Thank you, sir." He accepted a bottle of wine from Colonel Bliss and took a long swig. The guests applauded, and he waved the bottle.

"D'you know where this Hun crashed?" Milne asked.

"Oh, yes." Paxton thought about it. "More or less."

"Go and find the wreck. Get the guns and the crosses."

"Take my car," Bliss said. "I'll be here for a while."

"Of course you will, Bob," Milne said. "We're all going to play rugger after lunch." They began to walk back. "You played rugby for England, didn't you?"

"No."

"Oh, bad luck." They walked in silence as far as the camp. "Look, help yourselves to everything and have a good time," Milne said. "You don't need me, do you? I'm feeling a tiny bit tired. I might have a bit of a lie-down." Without waiting for an answer he headed for his room.

Bliss turned and watched the last of 'C' Flight make its landing and taxi past the Quirk towards the hangars. "What do you think?" he asked Dando.

"I think he's as well as can be expected."

"Do you? I think he's absolutely bloody miserable."

"Yes. Well, it adds up to much the same thing."

The red flare, the bad landing and the ambulance took some of the edge off the guests' cheerfulness. News of the kill put it all back on, especially when they learned that the ambulance hadn't really been needed – the pilot just got a bit of a knock on the head, soon woke up, no lasting damage. Paxton's back was slapped many times on his way to Colonel Bliss's car. As he was driven away, all he could see was a blur of smiling faces and waving arms.

'C' Flight got changed and cleaned-up and went to discover what the party was all about.

The padre was no help. "I was about to ask you," he said. They got drinks and wandered through the crowd and came across Gus Mayo. "I can tell you what it's *not* about," he said. "It's not about the latest news. Seen the papers? The Navy's had a fight at last. Big scrap in the North Sea."

"Did we win?" Ogilvy asked.

"Hard to say."

"Then we lost," Foster said. "Sailors always find it hard to say they didn't win. It's a speech defect they've got. I knew a captain who went down with his battleship, and his last words were: Don't be deceived by appearances – this is in fact a glorious victory, glug-glug-glug."

"Anyway, who cares what we're supposed to be celebrating?" Mayo said. "The fact is the old man's thrown a party and Paxton's got himself a Hun, so I'll drink to that."

"Balls," Essex said. "The archie got it."

"Really? Paxton didn't say anything about archie."

"We watched the whole damn thing," Foster told him. "God knows what an Albatros was doing so low over our guns, he must have been insane, but they plastered him thoroughly and in the end they nailed him. I saw it happen."

"Maybe they *both* got him," Mayo suggested.

"If Paxton was the gunner in that Quirk," Ogilvy said, "he missed every time. By a country mile. He might have hit France, but I wouldn't bet on it."

"Ah," Mayo said. "Well, now. Fancy that." He looked from their unsmiling faces to the laughter and enjoyment all around. "Let's not spoil everybody's fun with anything as awkward as the truth," he said.

They stood and drank, and watched the party. "Hey," James Yeo said, and they waited. "This sailor friend of yours who went down with his ship," Yeo said. "How d'you know what his last words were?"

"He sent a message in a bottle," Foster said. "Juggins."

Milne came out of his quarters, yawning and scratching, and saw Colonel Bliss sitting in a deckchair. "Bob, my dear chap, please forgive me," he said. "Shocking manners. You've been waiting for hours and hours."

"Twenty minutes. Are you awake?" Milne nodded, and he clapped his hands. The mule, Alice, stopped grazing and ambled over. "Then listen to me," Bliss said. "What am I going to tell my boss? He's worried. You don't send in half your returns, for a start. I know paperwork's a bore, and I know you all had a rough time a few months ago, but that's over now."

Milne patted Alice's neck. The mule sniffed his pockets,

searching. "Oh what a greedy girl you are," he murmured. All the time he was looking at Bliss, studying him. "You're turning grey at the edges, Bob," he said. "You're twenty-four and you're an old man."

"Twenty-five. Now look: if you pull yourself together you're in line for promotion and probably another decoration. If you don't, you'll get the sack."

"You leave me no choice, Bob." Milne swung himself onto Alice's back. "I shall fly home to England for tea and crumpets, and after that . . ." He dug in his heels, and the mule cantered away. "Tell your boss," he shouted, "that it will all be over by Christmas! That's official!"

Milne wandered on muleback amongst his guests, hatless, his tunic unbuttoned, ignoring anyone who spoke. He was looking for the officers from the Green Howards. He found them, and said to the one who was married: "Look here, I'm going to Brighton, now. Would you like to come? We'll be back by six o'clock." Everyone agreed that it was illegal and irresistible. Ten minutes later they took off. Bliss watched the FE2b fly north. "Suit yourself, Rufus," he said. "It's your funeral."

Paxton made himself walk across the field. He wanted to run, but it would be impolite to leave behind the gunnery-lieutenant who had guided him for the last mile. Also, running in flying gear might look inelegant.

The wreck had been roped off. It was guarded by a lance-corporal.

"Good Lord," Paxton said. "They must have hit the ground a fearful wallop." There was not much to see: a fire-blackened hole, with the tattered and shattered remains of the outer wings of the Albatros scattered around it. He picked up a bit of wood and poked about in the hole.

"That's the engine down there, sir," the lance-corporal said. "Petrol tank over here. One of the wheels is—"

"Thank you, thank you." Paxton did not look at the man. "I know all about this particular merchant. We have met before. The guns . . . I don't see the guns."

"We snaffled 'em," the lieutenant said.

Paxton snorted. Indignation pressed hard on his voice and

almost cracked it. "Well you can jolly well de-snaffle 'em!" he said. "Jolly well give 'em back."

"No fear. I told you: this was our bird."

"Bilge. I was nearest, I should know. It's mine."

"Come and fight us for it."

Paxton walked completely around the wreckage. All the German crosses had gone: no point in asking where. "Well," he said. "I think it's a jolly poor look-out, that's all I can say."

"You can have the bodies, sir, if you like," the lance-corporal said. "I suppose."

They lay about twenty yards away, side by side, half hidden in the grass, twisted and shrunken and blackened by the fire. Both faces had gone; only black smears remained. An arm was raised as if to shield the eyes of one body from the sun, but there were no eyes. By some fluke, the right foot of the other man had survived, white and intact. Perhaps the boot came off when the bodies were dragged clear. Paxton tapped the toes. "That's funny," he said. "His foot's the wrong way round. See? It's back-to-front."

"You find that funny, do you?" the lieutenant said.

Paxton wasn't listening. He had noticed a button on what had once been a chest. Perhaps a regimental button. He tried to work it clear with his stick, but succeeded only in making a deep scrape. "Blast," he said. His nostrils twitched, and he sniffed. "I say . . ." He swallowed, and sniffed again. "I say, isn't that . . .?"

"Mustard, or horseradish sauce?" the lieutenant said.

Paxton stared, and then roared with laughter. The lieutenant sighed and looked at the lance-corporal, who had the brains to look at a distant observation balloon.

"I want a picture of this," Paxton said. "There's a camera in the car. You can keep the guns, I'll take these gunners!" He smiled broadly and triumphantly.

The lieutenant said nothing until they reached the car. "I can walk from here," he said. "You fellows really enjoy that sort of thing, don't you? I suppose it's the only way you can do your peculiar job. Thank God I'm just a gunner." He didn't wait for an answer.

Paxton found the camera and walked back to the wreck. The lance-corporal took two pictures of him standing beside the bodies, one smiling, one serious. On the way back to the car he saw something purple lying in a little hollow. It turned out to be the tail unit. He collected the rudder, which had crosses on each side. It rounded off a very successful day.

Milne returned to Pepriac at about six o'clock. A car was waiting for his passenger. All the other guests had long since gone, including Colonel Bliss. Most of the pilots and observers were sitting outside the mess, drinking gin-and-tonics or – if they were due to go on patrol – tonics without gin.

Milne waved to them and went to his quarters. Captain Dando left the drinkers and caught up with him as he was opening the door. "You can come in but you're not going to examine me," Milne said.

"Suits me," Dando said. "I wouldn't find anything new anyway." He was about thirty, small, with a smooth, white face, and a rounded jaw, and neat, strong lips. "How was Brighton?" he asked.

Milne stretched out on his bed. He was still in his flying kit. "I had a damn good cry," he said. "Can you believe that? They were refuelling the plane and I went and sat under a tree. Oak. Enormous. I looked at it and I thought of all the people who've come and gone while that tree was growing, and hey presto – I got the weeps. Sergeant saw me, came over, thought I was drunk. Very embarrassing. For him, I mean. I couldn't give a damn."

"Perfectly natural," Dando said.

Milne turned his head and looked at him. "I expect you're accustomed to this sort of thing."

"It's happened before. I don't think you ever get accustomed to it."

Milne watched him for a long time. Dando rarely blinked. "The funny thing is," Milne said, "I sometimes have a great desire to go and blow a general's head off. One of ours, not theirs. Isn't that strange?"

"Well," Dando said thoughtfully, "it's certainly a sign of life." Milne laughed at that, and Dando joined in. Milne laughed until he exhausted himself. "Oh dear, oh dear," he said. "Dear oh dear oh dear."

"Sorry," Dando murmured. "Not meant as a joke."

"Write it down. Tell Bob Bliss. He thinks I'm a bad boy."

"He's going to have to know the truth soon." Dando took a seat. "I didn't tell him anything yesterday, because our tests aren't always completely accurate and anyway I wanted to see you before—"

"Very kind of you," Milne said harshly. "Just spare me the medical niceties, they're wasted . . . Oh, *bugger*," he barked. "I'm starting to bloody well cry again." He found a handkerchief and spread it over his eyes. "My manners are going to hell, aren't they? I should be ashamed . . . There was nothing wrong with your tests, old chap. They hit the bullseye. I've known for a month it wasn't dyspepsia. Such a rotten coward. Didn't want to do anything."

"There's not a lot that can be done," Dando said.

After a while Milne took the handkerchief away. "What a lovely evening." He got off the bed and went to the window. "I don't think I've ever seen such a marvellous evening. God must be getting good at it. Makes no sense, does it?"

"Nobody ever promised that anything would make sense," Dando remarked gently.

Milne sat on the bed and blew his nose. "I shan't lead the patrol this evening. Tim Piggott can do it. Would you tell him for me?" Dando nodded. He waited to see if Milne had anything more to say. Then he left.

'A' Flight took off about half an hour later. Milne, still sitting on the bed, heard the engines fade to nothing. He went out and found Alice. He rode the mule at a slow walk to the far end of the airfield. There was nothing to do there, so he did nothing.

The sky was slowly gathering its strength for another grand finale of a sunset. Milne had always seen the sky as his workshop: sometimes dirty and full of rubbish, sometimes clean and full of flying. The weather came from the west and the Huns from the east. Now, for the first time, he took delight in its colours and shapes: the clouds were dazzlingly white, the blue was inhumanly pure and deep. With a bit of imagination, the blue became ocean and the clouds were islands that drifted . . .

Alice looked around. The padre was bicycling towards them.

"I saw you out here all alone, old chap," he said. "I wondered if you planned to come and have some dinner."

Milne shook his head.

The padre dismounted. "You know me, Rufus," he said. "A bad ball hit for six beats the best sermon ever preached." He fed Alice a sugar lump. "Nonetheless, when a chap's spirit is troubled . . . Well, there's a trick I've learned that's worth a try." He handed Milne a Bible. "Open it anywhere you like and let your finger fall, and just see what verse you get."

Milne did this. "Numbers, Chapter 21, verse 9," he said. " 'And Moses made a serpent of brass, and put it upon a pole, and it came to pass, that if a serpent had bitten any man, when he beheld the serpent of brass, he lived'." He returned the book, still open.

"Stuff and nonsense," the padre said. "I don't believe it for a moment. Do you?" He studied the page, and grunted. "According to verse 6 the real serpents wouldn't even have *been* there if God hadn't sent them to bite the people. I must confess that there are times when it strikes me that the Almighty throws his weight about a sight too freely." He tore out the page and screwed it up.

"Bad luck," Milne said.

"Worse things happen at sea. Anything I can do for you?"

Milne combed the mule's mane with his fingers, teasing out the tangles and the burrs. He smoothed its ears until the animal had had enough and shook its head. The padre got onto his bicycle and waited. "There is one thing," Milne said. "You could tell them to start up my machine. And tell them to put ballast in the front cockpit."

"Ballast? Ballast." The padre pedalled away. "Ballast, ballast, ballast," he repeated, the words growing fainter each time.

Milne watched the sunset develop The colours became absurdly rich, vast sweeps of lemon yellow and rose and buttermilk and brick red, as if a drunken genius had been turned loose. It deserved a symphony, Milne thought, but what it got was a lone piper leading a company of Scots infantry along the road that flanked the aerodrome. In the distance an engine coughed and died, coughed again and roared. He nudged the mule with his knees.

*

After dinner the adjutant went to bed, hot with fever. "Waste of time, old boy," he had said when Dando offered to examine him. "You don't speak the lingo. This is an old Hindustani curse, this is." The padre and Dando settled down to chess in the anteroom. After five minutes, Paxton came over and looked. "Who's winning?" he asked. No answer. He went for a walk, and was watching some of the men playing football when Corporal Lacey approached. "You have been sent a box of cigars, sir," he said.

"Yes? From my uncle, I expect."

"And you may have noticed that we have no hot water."

"Nothing to do with me. Go and tell the adjutant."

"Mr. Appleyard generates his own heat. What's more he rarely takes a bath. However, with your agreement and your cigars I can get hold of a lorryload of coal this evening, thus guaranteeing hot water for the rest of the month."

Paxton stared. "Sounds very fishy to me. Why don't you just—"

"Why don't we just ask the Army for more coal? Because the squadron's had its ration." Lacey was calm, almost placid. "Why have we run out? Because the adjutant swapped a quarter of the coal ration for thirty cases of wine. Why was that a mistake? Because he forgot to give any wine to the officer commanding the fuel depot. Why should that matter? Because the officer hates his job, and if we tell him we've run out of coal he will enjoy greatly not giving us any more for as long as possible. How long is that? Until our next ration is due."

They watched the football. Someone scored a goal, and performed a handstand to celebrate. "But perhaps you like cold water," Lacey said.

"You want me to give my cigars to this wretched officer at the fuel depot," Paxton said.

"No fear. The sentry at the back gate gets the cigars. He's *reliable*. I wouldn't trust the officer with a bar of chocolate, the man's a scoundrel, an absolute rogue."

Despite himself, Paxton laughed. "Your idea sounds fairly crooked to me."

"In the Army," Lacey said, "the shortest distance between two points is a crooked line."

*

At eight thousand feet it was still as bright as mid-afternoon. The flood of sunlight coming from behind him meant that Milne could see everything to the eastward with astonishing clarity. Only one thing annoyed him: he had forgotten his silk scarf, and now every time he turned his head to search the sky, cold air whipped around his neck. That meant stiffness and aches. It was such a stupid mistake. He knew exactly where he had left the scarf; he could see it now, hanging over the back of a cane chair. Idiot.

Eight thousand feet was as high as this FE2b would climb. If he eased the stick back he immediately sensed the plane flirting with a stall: the engine simply couldn't shove the wings through the thin air fast enough. Even so, eight thousand didn't guarantee safety; plenty of Huns got a lot higher than that. Far to the south a tiny trickle of black archie showed itself. Probably a French patrol going home. Elsewhere, the sky was empty. Millions of men down below, all cramped and crowded and crushed together. Nobody else up here. What a silly war.

The German archie ignored him as he crossed the trenches. Maybe they agreed with him. Maybe they were all too busy eating their sausage and sauerkraut. He hunched his shoulders, trying to keep out that persistent, chilly draught. The pain that was not dyspepsia came out of nowhere and hurt and made him pound a fist on his knee and shout at it: "Shut up, you bloody fool!" It hurt so much that his eyes ran with tears. He took his goggles off and stuck his head in the airstream. For a few seconds he was blind. He pulled his head back and blinked hard. The tears went, and he saw a cluster of dots about two miles ahead and below.

They soon noticed him and turned to intercept. Milne was pleased to see that they were Roland C IIs, a new type of two-seater, big, heavily armed, valuable. There were five of them. They spread apart as the gap closed. No doubt they had all worked out their tactics for cross-fire. It made no difference to Milne. He pushed the throttle wide open. The leading Roland grew and grew until he could see the perforated barrel of the pilot's Spandau on top of the engine. It fired. The FE raced into the wandering line of bullets, soaking up damage, until the Roland veered away. Milne banked hard in the same direction. He kept turning and chasing until the eggshell smoothness of the Roland's fuselage magnified and filled his eyes and the rising drumroll of its engine deafened him. The impact of the collision welded the aeroplanes like mating insects. They fell in one piece for a thousand feet, and blew themselves apart. But by then Milne was feeling no pain.

Chapter 8

"When I was in 23 Squadron," Mayo said, "we had a pilot who could blow smoke through his ears."

"That doesn't make him dotty," Goss said.

"It might have kippered his brains," Jimmy Duncan suggested. "That's the way fish get kippered, you know With smoke."

"Has anybody ever seen the old man blow smoke through his ears?" Goss asked. Nobody had. "So much for that theory," he said.

Most of the squadron was sitting around in the mess anteroom. 'A' Flight's patrol had been uneventful, and nobody had seen the commanding officer's aeroplane. It was now more than two hours since he had taken off.

"I don't know what you're all worrying about," said an observer called Binns. He was teaching himself to be a cartoonist, and he was always sketching the others. "The old man's come down somewhere."

"I knew a chap who made twelve forced landings in a week," Duncan said. "He was always late back."

O'Neill nudged Piggott. "You're very quiet."

Piggott sighed. "I reckon he ran out of fuel ten minutes ago. So he's either crashed or forced-landed or something . ." He stirred his drink with his finger, and sucked it. "I'm wondering whether I should go and tell Frank Foster."

"What for?" Mayo said. "He's asleep."

"He's also senior flight commander. Which makes him acting CO "

That silenced them. Dando, glancing at their faces, caught glimpses of shock and even the foreshadowing of grief. Milne had always led Hornet Squadron. Now, suddenly, they might have to live without him. They felt damaged. The room was completely still.

Paxton came in, and strolled to the middle of the group. "You will be pleased to know," he said happily, "that there will be hot water for all in the morning." His smile was radiant, but when nobody looked at him it steadily burned itself out until there was nothing of it left. "I knew you'd be pleased," he said, peevishly. "I expect you'd like to know how I did it."

"I'd like you to stick your head up your arse," O'Neill said, "and take a close look at your brains."

Paxton glanced at them: sprawling, grubby, pouchy-eyed, defeated-looking. He sniffed, and said loftily: "Three cheers for the red, white and blue . . ." He never knew who picked him up. Someone seized him by the collar and the seat of the pants. His feet scrabbled against the floor as he was rushed to the door. It opened outwards. He was thrown into the night, which turned out to be made of gravel and quite painful. He crawled away and picked the bits out of his hands and face.

It had been a long day, and there would be more patrols tomorrow. One by one the pilots and observers left the mess. Paxton sat on the grass and watched them go. After half an hour he went up the steps and opened the door. "Oh, for Christ's sake," Piggott said. His voice was flat as spilled ink. He and Dando were standing at the bar.

"I just want you to know, sir, that I did not come to France to make friends," Paxton said. His voice was cracked, and he didn't know what to do with his hands so he took a good grip of a chairback. "I came here to fight, sir. I told you this afternoon that I shot down a Hun and you told me to forget it. Well, I can't forget it." Paxton could feel a nerve in his face jumping and tugging. "That was my Hun. My kill. I want it on my score. I'm entitled to it. Otherwise it's . . . it's . . . it's just not fair." He stopped because Piggott was nodding.

He went on nodding, gently, while he looked at Paxton, up and down and up again. "Yes," he said, "I think I can safely say that you are the tallest turd ever to join this squadron. We had a turd who was almost as tall as you, chap called Gallagher, but he died a long time ago, March, April, I can't exactly remember when. I said to Goss, 'Douglas', I said, 'that turd Gallagher won't last a week', and Gallagher went and copped it on his third day, didn't even have time to pay his mess bill. But you, chum, you out-turd Gallagher in all respects, including length, by a good ten per cent. You are the longest, strongest, thickest, heaviest, most stinking turd between the Somme and the sea. Pour me another large disinfectant, Collins," he said, "and one for the doctor, too."

"At least I got a Hun," Paxton muttered stubbornly.

"No. Not a hope. You got bugger-all."

"You weren't there."

"Captain Foster was. All of 'C' Flight was. You didn't notice them. There was a pair of Aviatiks in the sun. You didn't notice them either. They saw you, all right. D'you remember the sun? Big round yellow thing, quite bright?"

Paxton squeezed the chairback and glowered at Piggott's boots.

"Well, do you or don't you?" Piggott barked.

"Yes, I do. Sir."

Piggott grunted. "That's a bloody miracle, because you didn't see those two machines." He sipped his whisky, and grimaced at Collins. "Put more disinfectant in this disinfectant," he said. "Let me tell you why you're still here, stinking up this room. Captain Foster's flight saved your filthy skin twice today. First you got jumped by a wandering Albatros who would have blown you to blazes in ten seconds if one half of 'C' Flight hadn't seen him sneaking up on you and got behind him and made him nervous. The other half went and made sure the Aviatiks didn't interfere. Kellaway ran off and hid in the cloud. So did the Albatros, but he got confused and came out the bottom of it and made a perfect target for our archie."

"And for me," Paxton said.

"You missed. Why d'you think that poor bleeding Hun didn't try to get back up in the cloud?"

No answer. The only sound was a faint squeaking as Collins polished a glass.

"Because 'C' Flight was just above you, that's why. They kept him down, made him run for home, and gave the archie a clear shot. The archie hit him. Captain Foster saw the shell explode. He also saw you open fire when out of range. He says your gunnery was pathetic. He thinks you may have hit some of the men on the ground in the British gun pits. If that's true I'll have you court-martialled and I hope you get shot. Now go away." Piggott turned his back. Paxton, his legs weak and his knees stiff, stumbled on the way out.

O'Neill was squatting on Paxton's bed, cutting his toenails, when Paxton reached the billet. A paring sprang past Paxton's head and made him flinch. He saw O'Neill drag some grime from between his toes and wipe his finger on the blanket. "Poor little Kellaway began bleeding from the ears," O'Neill said, "so he's gone off to the hospital. Looks like the old man's a goner too."

"Kellaway was a tiny turd." Paxton felt almost too full of hate to speak. "The old man was a turd too." Then he noticed that the Albatros rudder was not hanging on the wall above his bed. "Look here!" he said, and pointed at the empty space. "Now look bloody here—"

"These need sharpening." O'Neill tossed the nail-scissors to him. "I gave that bit of Hun rubbish to the sergeants' mess. The colours clashed with the curtains. I wouldn't get a wink of rest with that up there. You ought to—"

"Bastard!" Paxton seized the bed and flung it onto its side. O'Neill hit the floor in a tangle of bedding. Paxton tramped over the heap to get his toilet kit from a shelf, and went out to the officers' bathhouse. He was amazed at his own strength. He brushed his teeth, savagely, until he made the gums bleed. But when he came back, O'Neill still lay wrapped up inside the heap of bedding, breathing slowly and deeply.

Paxton hurried out, found a full firebucket, came back and flung it over the huddled shape, which did not move or speak. He kicked it. His boot found nothing. Empty. O'Neill cleared his throat.

He was sitting on the floor in a corner of the room. "You can sleep in my bed if you like," he said, woodenly. "It smells a bit, but then so do I." Paxton threw the bucket at him, and

122

missed. "No wonder Frank said your gunnery stank," O'Neill said.

Hugh Cleve-Cutler improved his face considerably when he flew into a barn.

He had been born with moderately handsome features but the older he got, the gloomier he looked. Even as a child, his expression naturally fell into a slump. People treated him as if he were worried or grim, which made him *feel* worried or grim. He joined the Army largely because it seemed the right place for a young man with his outlook: stern, dutiful, joyless; then he transferred to the RFC because they seemed to offer a lot of fun, and he hungered for fun.

In May 1915 he was a captain, twenty-five years old, not having a bad time but still glum-looking and subdued and without many friends. He was stationed at Hazebrouck aerodrome. One day, as he was coming in to land, a Morane Scout took off across his path. Cleve-Cutler avoided the collision by banking his BE2a sharply to the right. Banking so steeply robbed the plane of its power to climb. Luckily the barn was elderly, frail and ramshackle, and he was lifted out of the wreckage with nothing worse than a broken leg and a slashed face. Next day he was able to hobble to the funeral of his observer who had broken his neck.

Long before the stitches came out, people began to comment on how chipper Cleve-Cutler looked. He went about with a jaunty smile and a rakish glance that quite took the nurses' minds off their work. He was literally a changed man: the doctors had sewn his face together as the pieces best fit, and now the left corner of his mouth was permanently hitched upwards, while the opposite eyebrow was always cocked. Cleve-Cutler looked a bit of a rogue. People warmed to him.

When his leg had healed he went back to France as a flight commander in a squadron that flew Gun Buses, pusher planes like FE2bs. Morale was poor. The older pilots had seen too many of their friends killed: they flew cautiously, not looking for trouble. Sometimes they didn't fly at all: the medical officer was kept busy treating inexplicable cramps and pains. Cleve-Cutler changed all that.

He called his Flight to a meeting and shut the door.

"I've just had a word with the CO," he said, which was not true, "and if any of you desperately wants a change of scenery, now's the time to say." He gave each of them a fair share of his crooked smile. One man nodded, or perhaps shrugged. "Right," Cleve-Cutler told him, "go and tell your batman to pack, toot sweet."

The man was startled. "Where am I going?" he asked.

"God knows. The trenches, I expect. That's where the rest of the army is. But don't hang around, old chap, because your replacement is going to need your bed tonight. Goodbye." Cleve-Cutler shook hands with him. "You will pay your mess bill, won't you?" The man left, looking dazed.

"I hate giving people the sack, don't you?" Cleve-Cutler said, looking jovial. "Much better this way. If a chap's unhappy . . ."

"I rather think he thought you were talking about compassionate leave," someone said.

Cleve-Cutler roared with laughter. It was a sound his Flight was to hear many times every day. "Compassionate leave! That's a good one." He wiped his eyes. "The CO warned me you were a mad lot of buggers. Which one of you was it who flew through that Jerry railway station while the troop train was unloading?" He roared again. They glanced at each other, half grinning, half guiltily. It was the first they had heard of it. Still, they felt flattered.

"Oh, one last thing," Cleve-Cutler said. "I'm sorry to see you all looking so disgustingly fit. It means I can't try out my Universal High-Altitude Cure-All Treatment. Doesn't matter what's wrong with the chap, I take him up to five thousand feet and chuck him out. By the time he's fallen four thousand nine hundred and ninety feet, the rush of air has completely cured him. Never fails. Marvellous, isn't it?" He beamed like a bishop.

Somebody had to ask, so someone did. "What about the last ten feet?"

"Well, he's fit and strong by then, isn't he? Strong enough to fall ten feet, I should hope."

"Actually, it's only the last six inches that hurt," someone else said. Cleve-Cutler roared with laughter, and this time they joined in. Cautiously. But it was a start.

During the next week, when they were not on patrol they visited all the BE2c squadrons within fifty miles. They learned what some of them had never known and others preferred to forget: that the average life-expectancy in those squadrons ranged from three to six weeks. Someone enquired about tactics. "I pray a lot," one observer told them. "And when that doesn't work I curse a bit."

Morale in Cleve-Cutler's flight improved. They scored a couple of kills and after that nobody went sick. It was lucky that the Fokker monoplane was in decline, but every good leader needs a bit of luck. Soon Cleve-Cutler became senior flight commander, then acting CO. Now, overnight, he was a major, posted to Pepriac as new CO of Hornet Squadron.

He arrived at noon. The first thing he did was assemble the officers in the mess anteroom.

"Major Milne is dead," he said. He was pressing a couple of fingers against the side of his mouth to hold his face in a suitably neutral expression. "It seems that he killed himself by ramming an enemy machine on the other side of the Lines last evening. One of our observation balloons saw him cross the Lines, and later saw the collision. My name is Cleve-Cutler and I now command this squadron." He released his face, and the roguish smile slowly restored itself. "Later on I shall meet each one of you individually. For now, all I shall say is this. There is soon going to be the most enormous battle near here, and the war will be over by Christmas. Which Christmas, God alone knows, and I personally don't much care, and if the lieutenant at the back doesn't stop picking his nose I'll come and pick it for him. Of course, all these umpteen infantry divisions camped around here could be just an elaborate deception. Maybe the real battle will be elsewhere. But in any case, the Hun can't ignore us, so there will be large numbers of Hun aeroplanes to be shot down, which is all they're good for. Finally, I invite you to sample Cleve-Cutler's Patent Pink Potion For Pale People, several gallons of which are now waiting at the bar. For convenience I think it ought to be re-named Hornet's Sting. That's all. Thank you."

Private Collins was at the bar, ladling out glasses of a blood-red drink from a small brass-bound keg. Frank Foster took a glass and sniffed it. "What's in here, Collins?" he asked.

"I'm allowed to mention the plum brandy, port, eggs, Cointreau, Cognac and linseed oil, sir, but not the special secret ingredients, I'm afraid."

"Why not?"

"Bombay curry and vodka, sir. You might develop a bias if you knew about them."

Foster took a sip. His eyebrows came together like shutters being closed. "Jesus wept," he muttered. "What a wallop."

"That'll be the rum, sir."

When everyone had a glass, Cleve-Cutler stood on a chair. "There is a very ancient squadron tradition which I have just thought of," he announced. "This drink must always be drunk with both feet off the ground to the words 'Hornet's Sting'." There was much scrambling onto chairs and sofas and tables. Cleve-Cutler raised his glass. Everyone shouted: "Hornet's Sting!" and drank. Mayo said later that it was like swallowing a whizzbang, only noisier. Douglas Goss fell off his chair, but that was normal, nobody paid any attention. He complained that he had broken his shoulder. Nobody paid any attention to that, either.

After lunch the new CO interviewed the officers one at a time. The interviews were short.

"Brigade want me to put up one of our flight commanders to be CO of another scout squadron," he said to Foster. "You seem to qualify."

Foster kept the shock from his face but Cleve-Cutler saw it in his eyes. "No thank you, sir," he said.

"Why not? Major Foster. Colonel Foster. Brigadier, even. Sky's the limit in this Corps."

"I honestly don't think the war will last that long, sir. One big push and the Boches will crack." Foster found it hard to breathe properly. He might get posted whether he liked it or not. Today, even.

Cleve-Cutler held his resolutely cheery smile until Foster had to blink. "This Etonian Flight of yours," Cleve-Cutler said. "Awfully cosy, isn't it? I'd better break it up, hadn't I? Then there's no risk of your chums trying to take advantage of you. Right?"

Foster hunched his shoulders as if to protect himself from further blows. "You must do as you think fit, sir," he said. "I can only say that I rate the value of friendship very highly."

"So do I. Just wanted to see how the idea struck you. Personally I think it stinks. If a chap can't keep his chums, what can he keep? Send in the next customer, will you?"

For a moment Foster's face tightened with resentment. Then he nodded and almost smiled, and went out.

Several interviews later, O'Neill was facing Cleve-Cutler.

"Australian," the CO said. "Waltzing Matilda and so on." O'Neill's file was on the desk in front of him.

"That was a long time ago," O'Neill said. "Before I got transported to England." All trace of his flat Australian twang had disappeared; he talked like an Englishman. "That's how the colonies get rid of their riff-raff, you know."

Cleve-Cutler chuckled. "I see you came here with a chap called Chivers." O'Neill was silent and expressionless. "In fact I see you *trained* with Chivers."

Long pause. O'Neill chewed his lip, but that could have meant anything.

"He's dead, of course," Cleve-Cutler said brightly, "so we can be quite candid about the bugger. Dirty, greedy, fawning little sodomite who sponged off his friends, hadn't the guts to go near a Hun, lied like a rug about his so-called kills, and did us all a service by flying into a Jerry shell. Yes?"

O'Neill, his face as stiff as a stone, gave that a lot of thought. "Well, it's not a funny joke," he said at last, "so you must have some other reason for inventing all that poison."

"Good!" Cleve-Cutler said. "Now understand this. It doesn't matter a hoot whether T. Chivers was shit or sunshine. He's dead. Agreed? But the entire squadron, including cooks and clerks, tell me that you refuse to accept that fact." The stoniness of O'Neill's face was becoming tinged with pink. "Every time you take off you're looking for Chivers," Cleve-Cutler said. "That's bloody silly, and if you keep it up you'll find him sooner than you think. When you do, remember to ask him what good it did either of you." He slammed the file shut. "Next!"

Paxton, being the most junior officer, was the last to be seen.

"You've only been here four days," Cleve-Cutler said, his

expression as jaunty as ever, "and everyone hates you. Mmm?" He cocked the other eyebrow.

That hurt. "I can't understand it, sir," Paxton said. Nobody had spoken to him all morning. "Whatever I do, nobody likes it, even when it's right, even when . . ." That was a low blow, saying *everyone hates you*. "I don't want to play cricket, I want to *fight*." He could very easily have cried. Tears were ready, waiting to leak out. He placed his right heel on his left toes and made enough pain to defeat the tears. "Nothing's gone right from the start, has it?" he said angrily. "I flew that blasted Quirk all the way from England, which was more than the others could do, and Major Milne burnt it. Deliberately! Set fire to it! Is that the way to win the war?"

"Yes. Give me your hat." Cleve-Cutler took it, and opened a penknife. He slit the fabric at the end of the peak. "What's wrong with Quirks?"

"Nothing. It's a topping machine. It almost flies itself."

"Exactly. It's not built to be dangerous, it's built to be *safe*. The bloody silly thing's so stable it stays straight and level when you want to chuck it all over the sky." He was tugging the wire stiffener out of the peak. "The Quirk isn't a fighting aeroplane, it's a pussy cat. Major Milne was right to burn yours." He squashed the peak with both his hands. "All the Quirks in France should be burned, then maybe we'd get sent something livelier." He sat on the cap, bounced up and down, then tossed it to Paxton. "Now you'll look more like a flier and less like a captain in the Church Lads' Brigade."

"I don't care about that," Paxton mumbled. But he did care. He liked his cap now that it looked properly broken-in, more like the rest of the squadron. But he wasn't going to say so. "I got an Albatros yesterday," he said. "That was from a Quirk. There's nothing wrong with Quirks."

Cleve-Cutler picked up a pen. "You're grounded," he said. "In fact you're undergrounded. Your flight commander told me you were a turd, so I'm putting you in charge of the men's latrines." The half-grin had hardened into a glittering scowl. "Start now." He pointed to the door.

A few moments later, Corporal Lacey tapped on the door

and came in, carrying a bundle of files and documents. "Good heavens, sir," he said. "What did you say to Mr. Paxton? He looks quite deathly."

"Suicidal?"

Lacey thought about it. "Murderous."

"That's all right, then . . . Look here, I'm not going to read all *that*."

"Certainly not, sir. There's a summary and conclusion on a single sheet." He placed the bundle on the desk. "I've kept everything as simple as possible."

Cleve-Cutler rocked back on his chair and put his pen between his teeth like a cigar. "I did go to school, Lacey. Quite a good school, actually."

"Yes, sir. Marlborough. Not noted for mathematics, however." The CO looked away. "Still less for fraudulent accountancy," Lacey added softly.

"Are you always as familiar as this with your Commanding Officer?"

"That depends how much he wants to borrow my Elgar records."

"My God, you're a spy. I should have you shot. Have you got the violin concerto?" Lacey nodded. Cleve-Cutler sighed. "Damn. I might compromise and have you lightly maimed instead. What the devil is that?" It was a distant popping, like the bursting of many balloons.

"It's the officers, shooting at empty bottles," Lacey said. "If the Hun ever attacks with empty bottles, we shall be ready for him."

About half an hour later, Cleve-Cutler telephoned the adjutant and asked him if he could spare a few minutes.

Appleyard splashed some eau-de-cologne on his cheeks and the back of his neck: it tightened up the skin and stopped him sweating for a while. He chewed a peppermint lozenge, sucked in his gut until he could tighten his belt, picked up his clipboard and set out. Tiny silver sparkles danced in front of his eyes, and his ears were singing. He thought of loosening his belt; instead, he went back and took a swig of medicine. He chewed another lozenge and set out again, eyesight and hearing clear. "Got a touch of the old Afghan Curse today," he said. Corporal Lacey paused in his typing and smiled sympathetically.

Cleve-Cutler gave the adjutant what seemed like a welcoming smile. "I make it just over a thousand pounds," he said. "On a captain's pay it'll take you about three years to repay that. But you won't be a captain, will you? You'll be a nothing, once you've been court-martialled. Isn't that right?"

Appleyard turned away from that appallingly jaunty expression. He could feel his gut slipping until it was below his belt. He opened his mouth, and then closed it. The singing in his ears had started again.

"It's too late to ask me what on earth I mean," Cleve-Cutler said. "That's a card you play immediately or not at all. Anyway, you're sacked."

"I can explain," Appleyard said.

"Start by telling me where it's all gone. Not even you could spend a thousand pounds on booze and still be standing."

"It's a damned lie." The adjutant was on the edge of a stutter. "Who's been feeding you these lies?"

"All this stuff came out of your office."

"I see. I see. I see." Appleyard took a quick trip up and down the room. "My office. My papers. This is what the British Army's come to, is it? Well, I'll fight it. I've fought for my country, I've fought the bloody Boers, the Afghans, the Zulus, black as your hat, bullets won't stop 'em—"

"No, I don't think you will," Cleve-Cutler said.

The adjutant shut his eyes and rubbed the lids with his fingertips, several times. When he looked again, the CO was still in the same place with the same expression. "All I can say is I'm glad you find it so bloody funny," he said.

Cleve-Cutler glanced through the papers again. For a long minute there was no sound but the soft rustle as he turned a page. "Tell you what," he said. "Let's forget all that's been said, and start afresh. You've stolen just over a thousand pounds from this squadron. Now where on earth did it go?"

"Horses," Appleyard said. "It went on the horses. There's still lots of racing in England. Chap in Amiens, used to be a bookie, now he's a lieutenant in the Signals, he runs a book on the English races. I lost most of it through him."

"And the rest?"

"Drank it."

"Now we know." Cleve-Cutler stood up.

"I don't suppose . . ." Appleyard blew his nose. "I mean, you wouldn't consider . . ."

"You're sacked, Uncle. Message ends." He held the door open for him.

Foster lay on the grass outside the mess, his head resting on a cushion, and studied the sky through binoculars. "Remarkable," he said. "Amazing."

Some of the officers were resting in deckchairs. Most were half-asleep. "There's damn-all up there," Ogilvy said drowsily. "You've got a pigeon-dropping on the lens, Frank."

"No, no. I heard it, and now I can see it. Definitely a Hun." That aroused them. Foster's eyesight was phenomenal: on patrol he was invariably the first to see the speck that turned into an aeroplane. An anti-aircraft battery stationed at Pepriac crossroads opened up and rapidly battered the afternoon quiet to bits. "Told you so," Foster said. "Daddy's always right, children." Two miles high the shells burst against the blue like little splatters of spilt milk.

"Any good?" Elliott asked.

"Well, they nearly hit a cloud. Not the cloud our Hun has gone behind, however."

Charlie Essex settled back and closed his eyes again. "Bloody nerve," he grumbled. "Probably a tradesman. Tell him to go around the back, Frank."

Dando said: "Can't you do anything? Go up and shoo him off?" Nobody bothered to answer. "I thought that's what you were here for," Dando said. "My mistake." He picked up his book.

"Oh, he's far too high for us," Foster said, still using his binoculars. "If I told Spud and Gus to go and chase him, now, they'd take ten minutes to get dressed and thirty minutes to climb up there and frankly I don't think he's willing to wait that long."

"So he's just going to get away."

"Don't get shirty with us, old boy," Mayo said. "It's his fault for not making an appointment."

"Hullo, he's dropped something," Foster said. "Parachute, I think."

The parachute took fifteen minutes to fall. The pilot had judged well: it landed in the next field. Several of the squadron were there waiting for it.

"Message-bag," said Ogilvy. "I bet it's booby-trapped. Where's the squadron booby?"

"Inspecting the latrines," Jimmy Duncan said.

Foster turned it over with his foot. "No, the German air force wouldn't be so crude," he said. "I know what's in here." He undid the drawstring. The bag held the scorched fragment of a British officer's tunic, two fire-blackened medal ribbons, a broken cockpit watch, half a shoe, and the remains of a cheque book. "That's that, then," he said.

"There's absolutely no doubt?" Dando asked.

"None. They knew where to drop it, you see. Their intelligence is pretty good."

"In that case," Dando said, "I'm free to tell you that he had cancer of the stomach. He probably suspected something for a month. It was pretty well confirmed a couple of days ago."

Foster shoved the bits back into the bag. "I wish I'd seen his last fight," he said. "You'd better tell the new CO about the cancer."

"Don't tell Dougie Goss," said Essex. "He'll think he's got it too." Nobody laughed. "Still, I suppose it's not infectious or contagious or whatever," he said. Dando didn't answer. They began to walk back to camp.

Later that afternoon, some of 'B' Flight returned from leave. The flight commander, Captain Gerrish, was tall and bony, with big hands and feet and a broken nose above a sprawling black moustache that did something, but not enough, to hide the absence of two front teeth, which had gone at the same time that he broke his nose in a small crash during training. His eyelids were heavy. He had been nick-named 'Plug', short for 'Plug-ugly'. It was dangerous to call Gerrish ugly. He was usually amiable, but sometimes he grew silent and gloomy and then he was liable to hit people who made jokes about him.

He was cheerful enough when he came into the anteroom. "Have a good leave, Plug?" Goss said. "Ah, new records!" He took them from him. "This is Dando, by the way," he said while he glanced at the labels. "That's his surname, he hasn't got a Christian name, I think it got amputated by mistake . . . I say: ragtime!"

Gerrish shook hands with Dando, and called for tea. "Anything exciting happen while I was away?" he asked.

"No, it's been very dull." Goss was winding the gramophone. "Fritz is being feeble. No fun at all."

Mayo put aside his newspaper. "Were you still here when Toby Chivers . . ."

"Yes. That was the day before I left."

Mayo grunted and went back to the paper.

Jimmy Duncan heaved himself out of an armchair, and stretched. "The old man went west last evening," he said.

"East, actually," Goss said, "and then west. Collision."

"Bad luck," Gerrish said.

"He wasn't very well," Goss said. "Tummy trouble . . . Okay, everyone, stand by for *Temptation Rag!*" He lowered the needle. Dando watched Gerrish stir his tea and tap his foot, slightly missing the beat all the time, and he saw Goss click his fingers and strut around the gramophone, and he realised that nobody would mourn Rufus Milne. People came and went. While they were here they mattered, more or less; once they'd gone they mattered not at all, so it was bad form to make a fuss about them. Foster had got it right, when he'd put the bits back in the bag and said, "That's that, then." That was that. Now this is this. Very English. Very sensible.

"I hear you've been sacked, Uncle," Piggott said. "Is it true?"

Appleyard nodded. He took down a framed photograph of a group of polo players and laid it carefully in a suitcase. "Surplus to requirements, old chap."

"But that's ridiculous. The old man must have given you a reason, for God's sake."

"Wheels within wheels." Appleyard tapped the side of his nose. "Ours not to reason why." He opened a drawer and searched it thoroughly. Piggott could see that it was empty. "My shoulders are broad, old boy," Appleyard said. "I'll carry the can, don't worry."

"Well, if you're definitely going, I thought I'd better collect that fiver you borrowed."

Appleyard closed the drawer and patted him on the arm. "I hope you profit from my example, old chap," he said. "Never do anyone a favour unless you've got it in writing. *And* witnessed." He took the photograph out of the suitcase and studied it, his head nodding. "This sort of thing wouldn't have happened when Brendan Lucas had the regiment. That's him in the middle."

"Yes . . . Can you let me have that fiver, Uncle?"

"Yes, yes, of course, of course . . . You've no idea how *awkward* they've made it for me. It makes a chap wonder just what's going on, it really does." He took out his fountain pen and unscrewed the cap and looked at the nib.

"What *is* going on, Uncle?"

Appleyard put the pen away and sat on the bed. He sighed, and looked glumly at Piggott. "Politics, old chap," he said. "Politics. Sometimes you have to run fast just to stay in the same place, as the White Rabbit said. I couldn't run fast enough."

"I think it was the Red Queen said that."

Appleyard blew his nose. "I didn't have your educational advantages," he said. "Just a simple soldier, me."

"I really could do with that fiver, Uncle."

"Nobody ever said I don't honour my debts. It's as good as paid."

"Yes, but . . . I meant *now*."

"Tell you what . . ." Appleyard took out his pen again. "I'll send you a cheque, *backdated* to . . . to whatever today's date is." He put the pen away and stood up. He looked under the bed and pulled out a cardboard box. Bottles clinked. He shoved it back. "Politics," he said. "I should have seen it coming. Too trusting by half, that's my trouble."

Piggott felt defeated. "You'll come and have a drink before you go, won't you?"

Appleyard shook his head. "Shakespeare understood," he said. "To everything there is a season, and so on."

"Yes. Isn't that the Bible?"

"You know best. Simple soldier, me."

On his way back to the mess Piggott met Binns and Mayo, who had only just heard the news. Appleyard owed them money, too. While the three men were talking, Duncan appeared. "I thought I was the only one," he said. "What on earth has he spent it on?"

"Politics," Piggott told him. "Maybe he's bought a peerage."

Chapter 9

Appleyard vanished. A month later there was a rumour that
he had been reduced to the rank of second lieutenant and
posted to a particularly tough Pioneer battalion, a dump for
all the thugs and wreckers in the British Army; a month after
that there was a rumour that his platoon had beaten his head
in one night and left his body in No-Man's-Land after an
argument over the rum ration; but by then there was hardly
anyone left in Hornet Squadron who remembered him.

A new adjutant arrived. His name was Brazier and it was
obvious that he too had recently been demoted: you could see
the unfaded shape of a major's crown on his epaulettes, which
now carried a captain's stars. He wore the ribbons of the DSO
and MC, which were enough to silence the squadron for a
start, plus various other ribbons that nobody could identify.
He was six foot four and very broad-shouldered. Doorways
were sometimes a problem, and he had developed a slight
stoop to keep his head down to conversational level. He had
the sort of face you see on a Roman coin, all chin and nose,
but his eyes were bright blue, very disconcerting at first.
According to Corporal Lacey, who looked him up in the
Army List, Captain Brazier was forty-nine. At first he was
rarely seen in the Mess. "He eats broken bottles for breakfast," Mayo said. "I've seen the corks in his out-tray." The
truth was that he was busy trying to straighten out all the
nonsense that Appleyard had left behind; but his absence
made him seem even loftier. "Spud called him Uncle," Mayo

said, "and he tore Spud's arm off, didn't he, Spud? It's in the goulash tonight."

"Anything's better than mutton," Foster said.

"You can tell it's Spud's by the dirty fingernails," Mayo said.

"If you don't like them," Ogilvy told him, "leave them on the side of your plate."

"Is that what they taught you at Eton?"

"Nobody gets *taught* at Eton," Foster said. "A certain amount of assisted learning takes place, when games allow, but nothing as crass as *teaching*."

Binns overheard this. "What's twelve times nine?" he asked him.

"I don't intend to go into trade, so it's of no consequence," Foster said.

Binns found that amusing. "What *do* you intend to do when the war's over?"

"James and I will form some kind of partnership," Foster said.

Yeo yawned and stretched. "No we shan't," he said.

"Partners in what?" Binns asked.

"Oh . . . lots of things. Motor-racing, perhaps. Or we might set up a film studio. Or maybe a jazz band. We haven't decided yet."

"I have, " Yeo said, opening a magazine. "I'm going to stay in the Army. I like the Army."

"Nonsense. You'd be wasted in the Army."

Yeo threw down the magazine. "I've told you before," he said. "Don't nag."

That killed all conversation for a moment. Then Binns decided he had been patronised by Foster, and so he said: "The answer's a hundred and eight. Just thought I'd tell you, now you haven't got a partner to count on."

"Remind me," Foster said, peering at Binns as if through fog. "Which school did you go to?"

"Clifton College."

"Clifton . . . In the West Country, isn't it? Last stop on the GWR. No tradition but excellent plumbing."

"Cor blimey," Yeo said bleakly, staring at Foster, "you're a right toff, you are, guvner, strike me pink if you ain't."

Again, the conversation died. After a few seconds he left the room, leaving Foster looking far from happy.

At first, nobody knew quite what to make of Cleve-Cutler. Now that 'B' Flight was back, there was rarely an hour of daylight when somebody wasn't flying, and the CO often led a patrol, even if it was only an escort for a bit of artillery observation. He knew his stuff, and anyone flying with him had to stay alert. Once, when O'Neill and Duncan were coming home with him at the end of a long patrol, Cleve-Cutler's machine suddenly disappeared.

It was still early morning, and O'Neill had been thinking of the second breakfast soon to be eaten – thinking of it for perhaps ten seconds, or forty, or ninety, he couldn't be sure, time played terrible tricks after a couple of hours in the air – when he glanced left at his leader and saw empty sky. Nothing to the right either. He flew a slow figure-of-eight, using his bank to search high and low. Duncan looked at him and gestured failure. Well, it wouldn't be the first time that a pair of aircraft had been cruising home when one blew its engine or bust a vital spar or snapped a control cable and went down so suddenly that its partner noticed nothing. O'Neill got back on course for Pepriac. He was beginning his final glide to the field when the sun was blotted out. It was Cleve-Cutler's FE, half a length above and behind. The CO waved. His machine sank, and vanished again.

O'Neill worked it out as he made his landing. The FE had an enormous blind spot directly behind its tail. With a bulky engine roaring at his back the pilot could neither see nor hear anything that followed him closely. And Cleve-Cutler must have trailed him very closely indeed. He must have duplicated every move, quick as a shadow.

Quite a clever bit of flying. Filthy with risk, of course. Cleve-Cutler's observer said afterwards that there were times when he could have reached out and grabbed O'Neill's rudder, but nobody believed that. Nevertheless, his face and goggles were black with exhaust smuts from O'Neill's engine. Cleve-Cutler said nothing about it.

He rarely talked shop. A couple of minutes' comments after the next day's Flying Orders had been read out, perhaps: an exchange of views on the probable weather, especially wind and cloud, or a change in the system of signals between aircraft, or reports of a new German machine. Then he would conspicuously change the subject, as if to say: *Enough is enough, I leave the rest to you, let's not allow the war to spoil the entire day.* He was very good at conversation, or rather at getting others to talk while he listened. He seemed to find everyone entertaining; even Jimmy Duncan made him grin. (But then so did the squadron dog, a mongrel that had turned up in the ration wagon one day.) After a week, almost everyone in Hornet Squadron began to believe that the old man – the new old man – was his especial friend. The exception was Paxton.

Paxton had decided to lie low for a while. There seemed to be some sort of conspiracy to blame him for everything and thank him for nothing. Nobody had thanked him for getting that load of coal, for instance. And of course he got no credit for shooting down the Hun; on the contrary he'd been *blamed* for it, as if it was his fault that the Hun had attacked them. He wrote a letter to his parents: *It is just my foul luck to have been sent to a squadron with so many wasters and drunks in it. On my first flight over the Lines we met a Hun and after a bit of a scrap I managed to shoot him down in flames.* Just writing those words excited Paxton. He had to pause and do some deep breathing. *But my flight commander, who is an absolute pig, refuses to approve my claim! What's more he is very ill-mannered and beastly about it. It is all so unfair that I sometimes wonder who is the real enemy out here.* The last line sounded a bit whining so he crossed it out. Next day he re-read the whole letter and tore it up. Everything he'd written was still true but he was eighteen; it was up to him to fight his own battles now.

He hadn't mentioned O'Neill because he couldn't put his hatred of the man into words.

The day after Cleve-Cutler and Brazier arrived, Paxton inspected the latrines (for the second time) and went back to his billet. He was braced for another fight with O'Neill. He had decided that the only way to cope with the Australian was to ignore him completely. Even so, his heart was kicking his ribs and his fingertips were prickling when he opened the door. The room was empty.

Ever since the business of the stolen book he had kept all

his belongings padlocked in his trunk. He found the key but even as be began to insert it the padlock swung open. He stopped breathing; the sound of his own pulse was as loud in his ears as the pounding of surf. When his lungs complained, he sucked in a huge breath and looked around the room as if his enemy might be lurking somewhere.

O'Neill had picked the lock. Paxton clearly remembered testing it, after he had turned the key. "Swine," he breathed. "Stinking, sneaking swine." He didn't really want to look inside the chest. His fingers were trembling when he opened the hasp and lifted the lid: God alone knew what that Australian pig might have done to his things. Lying on top was his book, *The Riddle of the Sands*, held together by a rubber band.

Paxton had given it up for lost since his first fight with O'Neill. Maybe there was a shred of decency in the fellow, after all. He took off the rubber band and thumbed the pages, but nothing gave way to his thumb. The book refused to open. All the pages were stuck together. It was as solid as a block of wood.

That chest had been Paxton's last hope. It was the keep of the castle into which he had retreated. Let O'Neill do his worst outside, Paxton had thought; as long as I have that one place which is safe and private and secure, then I don't care. Now he felt as if he had been raped. "Raped," he whispered, and played angrily with the padlock, making the shackle go in and out as fast as he could, just to prove its filthy treachery.

"Having trouble with your equipment, sir?" Private Fidler asked. He was standing in the doorway, holding a broom, "I find a touch of Vaseline sometimes helps."

"Oh, mind your own damn business." Paxton tossed the lock onto his bed. "If you want something to do, you can clean my boots again, they're filthy." He kicked the lid of the chest shut.

"Bust, is it, sir?" Fidler picked up the lock. "Oh dear. Look at this. My old grannie could open this with one wave of her feather duster."

"Thank you, I'm sure she could. I'm extremely grateful for your advice, Fidler. Most helpful. Perhaps I'll go round to Harrods and get something better."

"Well, I suppose you could do that, sir." Fidler swept a patch of floor, carefully redistributing the dust, fairly and evenly. "But if it was me I'd go and see Corporal Lacey."

Lacey had no padlocks but he knew where the best were stored and how to get one. "Good cigars are the most useful currency in the Corps," he said, "and as it happens another box of cigars arrived for you today."

"Good heavens," Paxton said.

"Yes. When the first box proved so valuable I took the liberty of sending a telegram to your uncle, nominally from you, asking for more."

"You did *what*? You've got a damn nerve, Lacey."

"But you do want the cigars? Five will get you the strongest padlock in France."

"Who from?"

"It's best that you don't know. Now if you'll excuse me, I must get back to my desk. Captain Brazier frets if I'm not at his beck and call."

Later that day, Lacey delivered the padlock. It was the size of a small pineapple and two keys were needed to operate it. "Specially made to protect gold bullion deliveries up the Khyber Pass," Lacey said. "Don't lose the keys or you'll have to dynamite your way in."

Paxton dropped the hasp over the staple and fitted the shackle through the slot. The two keys turned slickly, moving heavy and complex mechanisms. "That's one problem solved," he said.

Cleve-Cutler kept his squadron busy. Whenever the weather allowed, Brigade HQ ordered them up for escort duties or reconnaissance patrols. Each of the three flights was in the air at some time of the day, and Cleve-Cutler encouraged the pilots to practise low-level flying in their spare time. He also liked the observers to practise gunnery in the butts. What he didn't like was to see people standing around.

On his second day in command, 'B' Flight had been sent up to do the usual variety of jobs. Plug Gerrish, the flight commander, rendezvoused with a BE2c to give it protection while it directed an artillery shoot. Unusually, the plane quit and went home after half an hour, but by then Gerrish and his observer, a red-haired, sharp-faced, Scottish lieutenant called Ross, had seen and warned off a Fokker monoplane. It climbed and loitered. It seemed interested rather than aggressive.

Gerrish waited until the BE2c was safely out of sight before he went up and tried to catch the Fokker. No hope. It climbed as he climbed. At about eight thousand feet it levelled off. For some minutes they flew parallel, near enough to be able to see details: oil stains, patched canvas, the other man's goggles, machine guns.

Ross took out his binoculars and had a good long look. Either this was a new type or the Fokker was even smaller than he remembered. Really, it looked old-fashioned: just a plain cross, with square wings stuck on a square fuselage, not much better than the thing Blériot flew across the Channel. Strange to think that Fokkers had frightened the life out of everyone only six months ago. This one had twin Spandau machine guns on top of the engine, very wicked-looking, perforated like cheese graters, but obviously the pilot wasn't looking for a fight with anyone. Feeble, feeble. Gerrish banged his fist on the nacelle and Ross stuffed the binoculars away. Time to go.

Gerrish was bored. He put the tail up and the nose down and enjoyed plunging into nothingness. This was what he liked about flying: if you got tired of one place you could be somewhere else in no time at all. From the corner of his eye he saw the Fokker diving too. That was no good; he was fed up with this Hun. He steepened the dive, determined to out-race him; then changed his mind, opened the throttle until the vibrations made the instruments blur, and hauled the FE into a loop. The Fokker followed him. Gerrish looked out and saw the monoplane hanging upside-down just as he was hanging upside-down. They came out of the loop like brothers. It was a game now. Gerrish side-slipped left, then right, then developed a corkscrewing dive that widened into a lazy spiral. The German pilot copied everything, perfectly, instantly, levelled out as Gerrish levelled out, and waited to see what was next. Gerrish waggled his wings. He didn't look for the reply; he knew it was there. He flew home, feeling amused but also annoyed. Fun and games were all very well, but when were they going to start killing each other again?

Foster and Yeo landed together. It had been another dud patrol. Their observers trudged away to get out of their flying kit but Yeo had things to discuss with his fitter and rigger. Foster leaned on the wing of his plane and watched. It was hot and he began to feel sleepy.

Yeo's discussion ended. Foster heaved himself upright. They walked slowly and silently to the pilots' hut, scuffing their boots, sweating.

Yeo peeled off his sheepskin coat and let it fall. He slumped into a chair and got rid of his scarf. He tried to prise off one boot with the toe of the other but it refused to loosen.

"Hang on," Foster said. He took hold of the boot and dragged it off.

"Thanks awfully," Yeo said. Apart from formalities, those were the first words they had exchanged since the business with Binns.

Foster pulled off the other boot. "Are we friends?" he asked.

"We always were," Yeo said. "Sometimes good, sometimes bad. But always friends."

Next morning was wet but not windy. A soft, fine rain drifted across the aerodrome like smoke. Condensation dribbled down the inside of windows and when Tim Piggott got dressed his clothes felt clammy. 'A' Flight was due to be on patrol at 9 a.m. and he was not looking forward to it. Flying an FE2b through rain was like sitting on the sharp end of a schooner in a gale. The cockpit was open, with only half a thumbnail of a windscreen, and when rain arrived at seventy or eighty miles an hour it stung.

Talk at breakfast was subdued.

"They ought to call the war off on days like this," Charlie Essex said.

"You mean like Wimbledon?" O'Neill said.

"Exactly. The grass gets dreadfully cut-up if you fight when it's wet."

Goss got up and took his coffee to a window. At the far end of the field, the windsock almost came to life and then lost interest again. The adjutant walked past, under a large and brightly striped golf umbrella. It made him look ten feet tall. "I don't see how anyone at the Front can see anything through all this muck," Goss said.

The adjutant came in and gave the umbrella to Collins. "Porridge with plenty of salt," he said. The chair creaked as he sat down. "Reminds me of the day we counter-attacked at Mons," he said. "Same sort of rain. Perfect cover. Master Fritz never saw us coming. Scarcely a shot fired. All bayonet work. I encouraged thrift, you see."

"Nice to know we won something at Mons," Piggott said.

"No, we lost. The Hun brought up his guns and blew us all to blazes." His porridge arrived. "This is what the ground looked like after the barrage." He stirred it with his spoon. "Exactly like this."

"No good for mixed doubles, then," Essex said. Brazier raised an eyebrow. "Sorry," Essex said. "Family joke."

"Come on, let's go and do this bloody silly patrol," Piggott growled. Men stood, chairs grated, boots scuffed.

"Don't be late back," Brazier said. "There's to be a court of inquiry starting at eleven o'clock into the circumstances leading up to the death of a sergeant muleteer while driving a squadron tender when unauthorised so to do. You may be wanted to attend."

"What good's an inquiry?" Goss said. "He's dead. They're both dead."

"But not authorised so to be." Brazier looked for Collins. "More salt," he said.

The first three FEs took off one after the other, their propellers blasting the drenched grass and leaving a wake of spray that ceased as each machine came unstuck and began to climb. Douglas Goss was in the fourth plane, with an observer called Henley. Towards the end of his take-off run, with the aeroplane feeling ready and willing to stop jolting and start flying, the engine quit. In the sudden silence, the wings lost their lift and the weight of the aeroplane – nearly a ton, fully loaded – settled on the tricycle undercarriage. The FE took a hundred yards to run to a halt, squeaking and groaning all the way.

"What's wrong?" Henley asked.

"I think the wheels need oiling. Or maybe you weren't praying hard enough."

"I'm agnostic, you know that."

"Well, so's the engine. It certainly doesn't want to go to heaven."

"Suits me. We can play ping-pong instead."

A lorryload of ground crew came out and pushed the FE back to its hangar. "Sorry about that, sir," said Goss's fitter. Within two minutes he had found the fault. "Magneto's gone dud, sir," he said. "Can't understand it, I tested it three times yesterday and—"

"Never mind." Goss took the magneto and kicked it away, and hurt his foot. "Put another one in, and this time make sure it's brand new."

"The other one was brand new, sir."

"Charming. Just what I wanted to hear." Goss supported himself on Henley's shoulders and limped off. "I've broken several toes," he said.

"Frankly, Dougie, I think this war is going to be the death of you."

It took twenty minutes to fit and test the new magneto. Cleve-Cutler came out to see what the trouble was. "We've missed the rendezvous by now, sir," Goss said. "Anyway, I expect they cancelled the shoot and forgot to tell us."

"Don't hang about here. Get over the other side and make a nuisance of yourselves."

The new magneto worked. The cloud ceiling turned out to be less than a thousand feet, which was far too low for Goss's peace of mind. He kept climbing until they popped into sunshine. This was pleasant. Goss went up a few thousand feet, cruised idly from nowhere to nowhere and waited for business.

Nothing happened. Once or twice he thought he might have seen something but it was less than a dot, it was a pinprick and it vanished. After an hour he was getting sunburn and cramp and he wasn't at all sure that he knew where he was. Henley seemed to have gone to sleep, and then maybe died peacefully in his sleep.

Goss cut back the engine until it was ticking over and let the weight of the machine carry it down in an easy dive. Slicing into the cloud looked like falling into a bed of melting snow. The first thing he realised when they dropped into dull daylight was that the cloud base had gone a long way up in the past hour. The second thing was they were five miles behind the German Lines. He knew this because he could see three German observation balloons flying in the north: podgy, sausage-shaped bags tugging amiably at their cables. Goss opened his throttle. He probably couldn't get near enough to destroy any of them but he could make a bloody nuisance of himself. Henley was awake now, testing the Lewis gun with a brief burst.

Already the nearest balloon was on its way down. The Germans had high-speed winches and well-trained crews: in the time it took Goss to arrive, the balloon would be on the ground. Gunfire was flashing and flickering all around the balloon site and the sky was dirty with a protective barrage. The FE wallowed through the fading, acrid remains of a shellburst and Goss turned steeply away. The gunners chased him. There was nothing to do but fly the plane up to the cloud cover, but all the way he could feel sweat coating the ribs under his arms.

He flew north above the cloud for three minutes and circled for three minutes more to give them time to forget about him. Then he went straight down, as fast as he could. They had not forgotten about him. There was a balloon less than a mile off. He turned to it and frightened it but at the same time tracer began streaking up so he kept turning and saw the third balloon in the distance. Goss did a quick reckoning. He'd panicked two balloons and annoyed a mob of gunners To go for a third balloon would be reckless and idiotic. He felt reckless and lucky. He went for it. The winch crew began winding it down within twenty seconds. Goss laughed aloud. It was like driving fat cattle: you shouted and they ran. Quite bloody right, too. Teach them not to snoop.

He turned and flew east, away from the groping, barking archie, and climbed through the cloud yet again.

Nothing interesting happened on the way home. He found Pepriac, landed rather more neatly than usual and taxied to the hangars. As usual, Henley seemed to have gone to sleep, but appearances were misleading. Henley was dead. He had a firm grip of his Lewis gun and his eyes were open. He'd been killed by a burst of heavy machine-gun fire that came up through the floor. Dando took four bullets out of his chest.

Chapter 10

After ten minutes' walking along the lane Paxton had done enough saluting for one day. The roads around Pepriac were amazingly busy. He opened the first gate he found and set off across the fields.

Once, when Paxton first got his commission, saluting had been the greatest fun; he'd walked about town, seeking out private soldiers who must salute him or, if they failed, be reprimanded, which was almost more satisfying. But now, here, with so many units on the march, saluting had become a chore, no more exciting than inspecting the men's latrines, which he had already done.

He avoided an infantry camp, went past a silent and apparently deserted Casualty Clearing Station, and paused to examine a large hole, freshly dug, about the size of a tennis court. An experimental trench? Wrong shape. Something to do with latrines, perhaps? Unlikely. Paxton finally decided it was intended to be a swimming pool. He walked on, skirted a wood that was packed with stores, and passed an artillery battalion in camp.

By now it had stopped raining. The air was warm; steam was rising from the rows of khaki bell-tents. Paxton got a whiff of horse-dung. Somewhere out of sight, a blacksmith was making his anvil ring. A row of guns could be seen, lined up as if ready to fire a salute. Just the sight of them excited Paxton. He could visualize the flash from the muzzle, the recoil, the smoke blowing over the half-naked gunners slinging shells to each other, the distant flowering of an explosion as the enemy's position disintegrated in flying gobs of blood and mud. What fun! What simply ripping fun!

He walked on, and was leaning on a gate and thinking how pleased his parents would be when he won a medal (his father was an architect, and Oliver had always pitied him for leading such a dull life) when an elderly major came along. "You weren't thinking of crossing that field, were you, laddy?" the major said. "You might get your head chopped off if you do." His manner was distant rather than critical.

"Chopped off for thinking it, or for doing it, sir?"

The major lit a pipe and carefully broke the match in two. "You're Flying Corps, aren't you?"

"Yes, sir."

"Try not to be as big a bloody fool on the ground as you are in the sky."

"Very good, sir." Paxton felt too bouncy to be squashed. "Is something about to happen here, sir?"

"Cavalry charge. Ever seen a cavalry charge? No, of course you haven't. You were a dribbling infant in 1914." He pointed with his pipe. "There stands the enemy, that double line of stakes." They were about six feet high and each had a turnip stuck on top. "Any moment now a detachment of the Third Dragoon Guards will appear to my left. Then watch out."

Paxton glanced at him. The major's chin was thrust forward and his lower lip was twitching with eagerness.

The cavalry suddenly appeared, cresting a rise that Paxton hadn't noticed, in a solid-looking column of fours. At first the drumming of hooves was felt as a vibration, then it was heard. The column fanned out and formed two lines abreast, one well behind the other. Now Paxton could see clods of earth sent flying as the gallop began and the drumming was a soft, insistent thunder. Steel flickered along the line. Swords! "Golly!" Paxton said and wished he hadn't, but the old major was deaf and blind to anything except the Third Dragoon Guards. The first line swept past, tall men on big horses. Swords fell and hacked at the turnips on the poles, the line charged on. "I say!" Paxton said. The second line carried lances. Their targets were the fallen hunks of turnip. As each trooper bore down and thrust he gave a long rising whoop of triumph that did strange things to Paxton's testicles. "I *say*!" he said. The drumming faded. "What an absolutely splendid stunt!"

"That's what you'd call it, would you? A stunt?" The major carried a crop stuffed down the side of his right boot. He pulled it out and whacked his leg several times. "That stunt, as you call it, is going to cut the German army to ribbons and win this war in half a trice, if only we're given half a chance."

They climbed over the gate and walked to the scene of the charge. The major picked up half a turnip. "That's what Master Boche will look like after the Dragoon Guards have parted his hair," he said. "All we need is half a chance."

"I'm sure you're right, sir," Paxton said daringly, "but aren't there rather a lot of Huns?"

"Not just the Dragoons. Life Guards. Royal Horse Guards. Lancers. Hussars." The major ran out of fingers on his left hand, so he began prodding Paxton in the chest with his crop. "Second Indian Cavalry. That's the Deccan Horse, Hodson's Horse, Poona Horse. Canadian Cavalry. My God, man, we could finish the job with half that number. Just given half a chance." He gave Paxton the half turnip.

They walked back to the gate. "Pay no attention to me," the major said. "My impatience gets the better of me sometimes. The way things have been going, you chaps see more action in a week than we do in a year. What?"

Paxton nodded. "I had a scrap with a Fokker just the other day, sir. Managed to knock him down in the end."

"Good for you. Come and have a drink. Meet the chaps."

Paxton dropped the half turnip when the major wasn't looking. "People sometimes call us the cavalry of the skies," he said. "I must say I think that's the most enormous compliment we could have, don't you, sir?"

The RFC was very efficiently organised to provide replacements. The adjutant phoned the Officers' Pool at St. Omer and a new observer was delivered by tender to Pepriac in time for tea. He was Canadian and his name was Stubbs. He was built like a heavyweight and he had a face like a baby.

Gus Mayo had got permission to go to Amiens to get his

hair cut. When he came back he went to his billet and found his batman changing the sheets on Henley's bed. At the other end of the room Stubbs was playing darts against himself.

"Hullo!" Mayo said. "Henley gone?"

"Yes, sir," the batman said. "Shame, isn't it?"

"Oh." Mayo came to a halt. He watched him smooth out a creased blanket. "Gone for good, you mean."

"Funeral's tomorrow, sir. This is Mr. Stubbs, sir."

They shook hands. "You'll like it here," Mayo said. "Grand bunch of chaps. I don't suppose you brought any new gramophone records?"

"No. Should I have?"

"Dougie Goss trod on our one and only ragtime record last night, the silly sod. What about Mr. Goss?" he asked the batman. "Did he get pipped too?"

"No, sir."

Mayo grunted. "Bloody good pilot, Dougie. I just wish he'd watch where he puts his feet. Feel like a drink?"

The Court of Inquiry into the Circumstances Surrounding the Death of 2533409 Muleteer-Sergeant Harris J., Attached Royal Engineers, During the Night of 4–5 June 1916, While Driving RFC Tender No. 04379 in the Town of Breteuil, adjourned for lunch after two hours, resumed at half-past two and adjourned again at four, the Court (presided over by Colonel Bliss, supported by a major and a captain) having questioned everyone in Hornet Squadron it could lay its hands on and having discovered, in the words of its president, bugger-all.

That wasn't what went into the official record. It was what Bliss told Major Cleve-Cutler and Captain Brazier. "Personally I don't give a toss about Sergeant Harris J.," the colonel said. "None of this would matter if he hadn't utterly demolished a double-fronted grocer's shop. The owner is demanding a fortune in compensation. You know how the general hates grocers."

"Look, Bob," Cleve-Cutler said. "Isn't it obvious that Rufus Milne's your man?"

"The general won't wear that."

"Why not?"

"He doesn't believe squadron commanders go around at night swapping army tenders for mules. It's simply not the way they behave, in his experience."

"Milne was ill."

"Well, he doesn't believe that, either. He's never heard of someone that age getting stomach cancer. Milne looked perfectly all right the last time he saw him."

"And then went off and killed himself?"

"The general believes Milne died while battling against great odds. He thinks all these stories about Milne are in very poor taste."

"Jolly considerate of him."

"Rufus is going to get a posthumous medal," Bliss said. "Probably a bar to his MC. So I need a villain for my villain, not a hero. See you tomorrow."

With the arrival of Stubbs, Paxton no longer had the lowest place at dinner; in fact he was now third from the bottom, because Kellaway had returned from hospital. Kellaway had a black eye and some yellowing bruises on his forehead and a little thicket of stitches on his chin, but he seemed cheerful enough, although his eyes sometimes crossed without warning and he had to shake his head vigorously in order to uncross them.

Paxton was glad to see that Kellaway treated him in a friendly fashion. Evidently there were no hard feelings about the cold-bath treatment. When they had left the mess and were back in their billet, Paxton said: "You won't believe this, old man, but they've refused to credit us with shooting down that Hun."

"Who are they?"

"Captain Piggott." Kellaway looked puzzled. "Our flight commander, for heaven's sake," Paxton said. "And of course the CO backs him up. Isn't it a rotten shame?"

"What Hun?" Kellaway asked.

"The Fokker." Paxton remembered that Kellaway had seen the enemy plane. "The Albatros, I mean. It crashed. I shot the tail off and it crashed."

"I don't remember. If you say it happened, of course it happened but I don't remember anything for the last week. I don't even remember coming here."

"Yes, but . . ." Paxton felt swindled of his kill. "You remember me, don't you? We left England together."

"Dexter?" Kellaway suggested. "No. Wait a minute . . ."

O'Neill strolled in, eating an apple. "You want to stay away from the adj," he said indistinctly. "There's hell to pay in the men's latrines . . . Jeez, you look a sight," he told Kellaway.

"What's wrong with the latrines?" Paxton demanded.

O'Neill took three swift bites of the apple. "Better ask the adj, hadn't you? All I know is he wants your blood. Two men locked in a cubicle, not very nice, he's old-fashioned about that sort of thing, I never saw a man so angry, I'd wait until tomorrow if I was you . . ." But by then Paxton had grabbed his cap and gone. The adjutant didn't scare *him*.

Within a minute he was back. He came in quietly and didn't look at the other two, just sat on his bed and flicked through a magazine. He had never reached the latrines. Halfway there he had remembered that the cubicles in the latrines had no doors.

Beneath his apparent calm all his senses were pounding. O'Neill was chatting to Kellaway but it was a while before Paxton took in the meaning and realised that O'Neill was talking about him. "Personally, I put the peculiar smell down to the constipation," O'Neill said in that maddeningly flat, unchanging voice of his. "A lot of English people of his sort smell like that. We don't get it in Australia because Australians invented prunes, did you know that?"

If Sherborne had taught Paxton nothing else it had taught him self-control. This filthy sneering from O'Neill was painful, but Paxton had a trick which he used to deflect it: he repeated to himself the words of his commission: *George, by the Grace of God, of the United Kingdom of Great Britain and Ireland, and of the British Dominions beyond the Seas, King, Defender of the Faith, Emperor of India, Etc . . . To Our Trusty and well beloved Oliver Arthur David Paxton, Greeting. We reposing especial Trust and Confidence in your Loyalty, Courage and good Conduct, do by these Presents Constitute and Appoint you to be an Officer . . .*

"I offered him a pound of Australian prunes," O'Neill said, "but I think he thought they were extra large suppositories and you know he's not very big in that department. See these pyjamas?"

Paxton could not resist looking up. O'Neill was holding a pair of his pyjamas. He could see the monogram, OP.

"He threw these out," O'Neill said. "I had 'em washed in disinfectant, you can hardly tell where the stains were. Piece of advice. Never, ever touch that trunk of his. I don't know what he's got in there but he goes insane if anyone touches it." O'Neill picked up his sponge-bag and went out.

"I don't think he likes you," Kellaway said.

"I loathe and detest him. He's foul and disgusting and he steals everything he can lay his hands on. He stole my pyjamas. Wait a minute . . ." Paxton thought hard. When had he last seen those pyjamas?

"What was all that gibberish about your trunk?" Kellaway said.

Paxton, frowning furiously, was searching for his keys. "I had to buy this special padlock just to keep the thieving beggar out," he said. Kellaway came over to see. The keys turned sweetly. The shackle slid out of the staple. Paxton grunted with relief. "I've beaten the blighter," he said. He raised the lid and it fell to the floor with a crash that made him jump.

"Hullo!" Kellaway said. "What's happened now?"

Paxton picked up the lid and examined it. "Someone's knocked the pins out of the hinges," he said. "There's nothing holding the hinges together." He put the lid back in place and sat on it. "It shouldn't be possible, not when it's shut and locked, but . . ."

Kellaway delicately fingered the ends of the stitches on his chin. The cut itched, which was supposed to be a sign that it was healing. "Why don't you get your own back?" he asked. "Hit him, or something."

"I don't intend to sink to his level. The man's a cad, I shall treat him as a cad. Sooner or later the message will sink in."

"Well," Kellaway said. "You know best."

Next day the weather was lovely and the squadron's Flying Orders were cancelled. Everyone must be available for the Court of Inquiry.

This was unpopular, not just because it meant hanging around all day in one's best uniform but because it made people feel as if they were being treated like schoolboys. "What's all the fuss?" asked the Canadian, Stubbs. "The guy crashed a tender. Happens all the time."

"You don't understand how generals think," Foster said. "Planned destruction is one thing. You can have all the massacre and mayhem you like, at the Front. What they won't tolerate is accidental death behind the Lines. That upsets them. It's wasteful. Untidy."

"One of us should own up," Essex said. "Not me, I've got an alibi, I was smashing up a hotel in Amiens at the time."

After breakfast, Corporal Lacey sought out Paxton and handed him a diary. "I came across this when I was parcelling up Mr. Henley's belongings," he said. "I think somebody ought to read it."

The diary was the size of a pocketbook, with a scuffed green leather cover. "You think it might have something in it that would embarrass his family?" Paxton asked. He tried to remember what Henley had looked like. Something like a potato. Bland and harmless. "Not much chance of that, is there?"

"Somebody ought to read it, all the same."

"D'you mean you've noticed something?"

"Certainly not. Far be it from me to read the private and confidential papers of a commissioned officer. It's simply that with the Court of Inquiry in session, nothing should be overlooked, no matter how trivial." Lacey raised a finger. "Apparently trivial."

"I don't see what the devil the Court of Inquiry has to do with it." But Paxton opened the diary.

"June the fourth," Lacey said.

Paxton found the page, and read, and grunted, and read on. "Good God," he said, still reading, while his hand took a tighter grip of the pages. "What a pair of gibbering idiots."

"The adjutant is in his office," Lacey said.

Paxton showed the diary to the adjutant, who showed it to the CO, who showed it to Colonel Bliss when he arrived to reopen the inquiry.

Bliss read the entry three times.

155

"So," he said. "This fathead Henley got tight, pinched the keys of the tender from the CO when he wasn't looking, realised he couldn't drive, persuaded the other fathead Kellaway to drive, they got into an argument about its horsepower and decided to settle it by seeing how many horses they could swap it for, but what they thought were horses turned out to be mules."

"It was dark," Cleve-Cutler said.

"Of course it was. I expect Sergeant Harris thought he was getting a Rolls-Bentley. If it hadn't been so damn dark none of this would have happened. I blame everything on the blackout. In fact, considering this joker was writing his diary in the pitch black and falling-down drunk too, it's amazing he could put two words together. I'd like to congratulate him. Wheel him on."

"Can't," Cleve-Cutler said. "He copped it, yesterday."

"What bad luck. Never mind, wheel on the other idiot." Bliss checked the page. "Kellaway."

"No good either. He banged his head, lost his memory."

"Really? All of it? What a dangerous place this is. First you lose your CO, then your adjutant, then Henley, and now Kellaway can't find his memory. Honestly, it's getting so a chap daren't put anything down for a minute. What's behind it, d'you think? Magpies? Squirrels? Cat-burglars?"

"You don't believe this stuff in Henley's diary."

"Do you?"

"If it'll get us out of a hole, yes."

Colonel Bliss went off to telephone his boss, the general. When he came back he said: "The old buffer is satisfied. He knew Milne couldn't possibly have done anything so bloody silly, and now events have proved him right."

"So can we fly again?"

"Yes. In fact he's so pleased that he's put Hornet Squadron on double patrols for a week." Bliss returned the diary. "I liked the bit about the argument over horse-power," he said. "Somebody used his imagination there."

Kellaway and Paxton were among the pallbearers at Henley's funeral. There was no coffin; the body was in a neat canvas bag resting on a board. It lay on the floor of the tender that carried the funeral party to the graveyard at Pepriac church. Paxton was shocked by the absence of a coffin but he quickly forgot about it as he watched the body get jolted inside its bag by the bumpy ride. What fascinated him was the utter helplessness of this corpse, the way you could actually see the wobble of its feet or its head. All through the burial ceremony he kept thinking how easy it was to kill a man. You aim, you squeeze, and before he hears the bang of your gun he's dead. But even that wasn't the most exciting part. The real thrill was turning an aeroplane into a flaming wreck. That Albatros had looked so beautiful. And he had knocked it out of the sky. He, Oliver Paxton, not yet nineteen, never very brilliant at Sherborne although he'd got his rugger colours, couldn't master trigonometry to save his life but he could blast a Hun before lunch. He could count up to one! The padre finished speaking. Paxton hadn't heard a word. He glanced across the open grave at Kellaway. *He's smiling*, Kellaway thought. *What on earth is there to smile about?* An NCO shouted orders. Rifle fire crashed and echoed. Paxton smelled fumes, and tasted the scent of intoxication.

Paxton had no difficulty getting permission to leave Pepriac. Lacey fixed it with the adjutant. Now that Paxton had got his uncle to send a box of the best Havana-Havanas every other day it seemed that Lacey could fix anything.

At first he explored the land to the south, as far as the river Somme, the limits of the British Army. It was easy walking: gentle slopes, vast fields, well drained by the chalk that gleamed wherever a trench had been dug. Ten or twelve miles was nothing. And everywhere he went he met soldiers in camp, soldiers out training, soldiers on the march. The countryside was studded with regiments, and more kept arriving: not from the Trenches but from base camps, sometimes from England.

This military richness amazed and impressed him. Bugle-calls delighted him. Sometimes, when the air was still, three or four buglers in different camps would overlap and he stopped to admire the sheer cleverness of the organisation. He liked watching men on parade. He liked watching the wagontrains, sometimes six horses to a wagon, rumbling by knee-deep in white dust. But most of all he liked watching troops on the march behind a band of fifes and drums. The crunch of boots, the shrill of fifes, the thump and thunder of drumskins: all combined to make his chest swell and his legs twitch with suppressed energy. As the column marched away he felt a huge, patriotic pride mixed with a regret that he could do nothing to demonstrate that pride. He was an Englishman. That was Saint George's music. He wanted to slay a dragon or two.

One day he took the squadron dog, now named Brutus, with him for company. This worked so well that next day he asked Kellaway to come.

Dando had grounded Kellaway until he was sure he had recovered from his concussion. Kellaway was not keen on walking. "That's why I left the Somerset Light Infantry and joined the Corps," he said. "All that marching. You walk everywhere in the infantry. Awfully tiring. I've got small feet, too."

"Just a short stroll," Paxton said.

"Nice lunch somewhere?"

"Yes."

"I'm not absolutely sure it was the Somerset Light Infantry. Sometimes I think it was, sometimes I wonder. D'you ever get that feeling?"

"No. Come on, get your boots on."

It was another fine day. The fields were awash with poppies, and there was always a skylark high above, singing as if God were holding auditions. Paxton and Kellaway walked north. They visited battalions of the Royal Inniskilling Fusiliers, the Highland Light Infantry, the King's Own Yorkshire Light Infantry, the Scottish Rifles. They were offered lunch in the mess by some Northumberland Fusiliers, newly arrived. Only eggs and potatoes, for which the Fusiliers apologised, but lots of wine and cheese. Kellaway quickly drank two glasses of wine and became very jaunty.

"Your face seems to have acquired a few battle honours lately," one of the hosts said to him.

"Ah, yes." He felt his bruises. "But you ought to see the other chap."

"No, no." Paxton made a little melodrama out of it. "Not a good idea. Might put them off their food."

They asked him what had happened, as he knew they would. This was his party-piece. He was good at this. "Routine patrol," he said. "Four or five thousand feet. Above the clouds, anyway. You wouldn't have seen a thing from down here." That always impressed people. "Along came this Hun, two-seater, Fokker, nasty piece of work. Machine-guns fore and aft. One of their latest grids. Bigger than us, and faster. He knew it, too. You could tell from the way he charged at us. I reckon he must have been doing a hundred miles an hour." There was utter silence now. He took a sip of wine.

"Then we had a scrap and I shot him down," Kellaway said. "Pass the potatoes, old bean."

Paxton tried to grin and be a part of the laughter, but he felt sick with rage and hatred. Kellaway had not only pinched his story, he had pinched his Hun! And he was still chattering away. Paxton gave up. He chewed the tasteless food in order to make his face do something that hid his expression.

Kellaway was saying: ". . . but that one doesn't count because he ran away home, and it was downhill all the way so he went very fast. Anyhow, we made up for it next day. We caught a whale. *Huge* German aeroplane. When we searched the wreckage we found a billiard table and a genuine lavatory with a chain you could pull. I put three drums of ammunition through the Lewis before that Hun went down. The barrel was so hot it glowed red like a poker."

"So how many Huns have you shot down, in all?"

"Seven. Eight, if you count double for the whale."

Paxton made an effort to be cheerful but he felt both angry and ashamed. They left as soon as he could contrive it, which was not until Kellaway had drunk a lot of brandy. Neither of them spoke until they were out of sight of the camp. "I must say that was the most disgusting performance I have ever witnessed," Paxton said; but he was talking to himself: Kellaway had turned aside and was pissing on an old tree stump. Paxton walked slowly on, his face twisted in distaste, waiting for Kellaway to catch up and be condemned in style. But Kellaway didn't catch up. Paxton went back and found him asleep with his hat over his eyes. "Sod you, then," he said, and felt soiled by his own words. He walked away and spat to cleanse his mouth.

For half an hour he wandered about, watching troops erect tents. Then he decided to go home. Kellaway was where he had left him, still asleep. By now Paxton was too weary to be angry. "Come on," he said.

Kellaway awoke like a child, smiling, yawning and stretching. "Goodness, I'm thirsty," he said. "D'you know, I just had the most extraordinary dream. I dreamt I was back at school, and it was last summer, because I was captain of tennis – which I was, you see – only I was in uniform, and . . ."

Paxton let him ramble on as they walked back, until he lost patience and interrupted. "Why did you tell all those frightful lies?"

"Steady on. It's only a dream."

"I'm not talking about your dopey dream. I mean all the lies you told the Northumberland Fusiliers at lunch."

"Lunch?" Kellaway kicked at a dandelion. "Did we have lunch?"

"You told them you'd shot down seven or eight Huns."

"No! Really? What a spoof!" Kellaway was delighted.

"There is such a thing as honour, you know," Paxton said.

"Did they believe me?"

"Yes, of course."

"I don't see how anybody's honour has suffered, then. Do you?"

Paxton felt trapped. "It's just not good enough," he said.

Chapter 11

Flying two patrols a day was not unusual in 1916. Plenty of Quirks went up twice a day, coming home for lunch as if they were keeping office hours. But at least the crews of Quirks had specific jobs to do, and once they had done them they could quit, put the nose down and buzz off. FE2bs led a different life.

They were built to fight. The initial stood for 'Farman Experimental' but a lot of people assumed they meant 'Fighting Experimental', and some of the more gung-ho pilots actually called their machines 'fighters' instead of 'scouts'. Cleve-Cutler was one of these. When his flight commanders complained that they hardly ever saw enemy planes, and so two patrols a day were twice as pointless as one, he said: "Not at all. Now we own the sky. If Jerry wants it back he'll have to come up and fight us for it."

"I think Jerry's trying to bore us to death," Gerrish said.

"Then stir him up. You're supposed to be flying offensive patrols, so be more offensive. Be downright bloody disgusting."

"I couldn't do that," Foster said. "Nanny made me promise. However," he added as he saw Cleve-Cutler's expression, "I suppose I could always shoot Nanny first."

"And don't be so damned cocky," Cleve-Cutler said. "Remember what happened to that chap Dobson or Hobson or whatever his name was, at Lagnicourt last month." The meeting broke up in silence. Hobson had crashed in flames, caught by a low-flying enemy machine which shot him down when he was only fifty feet off the ground, thinking his patrol was over, probably thinking the other plane (if he saw it) must be British. Nobody knew what Hobson had thought. Nobody caught the other plane, either.

Flying offensive patrols was a wearying grind. There were the physical demands of going from ground level to the same height as the top of a small Alp and sitting there for an hour or more in a Force 10 gale. Do it twice a day for a week and your body starts to complain: the head throbs, or the sinuses burn, or the ears develop a persistent buzz. But that was trivial. The great strain was the search, and it grew worse when there was nothing to find. The sky became achingly empty. Impossibly empty. Some pilots and observers lost faith in their own eyes. The less they found the more they worried. After all, they were up there to kill someone. Where was the bastard? Stealing into their blind spot? About to kill with the shot the victim never hears? So they searched, and worried. A man would have to be crazy not to worry. On the other hand, worry was exhausting. Worry too much and you might end up too tired to search. It was something to worry about, was worry.

Little of this showed on the ground. They had the elasticity of youth, and in any case it wasn't the done thing to reveal one's emotions except on the subject of sport, or perhaps dogs. The squadron had a good spirit, better than it had had under Milne. The mess was much improved now that Appleyard had gone: better food in more variety, no more damn mutton, some decent wine and even occasionally a few crates of real English ale. A new cricket bat appeared, thought to be a gift from Paxton which was only right since he'd made Tim Piggott break the old one. The mess got a piano. It had three bullet-holes in the front and a dead pigeon deep inside, but it was a piano, even if the G below middle C made a twang like a departing arrow. Corporal Lacey had bought it with some of Paxton's cigars. Paxton also got part of the credit for two sofas and a set of cane chairs, none new but none badly broken. "I see the new boy has been making himself useful," Foster said to Piggott as they went in to dinner.

"Up to a point. Lacey wangled the stuff with his cigars.

162

Lacey can get anything. Paxton couldn't get wet in a rainstorm."

"I wouldn't mind a French virgin. Can Lacey get me a guaranteed French virgin?"

"I believe there's one left. Six years old, very ugly. Ten cigars."

"I'll think about it. Ten is a bit steep."

After dinner most officers took their coffee in the anteroom. Boy Binns could pick out a tune on the battered piano, after a fashion, and a group of singers and saboteurs clustered around him. Paxton sat by a window and watched the sunset. Others sprawled in chairs and read yesterday's newspapers. The adjutant sat in a corner and smoked a stubby briar pipe while he fed bits of cheese to the dog Brutus.

Eventually, inevitably, there was a fight between the singers and the saboteurs, and the piano swayed violently. Boy Binns quit. The fighters chased each other around the room until they made themselves so unpopular that they took their fight outside and the anteroom became almost silent.

Thus everyone heard Spud Ogilvy's grunt of surprise. He was reading his mail. "This'll interest you, adj," he said. Captain Brazier tossed a fragment of cheese. It was like a token opening bid with a poor poker hand. Ogilvy said: "Old friend of mine, chap I was in the trenches with, says he served under you. He says 'I hear you've got our old CO, the amazing Basher Brazier, fastest gun on the Western Front'. Did they really call you Basher?"

"It was a corruption of 'pasha'. That's what the Egyptians used to call me."

"Then he says: 'Too bad about the blue blood, but how can you tell what colour it is unless you make a few holes in the bag?' What on earth does that mean?"

"Can't imagine."

"And he ends with a bit of verse. 'Ashes to ashes, dust to dust, if Jerry don't get you then Basher must'."

"It rhymes," Brazier said, getting up. "Not much else to be said for it." He clicked his fingers and Brutus obediently followed him out.

"My word," Ogilvy said. "I must write and ask him what he meant."

"Another thrilling episode of this gripping yarn next week," Foster said. "Be sure to place an order with your newsagent."

Paxton paid a mechanic to make the hinges on his trunk tamper-proof. Next day he found the lock and the hinges intact, but the trunk was nailed to the floor. He had to borrow a crowbar, all the time wondering how O'Neill could possibly have got inside it again. He saw the answer when he prised it free. O'Neill had got under the floorboards and driven the nails upwards. Paxton, grim with determination, paid again to have the trunk encased in sheet steel. He had not known he was capable of such rage and loathing. He dreamed of doing things to O'Neill's helpless, squirming body of such a mounting ferocity that he startled himself. But when he saw the armoured trunk he felt a rush of glee. "That's the stuff!" he said. "That's the answer!"

"Yes, sir," said the mechanic. "Oh, thank you, sir. Thanks very much, sir. Very kind of you, sir."

The daft affair of Sergeant Harris and the mules had not been Major Cleve-Cutler's fault but he felt the squadron had come out of it badly and he wanted to do something to make up for it. He asked Captain Brazier if he had any bright ideas.

"Well now, look here, I'm no airman," Brazier said.

"No, but you're twice my size and twice my age and you've got ten times my experience of the British Army, so what would you do, if you wanted to score a few points at Wing and show them we're not a bunch of drunks and delinquents?" Cleve-Cutler's scars grinned at him.

"Not *quite* twice your age. Forty-nine this year."

"My father's only forty-seven."

"Lucky chap. When I was forty-seven . . ." The adjutant rubbed the spot where his eyebrows met, and decided not to follow that thought.

"They think *I'm* old, you know, some of them. I've overheard them talking. 'Not bad for his age.' That sort of thing. Very patronising. God knows what they say about you."

"Prehistoric," the adjutant said. "Fossilized. What's that doddering old fool doing around here? That's the view of the intrepid aviator. Seen from ten thousand feet, I suppose I am prehistoric. And all those muddy fools at the Front must look like cavemen seen by eagles. Except that cavemen almost certainly had much more comfortable caves, and they didn't have to keep their heads down all the time. I'm wittering on like this in the hope that you won't notice I haven't answered your question."

"Forget it, adj. Not important."

"I'll give you a piece of advice, though. Attack the enemy's strength, not his weakness. My very first CO taught me that."

"Um." Cleve-Cutler reviewed all his possible targets. "The toughest nut to crack is the German observation balloon, I suppose."

"The tougher the nut, the sweeter the meat," Brazier said.

Cleve-Cutler talked it over with his flight commanders. "The Hun wouldn't defend his balloons so heavily unless they really mattered, would he?"

"Given a good telescope, a man in a balloon can see forty or fifty miles," said Gerrish. "So they say."

"I shall never sunbathe again," Foster said.

"No future in just charging at the bloody things," Piggott said. "You'd need an icebreaker to get through the archie."

"Well, there has to be a way. This is not orders from the rear, you understand. I'd just like us to develop a reputation for something other than going on a binge."

Various suggestions were made: fly high and bomb the balloon, fly not so high and set fire to it with incendiary parachutes, tow a grappling iron on the end of long thin cable and rip the thing open (a French pilot had actually attacked German planes like that, in the days before machine guns were carried). None of these ideas excited anybody. Cleve-Cutler told them to go away and think some more.

Foster held a meeting of 'C' Flight pilots. "Balloon-busting," he said. "That's this month's fashion. You win a goldfish in a jar for every balloon you bust." He was chewing his nails.

"I wish you'd stop doing that," Yeo said. "It makes your fingers look pruned."

Foster sat on his hands. "Spud?" he said.

"Well, there's always the Milne Method," Ogilvy suggested. "Bit expensive, I suppose. And what d'you do for an encore?"

"Don't look at me," Charlie Essex said. "I can't spell balloon-busting. Can't even say it."

"It's a matter of finding some way to baffle the archie, isn't it?" Yeo said. "The problem's not the balloon, it's getting close enough to bust it."

"Bloody archie," Essex muttered. "I really hate the stinking stuff. It doesn't fight fair."

"Nobody's invented the perfect weapon yet," Foster said, chewing a thumbnail. Yeo sighed, and Foster sat on his hand again.

"We're not going to find the answer here," Ogilvy said. "Maybe if we go up and look . . ."

Nobody had a better suggestion. "All right," Foster said. "Next time the weather's right, James and I will study the problem from several angles."

"Keep your heads down," Essex said. "They can't see you if you can't see them. That's a scientific fact."

Pepriac was rarely silent. Engines were constantly being tested, and aircraft took off and landed all day. No matter how often he saw it, the act of take-off – the bellowing, bouncing charge across the grass, the instant of lift, the easy climb – never lost its magic for Paxton. He felt the cramp of envy, and a craving that no amount of tramping across the land of the Somme could diminish. He went to see Tim Piggott and asked to be allowed to fly again.

"It's not my decision. I didn't ground you." Piggott's rigger had extracted a ragged lump of shrapnel from his FE's undercarriage and it lay on his desk. He poked at it with a pencil. "Besides, there's no room for you. All the FEs are fully crewed."

"There's the Quirk."

"If it was up to me you could take it and good riddance to you both." Piggott frowned, hard. His left eyelid had started flickering again. He put a finger on it to make it stop. "The Hun loves chumps like you. Very sentimental, the Hun, very fond of children, he enjoys putting large lumps of red-hot metal through their stupid little heads." The point of the pencil snapped against the piece of shrapnel. Piggott looked at it bleakly. "Buzz off," he said.

Paxton told Kellaway about this exchange. "If you ask me," he said, "it's a clear case of professional jealousy. We knocked down a Hun and Piggott got hit by shrapnel."

"Sorry to hear that," Kellaway said. "Where was he hit?"

"Oh . . . I don't know. At the Front somewhere."

"A chest wound?"

"No, no, no. Piggott wasn't touched. For God's sake pay attention."

"I'm getting one of my headaches," Kellaway said. "I'd better go and lie down."

Paxton was not discouraged by Piggott's words. Sooner or later, he knew, the squadron would need a pilot. Every day there were forced landings because of engine failures – a cracked fuel line, a clogged-up carburettor, a broken electrical lead. The crew of a machine in 'C' Flight were lucky to survive when their propeller shattered and the fragments hacked through the control cables leading to the tail. The plane obligingly crashed into a small lake, the only stretch of water for miles around, and they waded ashore. Once, as an FE circled the aerodrome, smoke suddenly boiled out of the engine and Paxton thought his day had come; but this pilot deftly blew out the fire with a series of plunging sideslips, and he landed grinning. Another time, Paxton saw an officer fall out of a tree, and he sent a passing mechanic to get the ambulance. The officer turned out to be Douglas Goss (he had been looking for a lost cricket ball). He was a catalogue of pain and injury, but it was a walking catalogue, and he dismissed the ambulance and limped back to the mess. "Bloody branch broke," he told Dando. "Typical shoddy frog tree." Frank Foster picked a twig out of Goss's hair, and said: "Anyone who goes up in one of those things must be mad, that's my opinion." Next day Goss was flying as usual.

Paxton borrowed a motorcycle and explored the more northerly parts of the Somme. He found a fresh kaleidoscope of regiments, with more units arriving daily. It excited him to know he was part of the most brilliant battle-force the world had ever seen, he was in the prime of his life, and he was about to demonstrate his dash and prove his courage in the mightiest clash of arms ever known. And – most splendid part of all – *Britain was going to win!* Patriotism glowed in him like plum brandy.

The roads were dense with military traffic, endless supply columns feeding the infantry its meat and drink, its bullets and bags of mail and boots, and so Paxton often rode his motorcycle across country. It was a sign of the changing times that he was stopped by a military policeman at the entrance to a field, and made to prove his identity.

"If you wouldn't mind keeping to the side of the field, sir," the man said. "There's manoeuvres going on in the middle."

Paxton chugged around the edge and saw nothing going on in the middle. He was stopped by another MP, and then by a third, who was reluctant to let him continue. "You ought to have been given a special pass, sir," he said.

"Well, I'm certainly not going back to get one," Paxton said crisply. The man consulted his clipboard. Paxton looked too. "There it is, for heaven's sake," he said. "Air Liaison. Two from the end. Satisfied?" He rode off before there could be any argument.

A couple of hundred yards ahead stood a reviewing stand built of scaffolding poles and planks. Cars were parked nearby, and a crowd of officers lounged about. It was an odd scene: like the finish of a fashionable point-to-point, but without the horses.

He avoided the crowd and left his bike near the cars. This wasn't his sort of show; those were staff officers, colonels and brigadiers and generals; he shouldn't be here; he could get into very hot water. That's what made it irresistible. But did he have the nerve to walk over to those officers and join in their conversation? No. No, he knew he wasn't brave enough for that. Instead he walked over to a driver who was sitting on a running-board. The man came to attention. "Stand at ease," Paxton said. "Look here, I can't afford to stay long, I've got to get back to my squadron." He glanced wisely at the sky. "Routine patrol, but it's got to be done." How sweetly the lies flowed! "So when is this show going to start, d'you reckon?"

"Well, it's late now, sir. In fact—" An orange flare burst high in the air, half a mile away. The crowd began moving towards the stand. "Good man," Paxton said. (Always praise the servants, his father had taught, even when they haven't done anything; it costs nothing and they feel they have to work harder to deserve it.) He hurried to join the crowd.

Nobody looked twice at him. He found a space to stand at the top, in a corner, behind some Guards subalterns. Their gloss made him feel dingy.

A major appeared below, and announced through a megaphone: "One minute to zero hour." Paxton began to notice things. Two hundred yards to the right a long trench had been dug, in the correct military zigzag pattern; communication trenches led to it. Two hundred yards to the left, white tapes had been laid in a long line, parallel to the trench. A second set of tapes could be seen a hundred yards behind the first. Between the trenches and the tapes the ground was smooth and green. There was no breeze. Sounds carried perfectly: a few crows complaining as usual, a horse neighing somewhere out of sight. It was all very peaceful. "Zero hour in five seconds," the major said. Conversation ceased.

Whistles blew, dozens of whistles, and men popped up from the trench as if on springs. "The first wave will advance in extended line at walking pace," the megaphone informed. "They will cross No-Man's-Land in eight minutes and thirty seconds." Indeed the wave had set off and NCOs could be heard shouting, straightening the line. Very soon it was impressively correct. A lieutenant walked in front of each platoon, holding a revolver or a walking stick. "The men are spaced five yards apart," the megaphone declared. "Company HQ, comprised of company commander and six men, can be seen following." Whistles shrilled again, and the trench ejected another force. "The first wave having completed one hundred yards, the second wave commences the advance," explained the megaphone.

Paxton was puzzled. This was all rather slow. He expected troops to *charge* when they advanced, shouting hoarse defiance, terrifying the enemy into surrender or retreat. These chaps were just plodding. Then the first wave got close enough for him to see how heavily loaded they were. Equipment was strung all over them. Faces shone with sweat. "Full packs are worn," the megaphone announced obligingly.

"Two days' rations and water bottles are carried. Each man has his rifle with bayonet, two gas respirators, full ammunition pouches, two grenades, one spade, one pair of wire-cutters and other minor kit. Thus he can be sure of being ready to cope with any eventuality."

The first wave plodded past the reviewing stand. Whistles shrilled and the third wave appeared from the trench.

"At zero hour," said the megaphone, "our barrage lifted from the enemy Front Line, represented here by white tape, and moved to the enemy Second and Third Lines. No resistance is anticipated. However, for training purposes, some opposition has been allowed to exist." Sure enough, half a dozen isolated figures sat up behind the white tape and began firing blanks. The first wave kept walking. Eventually the megaphone admitted: "Minor casualties may be suffered." Here and there a man gratefully sank to his knees and lay down. A bugle sounded. Stretcher-bearers climbed out of the trench and trotted forward.

"You will notice," the megaphone said, "that some men carry poles with flags. These will be raised in due course to act as markers for our guns. Others carry wiring stakes. They will use these to fortify captured positions. Rockets and carrier pigeons are carried for purposes of communication. Machine-gun units are present."

By now a fourth wave of troops had come out of the trench. The first three waves were walking steadily across No-Man's-Land, five yards between men, a hundred yards between waves, the NCOs nagging at them to straighten their lines. Paxton was enormously impressed. There was something so calm yet so implacable about this attack. Unstoppable: that was the word. They looked as if they could walk all day, wading rivers, climbing hills, trampling the enemy beneath their steady tread, never tiring. He chuckled. "They really need a band," he murmured, "playing 'Land of Hope and Glory'." The Guards subalterns looked at him, looked at each other, looked away. *Go to hell*, Paxton thought cheerfully. *How many Huns have you shot down? Well, then.*

A green rocket went up. "The first wave has now reached and captured the enemy Front Line," the megaphone reported. "It arrived fifteen seconds late. Our apologies." The reviewing stand was mildly amused. "The fifth wave has now left our trenches." *My God!* Paxton thought. *Is there no end to them?* "This fifth wave will carry out mopping-up operations, if necessary. The sixth wave will act as reinforcements, preparatory to the seventh wave, which will consist of Battalion HQ including Signals."

There was a pause while the second wave trudged to the white tape and lay down. The third wave followed but crossed the tape and kept going. So did the fourth. A minute later a red rocket went up. "The enemy Second and Third Lines have now been captured," said the megaphone. "Our barrage had already lifted from them, of course." There was a flicker of ironic applause. "The opportunity for breakthrough has therefore been created," said the megaphone defiantly.

Everyone looked to the right. This was the climax, the clincher, the cream on the cake. Sure enough, a trumpet call brought a squadron of cavalry surging into view, and behind it a second and a third, all boiling up to a full-blooded gallop. The horses went streaming over the trench. Paxton stopped breathing. Bright pennants raced from the ends of lances, swords made streaks of light. It was a race between the squadrons. The infantry had scattered to leave a wide gap. As the cavalry hammered past them they cheered, a throaty, disciplined roar that made Paxton grin with delight. He breathed again, deeply and triumphantly. The cavalry raced out of sight. "The breakthrough has been achieved," said the megaphone. "Tea will now be served."

The reviewing stand slowly emptied. Everyone drifted, in a haze of talk, to a group of trestle tables. Paxton took half a cucumber sandwich, a slice of cake and a cup of tea. He found himself standing next to a middle-aged major who blinked a lot. "What did you think of it, sir?" he asked.

The major sipped his tea and stopped blinking. He said: "I think perhaps someone has over-egged the pudding."

"I meant the exercise, sir."

"So did I, old chap. So did I."

Potty, Paxton thought. "Excuse me, sir," he said, and sidled away.

Bunches of troops were walking back to where they had come from. He rode his motorcycle across the field, twisting and turning to dodge them, and going slightly too fast because he enjoyed it and because he envied the way the cavalry had been free to race like the devil. Some soldiers stopped and cheered him. That made him feel good. He celebrated with a bit more speed. The rear wheel skidded out of a turn, nothing dangerous, just enough to earn another cheer, so he purposely skidded out of the next turn, straightened up and charged into a little hollow so fast that he came out of it flying, three feet of air beneath his wheels. He landed almost perfectly; but almost wasn't good enough at that speed. The bike wobbled more and more as if it were shaking its head harder and harder until finally it fell over and flung him aside.

The nearest group of men waited and watched. When they saw him stand up, they walked on.

His lungs didn't want to work. That was the worst thing. No matter how hard he sucked, his lungs refused to fill. All the breath had been knocked out of them and now they seemed numb or dead or something. Not dead: struggling. Failing. Useless. He thought: *This must be what drowning is like*, and immediately thought, *What an odd thing to think*, and then miraculously squeezed a cupful of air into each lung.

After two minutes he had so much breath he could afford to laugh.

The handlebar was a bit skewed but the wheels went round and the brakes worked. Trouble was, the engine wouldn't start. No matter how hard he stamped on the starter, the engine wouldn't even cough. He laboured at it until his leg was weary and his face was sticky with sweat.

It was a long way to Pepriac.

He propped the wretched machine on its stand, and sat down to rest. "D'you know what you are?" he said to it. "You're a mechanical turd." A soldier was watching.

He was short, and made to look shorter by the packs and webbing and equipment hung about him. "Hullo," Paxton said. "I don't suppose you can make this damn thing go, can you?"

The soldier came over and stooped to look at it. His hands and wrists, grasping his rifle, were small. The cords at the back of his neck were not yet powerful enough to be those of a man. "I could try, sir," he said.

172

"Please do."

The soldier laid down his rifle and took off his steel helmet. He had a small face with neat and tidy features, like a boy's, and serious eyes. His black hair had been closely clipped. He sat on his heels to examine the machine; and Paxton, with a great rush of memory, saw who it was he looked like. The gardener's boy. Dick. The best friend he'd never had.

No, that wasn't strictly true. For a couple of weeks, in the summer holidays when they were both fifteen, he and Dick had been wonderful friends, closer than he had known it was possible to be, each totally trusting the other and each able to make the other laugh just by looking into his eyes. Dick was only the gardener's boy but he had something special, not just good looks, although Paxton envied his smooth skin and freckles (he used to count them) but a kind of charm that Paxton had never met before. For that couple of weeks he felt he wasn't fully alive unless he was with Dick. His parents noticed. They disapproved. Dick was barely literate and have you seen his fingernails? Paxton got packed off to stay with a seaside aunt until next term began. After that, it wasn't the same.

But he never forgot. And now this young soldier, no bigger than Dick had been, touched the same chord. "How old are you?" Paxton asked.

"Seventeen, sir. I think I've got it." He did something to some wires. "Your electricals was all loose, sir."

"Ah. I had a small crash, you see."

The soldier started the bike, revved the engine, let it stop.

"Splendid!" Paxton said. "You're a genius. Jolly good stuff." He stood up. "What's your name?"

"Watkins, sir. Private Watkins."

"Jolly good." The more Paxton looked at him, the more he remembered Dick. He very much wanted this man to smile, the way Dick had smiled. "Aren't you awfully young, to be in the . . . whatever it is you're in?"

"Bradford Pals, sir. There's younger than me." Still no smile.

"Bradford Pals? That's one of those battalions full of chaps from the same place, isn't it? I met one the other day, in the Highland Light Infantry. Glasgow Tramways, they call

173

themselves. I couldn't understand a word they said." Paxton chuckled. Still no smile. "It must be great fun, being with your pals."

"The whole street joined up, so I joined up too. Didn't know what I was doing. Just followed the others. Didn't want to be left on my own."

"Good man." Paxton straddled the bike. "I expect you're looking forward to the Big Push, aren't you?"

"No, sir."

"No? Why not?"

The answer unrolled like dirty puttees. "Fucking trenches, fucking lousy food, fucking sergeant hates my fucking guts, fucking fritz is going to blow me to fucking bits." He picked up his rifle and helmet. "Sir."

Paxton was shocked. Watkins clearly meant what he said. Briefly, Watkins was in command: he spoke from authority, greater authority than Paxton had. "Perhaps I see things differently," Paxton said, "but believe me, from upstairs it's pretty obvious that the Hun is on the run, so you've got nothing to worry about."

Just when he least expected it, Watkins smiled. "I wish I could fly," he said. "I'd give anything to be able to fly."

"Would you? Well, come and see me, and I'll give you a flip in my plane." Paxton started the bike. "I'm at Pepriac," he shouted. "Lieutenant Paxton." It was a reward for Watkins' smile. Watkins would never be able to claim the reward, but it's the thought that counts. He roared off, zigzagging until he got the hang of the lopsided handlebars.

Chapter 12

It was like trying to sneak up on a guard dog. At a certain point the dog began to snarl. Get closer and it barked. Push your luck and you'd probably get bitten. Back off and the dog would shut up. But it was always watching.

Frank Foster in one FE and James Yeo in another had crossed the Lines to see how near they could get to an observation balloon before the dogs barked and bit. Only one balloon was flying that day, opposite the southerly end of the British sector, near the river Somme. The wind had probably grounded the others. It was strong and gusty. Even from a distance Foster could see the basket swinging as the balloon wallowed. What was worse, the gusts sometimes forced the balloon sharply down, making the cable go limp; then as the wind eased, the balloon leaped again. The observers must have had strong stomachs and their observations must have been urgently needed.

At first the two FEs had pretended to bypass the balloon, as if they were flying from north to south on some other business and the prevailing westerly wind just happened to push them near to it. It was a poor excuse and nobody believed it. A few ranging shots came and went, high and low, looking as harmless as tufts of black wool. Within twenty seconds the German batteries had adjusted for height. A string of shells burst in quick succession, starting wide and racing in for the kill. The last missed by less than fifty yards. Foster heard their gruff barks. The closest was as loud as his engine. Maybe its blast shook the plane, maybe the wind gusted. He dropped a wing and turned away. Yeo left by a different route, just to divide the targets.

For the next half-hour they tested the defences. Nothing made any difference. Come too close and you got shot at.

Yeo loathed archie. The FE gave him a lovely view of the world but no protection in front. Other planes had a big heavy engine in front, something to hide behind when the shell splinters came fizzing through the air. Nothing to hide behind in the FE, not even your observer, who was sitting in the stalls while you were in the balcony. It wasn't the risk of death that upset Yeo. Where would the Army be without death? Like roulette without chips. You had to have something to lose, otherwise what's the point? Nothing wrong with killing people in war. That was the only way to win medals, and Yeo accepted pain and mutilation and blindness and all the other unpleasantnesses as unavoidable side-effects of the process. But what he loathed and resented about archie was its stinking ugliness. It was worse than being attacked with a filthy bayonet by a chap who needed a bath. It was squalid. It was unmilitary. He despised the Hun for having dirty archie. British archie was white, or at least off-white.

Foster waggled his wings and pointed upwards. Yeo looked up and saw, very high, a formation of aircraft, at least six. How odd. He had never seen more than four planes together over the Lines before. Six was a crowd. It was like seeing six bishops or six Red Indian chiefs: you wondered what on earth they were up to. His observer put down his binoculars and shouted: "French." Yeo nodded. "Nieuports," the observer shouted. So that was all right. Clever little plane, the Nieuport. Came to pieces in a long dive, sometimes, but that was because the frogs were too cheap to tie it up with really strong string.

Foster gave a signal and the FEs separated again. There was one final test to be made: they would approach the balloon from opposite sides at the same time and see how the archie liked that. Then home for tea.

It took three or four minutes to get into position. When Yeo saw Foster's FE lined up with the balloon he opened his throttle to the full, and turned. The six-cylinder Beardmore vibrated like a threshing machine and everything Yeo saw was blurred. *Bloody awful engine*, he thought. *Why don't they give us decent engines?* He began worrying, in a remote, detached sort of way, what would happen if a piston snapped or a crankshaft broke, here and now. Collapse of stout party. Prisoner-of-war camp. He'd forgotten to bring his shaving kit, too. Parents would get a War Office telegram, *Missing, believed killed*. Hullo, hullo! Where was the German archie? Surely he must be within range by now. This was odd. He throttled back to cut the vibration and something hit him an almighty blow in the back, a huge thump that flung his body forward and jerked his head back. He crashed into the joystick and made the plane dive. His head slammed against the instrument panel, shattering glass and turning his face into a red ruin. Not that it mattered. Yeo was dead.

The observer did his utmost to reach him and shove him off the joystick. The FE was diving almost vertically, its wires screaming, its engine working hard to help it on its way. The observer was young, strong and fit, but it was like trying to climb up a cliff face and lift a rock that weighs as much as you do. The wires screamed, and in the end the observer screamed with them not from fear but from rage and frustration. He never knew what killed Yeo, and he was facing the wrong way to watch the ground come hurtling up to kill him.

"D'you know," Paxton said, "that's the fourth swimming pool I've seen being dug in the last week." He aimed his mug of tea at a gang of Chinese labourers working a few hundred yards away. "Good show, isn't it?"

He was talking to a captain in the Medical Corps. They were standing outside a new Casualty Clearing Station. "Is it?" the captain asked. He sounded doubtful.

"Well, I bet the Hun doesn't look after his troops like that. I think it's jolly thoughtful. It could get pretty hot this summer."

"Oh, I think it will. Extremely hot."

"There you are, then. I know the chaps at the aerodrome wouldn't mind having a pool as big as that."

"Give those Chinks a dozen loaves of bread," the doctor said, "and they'll dig night and day for you."

Paxton laughed. "It takes a war to get things going, they say."

"It's certainly done my career a power of good. I've learned more about heroic surgery in a year than I would have done in a lifetime. Lucky old me. At this rate I'll be the world's greatest expert at high-speed multiple amputation. Did you know that the record for lopping off all four limbs is twelve minutes ten seconds?" He ditched the dregs of his tea.

"Good Lord."

"It's not good enough." The doctor looked Paxton in the eye. "I can get that time down to eight minutes dead *and* throw in an appendectomy, if only they'll let me use my surgical axe. You see," he said, flexing his elbows, "it's all in the follow-through. If this war has taught us doctors anything, it's the need to use the wrists and follow through." He lifted Paxton's right arm and fingered the shoulder. "Otherwise it's all chopping and hacking," he said. "Which is not only distressing to the patient but also very, very time-consuming."

"Good heavens."

"You've nothing to worry about." He let the arm fall. "I could whip through that joint in half a minute. Be sure to ask for me, won't you? Don't let those butchers start hacking at you."

Paxton wondered about this conversation all the way back to Pepriac. There had been a combative glint in the doctor's eyes. Could have been drunk, of course. Except that he'd sounded so utterly clear and sure of himself. Queer coves, doctors.

"They could have been hit by archie," Colonel Bliss suggested.

"No, sir," Foster said. His face looked frozen.

"I mean you were both deliberately trying to provoke their guns. You went in until they forced you out. Isn't that right?"

"I've seen planes hit by archie. I know what it looks like."

Cleve-Cutler said: "You were a mile away, Frank."

"What's a mile? I could paint a picture of it all." His voice was dead level. "The Nieuports came down in single file, steep dive, going for the balloon, that's what I thought and so did the Hun. He turned all his guns on the frogs. Archie all around them. The frogs swung away, kept diving, passed behind Yeo's machine. The last Nieuport was closer than the rest. I saw it fire, I saw the tracer, I saw it hit the FE, I saw the FE tip up like a . . . like a wheelbarrow. I saw it crash."

They were in Cleve-Cutler's office. Bliss picked up a pen and examined the nib from different angles. "Perhaps we ought to wait and see what the Hun drops over our Lines. By way of confirmation, I mean."

Cleve-Cutler saw the look on Foster's face and rapidly put himself between the two men. "Captain Foster is a most experienced and capable flight commander," he said. "If Captain Foster says it was a fatal crash, you can be sure it was exactly that. Captain Foster is an officer I have complete and utter confidence in."

"Of course, of course," Bliss said. He was on his way out. "It's a shocking business. The French Air Force will be given hell, believe you me."

"They'll get more than that," Foster said.

Bliss pretended he hadn't heard. "Absolute hell," he said. "It's too bad you weren't able to spot the identification letters on those Nieuports."

"We got them," Foster said. "It's all in my report, for God's sake."

"Is it? I must have lost the file." Bliss remembered that he was holding the pen and gave it to Cleve-Cutler. "No, it really is too bad, because otherwise I might have been able to tell you that they belong to the 27th *Escadrille* of *avions de chasse* stationed at Selincourt. Shame, isn't it?"

They walked with Bliss to his car, and then went to the mess. It was the end of the afternoon, a grey day, no wind. Cleve-Cutler sent Private Collins to round up all those pilots and observers who were on the aerodrome. He went behind the bar and began opening bottles. "I'll make a few gallons of Hornet's Sting," he said to Foster. "You'd better hurry if you don't want to miss the party." Foster nodded, and went out.

Paxton went to his billet to change and found that his chest had been painted bright red.

Well, it was just another insult. He could tolerate it. He

moved the chest and found that the paint was wet. His hands were red. He shouted for Fidler, and sent him to get petrol and rags.

While Paxton was standing waiting, holding his hands as if supporting an invisible tray, Kellaway came in from the bathhouse. "Hullo!" he said. "You've got red hands."

"Shut up before I kill you."

"Please yourself." Kellaway began to dress. "There's a party in the mess, you know. CO's party. Remember Yeo?"

"Of course."

"Well, you can forget him."

At first Paxton was amazed by Kellaway's coldblooded announcement; then he realised that it meant another move up the table. To make sure, he said: "What about his observer?"

"Gone west too. The frogs did it."

Paxton didn't know whether to believe that or not. The more he thought about it, the less it mattered.

Kellaway put his cap on. Paxton said, distantly: "You might give O'Neill my compliments and ask him to spare me a few minutes."

Kellaway left. Paxton walked up and down. He found a loose floorboard and made it creak. O'Neill arrived, whistling. Paxton showed him his red hands. "If you are a gentleman, which I very much doubt," Paxton said, "you'll put your fists up and we'll settle this affair here and now." His lungs were pumping double-time, ready for the fight.

"You first." Nothing seemed to excite O'Neill.

Paxton clenched his fists and raised his arms and put one foot forward.

"Your lace is undone," O'Neill said. Before Paxton could look down, O'Neill had knelt and was retying the lace. He seized Paxton's ankle in both hands and heaved it waist-high. Paxton staggered. O'Neill turned and walked him out of the room. Paxton hopped behind, shouting and windmilling his arms. O'Neill led him to the mess, passing Fidler as he returned with a can of petrol. By the time he hopped up the wooden steps of the mess, Paxton's working leg was so exhausted that when O'Neill let go he fell over. He tried to stand on the other leg and fell over again.

A loud and violent race was going on inside the mess. It

involved jumping from one piece of furniture to another, while holding and drinking a tankard of Hornet's Sting. Paxton lay on the floor and watched furniture collapse and splinter, and heard the raucous howling of his fellow-officers. Collins gave him a full tankard. He got red paint all over it. Nobody cared. O'Neill had vanished. Paxton didn't care. He drank the filthy muck. It didn't taste too bad. He finished it and threw the tankard at Collins. Collins caught it, one-handed. Somebody went through the piano with a noise like a harp having a nightmare.

Foster reached Selincourt and remembered nothing about the journey. He had climbed to three thousand feet; he remembered nothing of that either. He circled Selincourt. It looked just like any other aerodrome, from the air.

He had to wait twenty minutes for a Nieuport. A monoplane took off, probably a Morane, and a big heavy biplane flew by. He ignored them both. The Nieuport came out of the east, as expected. It carried identification letters and numbers on its fuselage but he didn't look for them because he didn't care what they were. He dropped, turning his height into speed, and followed the Nieuport down to the field, gaining on it all the time, until the FE was bouncing about in its wash, only a couple of lengths behind.

That was when the French began firing off rockets, to warn the pilot. Foster's observer killed him before he could look around to see what they meant. Foster's observer shot him dead, in the back, as Yeo had been shot. The Nieuport tumbled as if it had tripped over its own feet. Foster climbed away and watched it crash and burn.

He flew home, and remembered nothing about the journey. If the French tried to chase him they took too long getting off the ground because they never caught him. He landed and gave the machine to his groundcrew.

Cleve-Cutler was waiting. "Well, that squares the account," Foster said. "Now maybe we can get on with the war." In the distance the racket from the mess rose and fell.

"I've kept it warm for you," Cleve-Cutler said.

*

181

The noise of snoring woke Paxton, and hatred flared like a fire in sudden wind. It was a primitive, grunting snoring, typical of O'Neill. Paxton snarled. The snoring stopped. Too late, of course: sleep was impossible now. He sat up. The billet was empty.

Kellaway came in, swinging his sponge-bag. "I can't tell you how unspeakably filthy you look this morning," he said.

Paxton tried to speak but his mouth seemed to be stuck together. He was wearing his uniform, including shoes. He must have slept in his clothes. He got his lips apart and cleared his throat. The effect was nothing to be proud of. "Unspeakably filthy," Kellaway said.

Paxton got to his feet and walked to the foot of the bed. His knees wobbled as if taken by surprise and he had to clutch at a chair. For a few seconds the floor receded enormously until he felt as if he were looking down from a mountaintop. His ears made a note higher than any violin could reach.

O'Neill kicked the door open and came in whistling. Paxton had to sit down.

This whistling was slow torture. It was never loud and it never stopped; it just warbled on and on, endlessly, like the whistle of a kettle always coming to the boil but never making it. Half the time O'Neill was flat. If he had been flat all the time Paxton could have accepted it but instead O'Neill's whistling slipped off-key and then, after a bar or two, found it again, for a short while. He often skipped a beat; sometimes he skipped whole bars and picked up the tune at odd and disturbing places. His whistling never paused but it was always sluggish. It dragged. It was slipshod. It drove Paxton mad. He hunched his shoulders and clenched his teeth.

"Hard cheese on Jimmy Yeo, wasn't it?" Kellaway said.

O'Neill stopped whistling. Paxton slowly relaxed. "Oh well," O'Neill said. "There are worse ways to go. Bloke I knew caught the Queensland potato blight. His name was Lewis. He looked so bloody awful he had to go round with his head in a sack. Five years he lingered. They called him Lingering Lew."

"You do talk a lot of balls," Kellaway said.

"Mind you," O'Neill said, "he never looked as bad as *that*."

They gazed at Paxton. "A cold bath would do you a world

182

of good," Kellaway said. "The CO wants to see us all in half an hour." Paxton tried to stand, but one leg was much shorter than the other. Either that, or the floor was cockeyed.

Cleve-Cutler assembled his officers in the debris of the mess and held up a canvas message-bag with a German eagle stamped on it. "The enemy dropped this behind our Lines at dawn," he said. "It's addressed to me, here. Full marks to German Intelligence. It contains some personal items found in the wreck of Yeo's FE, and there's a note saying both men will get a military funeral. I'm glad about that. The padre's going to say a few words."

There was some shuffling of feet. Broken glass tinkled.

"The squadron has lost two good friends," the padre said. "Two thoroughly decent sportsmen. I know you will agree when I say they each played a straight bat, often on a bumpy wicket, and indeed they had assembled a very creditable score when, out of the blue, the Great Umpire in the Sky decided that both their innings were closed, as one day He will for each and all of us.

"If his decisions sometimes seem hard to understand we always have the Bible to turn to for help. It has never failed me, and it did not fail me now. Last night, I admit, I was sorely puzzled by the actions of our French allies. I prayed for guidance, and when I awoke this morning the answer came to me immediately: Exodus eight." He opened his Bible. "Verse 8. Pharaoh says to Moses: 'Entreat the Lord, that he may take away the frogs from me, and from my people'. And verse 13: 'And the Lord did according to the word of Moses; and the frogs died out of the houses, out of the villages, and out of the fields.'" He closed his Bible. "They had a plague of frogs, you see. Well, in a sense, can we not say that we too, yesterday, suffered from a plague of frogs? And that our remedy was very similar? The Lord smote the frogs of Egypt, and we smote the frogs of France. In both cases, the godly people were not plagued by frogs any more. The message of God's holy word," he said, waving it above his head, "is here for all to see, if only we look hard enough. In the name of the Father, and of the Son, and of the Holy Ghost. Amen."

They mumbled their amens.

"Thank you, padre," Cleve-Cutler said. His fixed half-grin glittered with an amusement that perhaps he really felt. "As far as I'm concerned a plague of frogs consists of one, and in future if one frog pilot so much as looks at you sideways, blow his head off. Okay, that's all."

As they dispersed, Goss said to the padre: "I never knew all that stuff about frogs. How on earth did they get into the houses?"

"It's rather a complicated story, Douglas. You see, God wanted Pharaoh to let the Israelites go out of Egypt, and when he refused, God sent this plague of frogs to show Pharaoh that he meant business."

"And did it work?"

"Well, no, it didn't, so God sent a plague of lice to Egypt, and when that didn't work He sent swarms of flies, but Pharaoh still refused to let them go."

"What a bally nerve."

"Yes. So God sent a murrain upon all the beasts of Egypt. That's a disease like boils, very unpleasant. Then he sent plagues of hail and locusts, and a plague of darkness."

"My stars. Not very nice for Pharaoh's mob."

"No."

"And I expect God got His way in the end."

"Yes."

"He usually does, doesn't He?"

"I suppose so."

"In fact Pharaoh was a bit of a chump to think he could win."

"A bit of a chump. Yes."

Cleve-Cutler was sitting on his bed, reading a letter from a friend in his old squadron and grinning because it was a very funny letter, when Foster knocked on the door.

"Want a whisky?" Cleve-Cutler said. "You look absolutely frozen." It was not a cold day.

"No thanks." Foster sat in a chair, didn't like it, got up and sat on the floor in a corner of the room. "The other day you offered me a job in another outfit. Acting CO."

"It's gone." Cleve-Cutler found a couple of glasses and wiped them with a towel. "D'you want to move, Frank?"

184

"Yes. Now."

"Can't be done, old boy. I need you here."

"Oh well." Foster found a long, thin splinter of wood in the wall of the hut and began pulling it free. "Doesn't matter. I don't deserve to be given a squadron, I'm too stupid. I've been incredibly stupid."

Cleve-Cutler poured whisky and gave him a glass. "Yes?" he said.

"I can't believe how dense I've been. I really, honestly did think it would all be over soon. Then we'd all go home and . . ." He stirred his whisky with the splinter. "It's going to go on for ever, isn't it?"

"Look on the bright side, Frank. Lots of lovely promotion waiting for chaps like you."

Foster aimed the splinter like a dart and tossed it across the room. "Stupid and blind," he said. "I thought I'd never cop it. Other people go west. Not me. Now I know better. Or worse."

"Oh, tosh!" Cleve-Cutler said. "Your chances *improve* with experience, everyone knows—"

"Flamer," Foster said. "I'll be a flamer. Quite soon."

"Bet you won't. Week's pay. How's that, Frank?"

"It's bound to happen." Foster made a sour face. "Doesn't matter."

"It matters to me. I need you."

Foster stood up and drank the whisky. "Incredibly stupid," he said, and went out.

Nothing was heard from the French about Foster's revenge. It was assumed that the incident was closed. Brazier told Cleve-Cutler of an occasion late in 1914 when English artillery had accidentally dropped a few shells on a French position. Before the French protest could be translated the same number of French shells had fallen among English troops. "Nothing left to be said, after that," Brazier remarked. "Or written. I gave our gunners a damn good rollicking but you won't find a whisper of it in the regimental history. Now then: what d'you want me to enter in the squadron diary regarding the loss of Yeo and his observer?"

"Killed while attacking an enemy balloon," Cleve-Cutler

said. "You might chuck in a 'gallantly'. That never did any harm."

"And Foster's business?"

"Exactly. It's Foster's business. Nothing to do with us."

Nevertheless, Cleve-Cutler knew that Foster's state of mind was something he could not ignore. The man still did his job well but off-duty he could be touchy and unpredictable. Sometimes he was as debonair as ever; at other times he laughed when there was no joke to laugh at; and once or twice he withdrew into a kind of frozen silence while conversation went on around him.

"You know him better than I do," Cleve-Cutler said to Piggott. "Have a quiet word with him."

Piggott had a chance for a quiet word when he found Foster sitting alone at the end of the bar, holding a fly-swat. He seemed to be in a cheerful mood. "See that fly, Tim?" he said. At least a dozen flies were circling nearby. "That one on the left . . . No, it's in the middle now . . . There he goes . . . I'm going to kill that fly, Tim. Sooner or later he'll wander over here and then . . ." Foster demonstrated a brisk swat, and smiled. "One dead fly."

"I see." Piggott got himself a bar stool. "Does it have to be that particular fly?"

He had asked the wrong question. All Foster's cheerfulness faded away. He looked saddened and weary. "Probably not," he said. "I suppose one dead fly is worth just as much as another. What's the price of a dead fly nowadays? About a thousand pounds, isn't it?"

Piggott was baffled, but he decided to go along with what might turn out to be an elaborate joke. "It depends who's buying," he said.

Foster got off his stool, thrashed about with the swat, and drove all the flies away. "They'll be back in two minutes," he said, "so I don't see the point of it all. Do you?"

"Maybe there isn't a point." Piggott's threshold of tolerance for foolishness was low and he had almost reached it. "Listen, Frank," he said, "we're all as cheesed-off as you are about what that murdering frog did."

Foster frowned hard. "I don't follow you, Tim."

"That awful business with Yeo."

"Oh, that." Foster tossed his fly-swat in the air and deftly caught it. "Doesn't matter."

Cleve-Cutler listened to Tim's report. "Oh well," he said, "he'll get over it, I expect. Whatever it is."

Chapter 13

All the FEs were up on patrol. Kellaway had gone to hospital to have his head examined. The aerodrome was dull. For ten minutes Paxton threw an old tennis ball for Brutus to chase. Then he went to the adjutant and asked permission to go to Amiens for a haircut. "Get me some decent ink while you're there," Brazier said. "This Army stuff's like gnat's piss."

A wagon was leaving the transport section. Paxton waved it down. Corporal Lacey was driving. "I have a few calls to make *en route*," Lacey said as Paxton got in. The cab was stacked with boxes of Havana-Havanas. "I want to collect some new old furniture to replace the old old furniture in your mess, for instance."

"Sorry about that. Childish way to behave. Mindless destruction."

"Do you think so? I'm surprised. The apparent vandalism of squadron parties and mess nights is squarely in the Western tradition of emotional relief through the exercise of seemingly primitive orgies of self-indulgence which are actually very tightly contained."

"Tightly contained?" Paxton scoffed. "Don't talk rot. We smashed everything in sight."

"Exactly. Everything in sight *in the mess*. It was like Carnival, or Mardi Gras, or New Year's Eve in Glasgow. A beano as an essential corrective to the restraints and restrictions of the rest of the year. With all due respect to the Duke of Wellington, the battle of Waterloo was not won on the playing-fields of Eton. It was won in the shambles and wreckage of the Fourth of June celebrations, when the Old Etonians proved they were as happily violent as any, and far more so than most."

"Tosh," Paxton said. It wasn't an adequate answer, but Lacey engaged the clutch and revved the engine and after that it was too noisy to talk.

They drove over washboard *pavé* and rutted side roads and potholed farm tracks, calling on depots where stores were heaped in small pyramids of boxes that could be seen a mile away. Sometimes Lacey stopped at the main entrance; more often he went to the back and talked to a shirt-sleeved NCO who lived in a small guard hut with a large guard dog. Cigars changed hands; goods were loaded into the wagon: timber, carpet, drums of olive oil, bits of plumbing, rolls of canvas, a cinema projector, much furniture, a piano, a hip-bath, and more that was hidden inside wooden crates. He also collected items at military storehouses in requisitioned barns and farms. There were so many stops that Paxton lost interest until he saw Lacey and a sergeant discussing a cow. Lacey didn't take the cow but he did come away with a box of live hens. "What's wrong with the cow?" Paxton asked, sarcastically. "Too heavy?" "Too pregnant," Lacey said.

At last they drove into Amiens. Occasional gaps in the streets showed where bombs, or perhaps long-range shells, had fallen, but the town was full of life, most of it in khaki and all of it with francs to spend. Lacey trundled through the centre, pointing out the good places and the bad. "*That's* the only shop to go to for handkerchiefs . . . This little restaurant on the corner iš very sound on fish . . . I can't recommend that café unless you're desperate for company . . . Stay away from *them*, they're so overpriced it's quite criminal . . . Excellent *pâté* here . . ." Eventually he ran out of shops and increased speed.

"Where are you going?" Paxton complained. "I came here to get a haircut, you fool."

Lacey stopped the wagon. "Surely you don't want to have your hair cut *back there*, do you?" he asked. "They're all barbarians. I wouldn't let them cut the grass. I assumed you would want to go to the place that I go to." For a moment they stared at each other. "It's tucked away behind *l'église St.-Jacques*," he said. "It's called Leroux Frères."

"You're M.N.T. Lacey," Paxton said in a voice that was not much more than a whisper. "You played Hamlet in the school play."

"Yes. I thought you knew."

"You were years and years ahead of me. I was just a kid. In fact you must have been in your last year when I was in my first."

"Probably."

"And the moustache . . . It completely changes your face."

"I recognised you immediately. But then, yours is a much smaller moustache."

Paxton looked away. "You were a prefect," he said. "You beat me, once."

"Did I? Why?"

"For fighting."

"Ah. And did the beating hurt?"

"Not much."

"No. My heart wasn't in it, even in those days."

They drove to Leroux Frères. From the outside it could have been mistaken for a town house. A very old man opened the door and silently took their hats and Paxton's cane. The place smelled faintly of sandalwood soap. He led them to a room that was all marble and mahogany except for a pair of barber's chairs placed back to back. Two men, black-suited, grey-haired and silent, helped them out of their tunics and into the chairs. These, Paxton thought, must be the famous *frères*. His mind was still fluttering around the discovery that Lacey was an old boy of Sherborne. "Um . . ." he said. "*Je voudrais que vous . . . um . . .*"

"Don't bother," said Lacey from the other chair. "They know what's best for you."

Paxton gave up. It was all too much. A hot towel was wrapped around his face below the eyes and the chair smoothly reclined. He found himself looking at the ceiling. It was covered in frescoes, skilfully drawn and delicately coloured and so erotic that his stomach muscles jumped like hot chestnuts. A small gathering of men and women, none with clothes on and all splendidly athletic, were doing amazing things to one another as if it were all great fun. There seemed to be some kind of sequence to the pictures. One led to another. Heavens above! Paxton's eyeballs rolled around in their sockets while the scissors snipped.

When he was back on his feet and in his tunic, nicely brushed down and buttoned up, he suddenly remembered the need to pay. "Don't bother," Lacey said before Paxton could reach his francs. "I have an arrangement." Lacey shook hands with the man who had cut his hair. Paxton did likewise. The very old man showed them out. *Fancy shaking hands with your barber*, Paxton thought. *No wonder the frogs are in such a pickle.*

"Quite a deçent haircut," he said.

"Thank you."

Paxton jutted his chin. He felt in danger of being patronised. "Mind you, I'm not sure I believed it all," he said.

Lacey looked amused. "These things can always be tested. It's early in the day, but there are a couple of places you might like to try. For instance . . ."

"No." Paxton felt his face going red. "No thanks. Lunch is what I need."

Lacey drove him to a serious-looking hotel called *Voyageurs*. "Their *terrine de canard* is not to be despised," he said.

"Aren't you coming in?"

"It's officers only. I wear mufti when I come here. Feel free to mention my name. I shall go off to a rude, crude *cave* and eat half as well as you for a tenth of the price."

Paxton climbed down and watched the wagon clatter away. He felt suddenly quite lost without Lacey. But that was absurd. Lacey was one of the Other Ranks, while he was Our Trusty and well beloved Oliver Arthur David Paxton, in whom King George reposed especial Trust and Confidence . . . He looked at *Voyageurs*, and it seemed even more serious and costly and overwhelming. He breathed deeply and ran up the steps as if he owned the place. When in doubt, get on or get out.

The restaurant took up almost the whole of the ground floor. It was busy; very busy. The head waiter was fussing with a party of staff officers who had just arrived, and when at last he came hurrying over to Paxton his flurry of apologies

191

and welcomes went straight past him to yet another high-ranking group, all spurs and red tabs, who got steered to an empty table. Paxton felt exposed and ignored. The head waiter eventually found time for him, took the news that he was alone with tightened lips, and did a lot of muttering and standing on tiptoe before he found him a small table in a dim corner and disappeared.

The menu was as long as a short story, and Paxton understood about six words of it. He couldn't see *terrine de canard* anywhere. He began to loathe Lacey.

Waiters hurried by, blinkered in their devotion to duty to others, until he lost patience and tried to stop one. Total failure. The man shrugged, said something in the usual gabbling gibberish and laughed, *actually laughed* as he went away. Paxton sat and steamed. He was helpless. He hated being helpless. He hated these arrogant frog waiters and these fat and greedy colonels and brigadiers. He was hungry. Ravenous. And still nobody came.

When he had lost all hope, and given up, a waiter did actually arrive. He placed a tulip-shaped glass of champagne in front of Paxton. Beside the glass he placed a card. Then he stood back and waited.

Paxton tasted the champagne and drank the lot in one go. The card was embossed in gold with the name *Judith Kent Haffner*. Extraordinary. He looked at the waiter, who shrugged, but then what else could you expect? He turned the card over. *Join me before you starve to death*. Green ink. Firm, confident handwriting.

There were eight or nine young officers seated at her table in the middle of the room. The oldest was a major in the Royal Sussex with a badly scarred face; he looked about 25. The rest were captains and lieutenants of Paxton's age or a year or two older. Most wore medal ribbons. It was a noisy, jolly party; everyone was talking and pointing and telling the others to shut up and listen, and failing, and laughing. Judith Kent Haffner was listening and talking and joining in the jokes too, but mainly what she was doing was smiling at Paxton as he followed the waiter. And Paxton, who was not much good at smiling and who fundamentally disapproved of strange women sending him drinks, found himself smiling back. She was not the matron he had expected. She was young and she was startlingly pretty in a way that reminded him of the pictures of girl elves in the fairy stories read to him by his nanny: big eyes, big mouth, shiny black hair cut short and swept forward in twin curls that touched her cheekbones. She reached out a long, slender and almost naked arm and took Paxton's hand. Her fingers were firm. "Buzz off, Henry," she said. The cavalry lieutenant sitting at her left immediately got up and cheerfully moved away. A waiter scooped up Henry's plate and held the chair for Paxton to sit. "You're one of those golden eagles, aren't you?" she said. "I can tell from your wings."

"I potter about the sky occasionally."

She found that very funny, and he felt flattered. "What's your name?" she asked.

"Paxton. Oliver Paxton. And you must be Mrs. Haffner."

"No, no. Everyone calls me Judy. I don't like Oliver. Haven't you got another name?"

Paxton didn't like Arthur. "There's David."

"Bring my friend David a lovely steak," she told a waiter.

His glass was filled with wine. The cavalryman, Henry, had been found a place elsewhere at the table. A steady shuttle of waiters came and went. The only person not eating was Judy. She seemed able to follow half a dozen conversations at once. Occasionally she stroked Paxton's hand, even tucking her little finger inside his, and when his steak came she watched him eat and she shared in his enjoyment; he looked at her and she made a happy pout, so he sliced the most tender piece of the steak and carefully put it between her lips. She shut her eyes as she ate. For no reason at all he felt a little weak, and drank some more claret.

Everyone chatted to him; he chatted to everyone. Judy ordered apple pie for him, and it was a revelation: sweet and tangy, crisp and flaky. Apple pie at Sherborne had been stodge in stodge. How right he had been to leave school! He could easily eat another piece of apple pie but he wasn't sure if that was the done thing. In any case she took his hand, and squeezed it, and said, "Now you're going to protect me against all these hulking great thugs, aren't you, David?"

"But of course." He felt like St. George with a freshly ground and sharpened sword.

She took his arm as they all trooped out. He realised that nobody had paid. Money didn't seem to matter to these people; this was a refreshing, exhilarating experience; an introduction to a higher level of living. He cocked an eyebrow at the smiling head waiter as they went by. The man saw it, and cocked an eyebrow in return.

Two chauffeur-driven Buick limousines were waiting. They drove out of Amiens to the west, quite fast. "This must seem awfully *slow* to you," she said. She had an appealing way of drawling one word in a sentence; apart from that her voice was light and only faintly tinged with Irish. At first, when he saw that elfin face, he had assumed she was delicately built, even fragile, but now he saw that she was slim – unfashionably slender, in fact – but very well put together. Jolly nice legs, and a jolly good chest, or whatever it was that girls called it. "I'm just glad to be alive," he said. She opened her eyes wide. "Death by starvation," he said. "Deadly dreary." She laughed, and imitated his clipped style: "Deadly dreary," and laughed again, all of which made him feel good. "Want to play a little tennis?" she said.

They were passing some grass courts. Beyond them a lake glittered in the sunshine, with a wooded hill overlooking it and part of a big, honey-coloured house visible through the trees. "Don't you lose a lot of tennis balls in the lake?" he asked.

"Hundreds!" she said with a childlike gusto. "Thousands!"

Jimmy Duncan knew he'd already killed the gunner of the Aviatik when he saw a red streak shimmering along its side. That was during the third attack, when he fired two short bursts but the German pilot jinked so hard that Duncan missed with both; however, there was no return fire and he saw the long streak behind the rear cockpit. It stood out against the Aviatik's camouflage, a pattern of green and yellow cubes, like expensive gift-wrapping. Maybe a bullet had nicked an artery. If the gunner wasn't dead he was dying fast: Jimmy Duncan knew that for sure. Now was the time to get in really close and blow the Aviatik to bits. Now. Fast.

Frank O'Neill wasn't so sure. He hadn't noticed the blood

and he thought maybe the gunner was reloading, or clearing a stoppage. Rush in now and he might pop up and make holes in them both. Besides, there might be another machine lurking high above, in the sun. It was a dazzling afternoon and he couldn't search that part of the sky but something in his gut said somebody was up there. They were three miles on the wrong side of the Lines and they'd been bloody lucky to catch the Aviatik, so lucky that he wondered whether it was a decoy and he was about to be jumped from a great height. It was late in their second patrol of the day and O'Neill was tired.

On the other hand the Aviatik was slow and probably damaged. It couldn't get away. It should be an easy kill.

He flew the FE parallel to the Aviatik, just outside the range of its gun, and tried to squint up into the semi-glare around the blinding disc of the sun. Splinters of light danced in his eyes until they were lost in the wash of tears.

"I got the gunner," Duncan bawled. He was kneeling on his seat and facing O'Neill. "Gunner's dead."

"Says you," O'Neill shouted.

"Let's go, let's get the bugger." Duncan tried to reach into O'Neill's cockpit and grab the joystick. "He's mine, I want him."

O'Neill batted his hand away. "Okay!" he shouted. "Sit down, for Christ's sake!" If Duncan had knocked the joystick he might have been thrown out. It was a measure of Duncan's hunger for a kill after dozens of barren patrols.

Duncan sat. O'Neill nudged the throttle forward and eased the joystick across. The horizon swung like a seesaw. A touch of rudder brought the nose around until the Aviatik was dead ahead, chugging along, pouring smoke from its upright exhaust, its pilot praying for rescue, or a cloud, or a miracle. When it was obvious that none of those was going to appear he despaired and stuck his nose down.

To dive was the only thing left to do and also the worst thing to do. The FE could outdive an Aviatik, which meant that O'Neill would catch him, and when he did the German pilot would no longer be so free to jink and dodge and swerve. On the other hand it could be dangerous down there. German ground fire was notoriously lethal. All these thoughts chased each other through O'Neill's mind when it was already too late. The FE was howling and vibrating as its dive steepened.

He caught the Aviatik after they had fallen about a thousand feet, and the strain on the German plane's wings was such that O'Neill could see them fluttering and distorting. If his FE was doing the same he didn't want to know, so he didn't look behind him. He manoeuvred so as to give Duncan a slightly upward shot. When the Aviatik exploded or fell to pieces he wanted to be out of the way. They were four lengths apart. France lay in front like a map. Duncan fired. Every third shot was a tracer. His bullets went skimming over the Aviatik's top wing. He adjusted his aim and fired again. The Lewis gun jammed.

Duncan had never before cleared a jam when he was hanging in a dive with a hurricane battering at his arms. The Lewis often jammed; he knew just what to do; but it demanded strength and skill to force the gun to reject the faulty round wedged in its breech, and then to accept a fresh round, properly cocked, while the FE rocked and shuddered. This jam was a bad one. Duncan heaved and thumped until in the end he had to fumble under his seat for the leather mallet and give the gun an almighty wallop, and then another. The third bash did the trick. He gasped for breath and relaxed. The FE lurched, and the mallet swung and knocked the ammunition drum off the top of the gun. He grabbed and missed. The drum bounced off his chest and vanished. Fear made him shout: that drum could have smashed their propeller! Maybe it sailed wide. Maybe it went clean through the disc. What difference? By the time he had unclipped a spare drum and banged it into place the dive was over. Duncan looked up and saw trees higher than his head. O'Neill was chasing the Aviatik up a valley.

The German was dipping and rising, working hard at making himself a poor target, but the valley was narrowing and O'Neill was steadily gaining. Duncan fired a couple of short bursts. The Aviatik seemed to stagger. It dropped until its wheels were parting the tall grass. O'Neill held the FE steady to give Duncan a good, final, downward shot. Both men were looking at the Aviatik. Neither of them saw the telegraph wire strung across the valley. It took Duncan's head off as cleanly as a grocer cutting cheese and then it snapped. O'Neill felt the FE shudder. At first he thought a cylinder had blown, but the engine note sounded true. Duncan wasn't firing. Why the hell wasn't Duncan firing? Another jam? O'Neill half stood and looked down into the front cockpit. Duncan's body was flopping about and blood was jetting out. The body flopped again and O'Neill got a hot squirt in the face. He sat down and hauled the joystick into his stomach and spat. As the FE climbed away, below it and behind, the Aviatik came to rest with its tail in the air.

They all drank coffee and cognac on the terrace of the honey-coloured house. Servants brought the coffee but Judith Kent Haffner served it, strolling amongst the men with a silver coffee pot that had a neck like a swan's, while two maids followed carrying cups and sugar and cream. Paxton stood at the edge of the party and pretended to be examining the house but really he was watching her. There was a rose garden nearby; sometimes the breeze carried its scent. She reached him and now he could look without pretending. "I want to know something," she said as she filled his cup. "I want to know how big your machine-gun is. Now be honest, David."

"I'm not allowed . . . I mean, I'm pretty sure that sort of thing is, you know, secret."

"Wow," she whispered. "Holy smoke."

Later the men played tennis. Paxton had no tennis shoes, of course, so he played barefoot and beat Henry, who didn't try terribly hard. The breeze had dropped; the afternoon was baking hot. "Fancy a swim?" Henry said. "There's an hour till tea."

They undressed in a boathouse that overhung the lake and smelt of tar. Several costumes hung on hooks; all were too big or too small. "Oh, forget them," Henry said, and ran and dived in. Paxton followed him before he had time to think about it. The water was superbly cool and smooth; when he looked up he could see the surface, glowing greenly. He swam underwater as far as he could and burst up into the sunlight, gasping for breath.

They fooled about for a minute or two and then swam to a small island, little more than a huge boulder with a couple of trees growing out of it. The rock was smooth and hot. Paxton stretched out on his back and felt the heat soak into him. "D'you do this sort of thing often?" he asked.

"Now and then. Judy keeps more or less open house. Once you've been invited you're free to pop in whenever you like."

"Very generous."

"Damn good billiards room, too."

Paxton waved at what could be seen of the house. "She's awfully young for such a whacking great place, don't you think?"

"Awfully young and awfully beautiful."

"What I mean is, how does Mr Kent Haffner fit into the picture?"

"Ah. Well, we don't see much of him. He's American, she's Anglo-Irish. I don't know all the facts, but I think she's his second wife and he wants to be the next American ambassador to Paris, so he's got himself appointed special consul or something, to prove how good he is. Apparently he spends all his time travelling around France and buttering-up people. Getting Yankee war material sent over. That sort of thing. Stinking rich, obviously." Henry closed his eyes.

"I see. So Judy has to find her own friends."

"She likes goodlooking young men. She's probably up in her bedroom right now, watching us through a telescope."

Paxton laughed. "Don't be absurd." But he sat up and raised his knees.

"Don't worry, old man. You've nothing to be ashamed of." Henry got to his feet and waved in the direction of the house. "Her husband's a hundred years old," he said. "Fifty, at least. Doesn't seem fair, does it?"

Tea was served on the terrace. It was lavish and Paxton was hungry. The jams and jellies were English; the scones and cakes were made English-style; there was even a genuine sherry trifle. Judy knew how to please her guests. Paxton took his time and ate his fill, and watched her dance as the gramophone played jazz. She made a game of it, dancing through and around the guests and changing partners whenever the whim took her, which was often. Eventually, inevitably, she released her partner and took Paxton's hands. "Bad mistake," he said. "I'm dreadful." But she was already dancing and he did his clumsy best to match her steps. Fortunately they moved into an empty part of the terrace so he didn't have to worry about colliding with chairs and tables; nevertheless he was frowning furiously. She stopped and hugged him. "You're not dreadful, David," she said. "You're *appalling.*" He stood, shocked and delighted, and waited to see what happened next. She led him to a stone balustrade where they could pretend to admire the view and no one could hear them. "You're as stiff as one of those great big machine-guns of yours," she told him.

"I never said I was a dancer."

"Absolutely right. You never did. How many German aeroplanes have you shot down?"

"One. One big one. Two-seater Albatros."

She had linked her little finger with his. Now she tightened it. "Tell you what. You shoot down another German plane and I'll teach you how to dance."

"That's a bargain."

Yeo's replacement was an eighteen-year-old called Peter King who should never have been given his wings. He had impressed the interviewing officer at the War Office with his games record at Winchester and his fresh-faced keenness to get stuck into the Hun. He survived pilot training because he was lucky and because the aerodrome was so big that it disguised his faults. His instructor was a man who had been sent home after too long in France; he despised instructing and he disliked King because he was such a bad pilot, so he ignored him whenever he could. A lot of instructors were like that. They called the trainee pilots 'Huns' and were glad to see the back of them.

Cleve-Cutler looked at King's logbook. "Twenty hours," he said. "Eight solo." He passed it to Foster.

"Yes, sir," King said.

"You've never flown an FE."

"No, sir."

"Now's your chance. Go and get some kit."

"Thank you, sir." King went out, looking as if he had won several medals.

"Give him the worst machine we've got," Cleve-Cutler

said, "I don't want him smashing anything new. He goes up alone, of course."

"All right." Foster paused on his way out. "He reminds me of someone," he said, "but I can't think who."

"He reminds me of everyone who comes here. Boring, isn't it?"

Foster walked with King to the aeroplane and briefed him on the take-off routine and what speeds to aim for. King nodded all the time. "You know about torque?" Foster asked. "Slight tendency of the plane to rotate the opposite way to the propeller?" King nodded. "Apply a bit of opposite rudder to cancel the torque," Foster said. King nodded. "The main thing is to keep your revs up and give yourself plenty of height," Foster said. King nodded. "And no violent manoeuvres, no stunting." King nodded. "And your crab sandwiches are under your seat," Foster said. King nodded. Foster stopped and looked at him. King blinked, and smiled. "You don't have to do this, you know," Foster said. "It's not compulsory." King nodded.

He took off without difficulty. It was the ropiest FE in the squadron, heavily patched and splinted, but the engine was sound. King loved the pusher-propeller arrangement. It was a thrill just to sit in the open and enjoy the rushing air and the panoramic view.

It took him forty painstaking minutes to climb, in wide and easy circles, to three thousand feet. This was the happiest moment of his life, and the shock was all the more severe when the engine coughed and faltered. King panicked. The engine spluttered. One petrol tank was empty; it was time to switch to another. Foster had warned him of this. A good pilot – even a mediocre pilot – would have had the sense to let the nose drop, let the aeroplane make its own speed. King clutched the joystick and the FE stalled. It fell sideways, clumsily, and dropped into a spin. King kept his frantic grip on the joystick. The FE went on spinning down, chucking its tail from side to side, until King felt as dizzy and breathless as if he were in a runaway fairground ride. He clung to the joystick like grim death.

Everyone stopped to watch the plane fall. Several battalions of infantry camped nearby saw it. So did a couple of squadrons of cavalry, and a unit of sappers, and some gunners. Not many French farmers looked up: they usually got on with their work and let the war go by. Still, King had the biggest audience of his brief life as his FE tumbled from the sky, twitching like a scrap of paper.

"Oh, Christ Almighty," Foster said, in a voice like cracked leather. "What a waste."

"Not your fault," Cleve-Cutler told him.

They saw the FE hit the ground about a mile away. A second later the sound reached them. It was like a wooden hut collapsing. They saw flames, and then the bang of the exploding fuel tank made the windows rattle.

Cleve-Cutler stood and stared at the smoke. There was nothing he could do at the wreck, and in any case other men were already on their way to it. "I'll write to the parents," he said. "What was his name? King, wasn't it?"

No reply. Foster had gone.

Five minutes later he found Foster in the anteroom, scribbling with chalk on the blackboard that normally carried Flying Orders for the day. Foster had cleaned the board and covered it with algebraic equations. He was still writing, writing so hard and so fast that bits of chalk went flying. He reached the edge of the board and stopped.

"Doesn't add up," he said. "I can't make it add up."

"That's because it's all junk, old boy," Cleve-Cutler said.

Foster took a pace back. They examined the mass of algebraic nonsense for quite a long time. "Well, of course it's junk," Foster said. "That's why it won't add up! That's the whole problem, don't you see?"

Cleve-Cutler found a cloth and wiped the board clean. "Come on, Frank," he said. "I'll buy you a nice big drink."

One of the Buicks delivered Paxton back to Pepriac in good time for dinner. He sought out Kellaway and found him lying on the grass, watching a game of cricket. "Hullo!" he said. "Guess what?"

"The Kaiser's had a baby," Kellaway said without looking up.

"No, no. Nothing like that." He began to describe his meeting with Judith Kent Haffner. He got as far as coffee on the terrace when O'Neill sat next to him. "CO wants you," O'Neill said.

Paxton couldn't stand being close to O'Neill, so he got up. "I don't believe you," he said.

"You're right, the old man's lying, he doesn't want you." O'Neill lay back and closed his eyes. "Don't let him toy with your affections like that, get over there and gouge his eyeballs out."

"Excuse me." Paxton walked away.

Kellaway applauded a big hit by Gus Mayo. "Why do you keep pestering him?" he asked.

"It's a dirty job, I know," O'Neill shouted at Paxton, "but somebody has to do it."

Kellaway didn't understand, but he didn't really care. "You're looking a bit pale, old chap," he said. "Been sick?"

"Paxton took my rouge, without asking." O'Neill's face was as blank as ever. "He wants to humiliate me in front of the entire German Air Force." Kellaway gave up.

Paxton went to his billet. He was looking at his haircut in a mirror, and thinking how desirable it would be to go back and get a trim in a week or so, when Fidler arrived. "Mr. Cleve-Cutler's compliments, sir," he said, "and could you report to his office immediately."

Paxton forgot haircuts, forgot Mrs. Kent Haffner, forgot O'Neill and Kellaway and all. This was the call. He was going to fly again.

The CO and Captain Piggott were looking at a short length of telegraph wire. Paxton saluted and waited. "Where exactly did they find this?" Cleve-Cutler asked Piggott.

"Outer strut, left-hand side. Sawed the strut nearly in half."

Cleve-Cutler tested the strength of the wire until he hurt his fingers and grinned with pain. "Cheap and nasty . . . Where have you been all day?"

"Amiens, sir," Paxton said. "Haircut."

"Didn't O'Neill tell you I wanted to see you?"

"Yes, but . . . I'm afraid I don't trust him, sir."

"Really! You don't trust O'Neill." Cleve-Cutler blew his

nose: one short foghorn blast. "And how does O'Neill feel about you?"

"Well . . . he's not friendly, sir."

"Not friendly. How odd. Everyone else finds him friendly."

Paxton turned his head and looked out of the window. This wasn't what he'd expected but he was quite willing to reveal the truth. "From the start, sir, O'Neill has had his knife into me."

"And how do you feel about him?"

"I detest him."

"That should be interesting. Starting now, you're O'Neill's observer."

For a few seconds Paxton's brain refused to accept these words. They made no sense; they didn't fit. Yet the squadron commander and the flight commander kept looking at him as if they made sense. "I'm a pilot, sir," he said. "I'm not an observer."

"Then you'll just have to do your best, won't you? I've got too many pilots and the Pool's run out of observers."

"But O'Neill . . . I mean isn't there anybody else—"

"No, there's nobody else," Cleve-Cutler said jauntily, "and I know you're the worst air-gunner in the Corps and you couldn't hit Immelmann himself if he came up and sniffed the end of your gun, and it's certainly rough luck on Frank O'Neill, whose life-expectancy with you guarding him is now a minus figure because you'll probably shoot him the very first chance you get, thus causing the plane to crash and kill you both, which will be an enormous relief to me. Now go away."

Paxton went away, looking dazed.

"I thought he might learn something if he kicked around the squadron for a few days," Piggott said. "He hasn't learnt a damn thing, he's just as stupid as ever. I wonder what he did to get on O'Neill's tit?"

"Doesn't matter any more. Once they start fighting, they create more reasons to fight."

"Childish, isn't it?"

"I hope not," Cleve-Cutler said. "It's what we've all been doing for the last two years." He made a coil of the wire and released it, so that it bounced across his desk. "He didn't ask what had happened to Duncan."

"No. Self-centred and selfish. Doesn't give a damn for anyone else."

"So all he needs," Cleve-Cutler said, "is brains, guts and a ton of luck and he might make a good fighter pilot one day." Piggott stared. "Just a little joke," Cleve-Cutler said.

Paxton searched the camp until he found O'Neill. He was strolling around his FE, whistling in his peculiar tuneless fashion.

"Shut up that racket and listen," Paxton said. O'Neill went on whistling. He took a close look at an oil stain. "I don't know what I've done to deserve this," Paxton said, "but it seems that I am your observer."

O'Neill stopped whistling. For the first time, Paxton saw emotion show through that usually wooden expression. Surprise, certainly. Perhaps even alarm. It lasted only a few seconds.

"Or perhaps it would be truer to say that you are my pilot," Paxton said.

"You'll like flying with me. It's better than prunes." O'Neill was back to normal.

Cleve-Cutler mixed up a batch of Hornet's Sting in memory of Jimmy Duncan but there was no squadron party. It seemed wrong to smash up the new old furniture as soon as Lacey had had it unloaded, and in any case tomorrow's orders had come through and 'A' and 'B' Flights were on dawn patrol. All the keys worked on the replacement piano, so Stubbs played and everyone sang. Even Paxton stood at the edge of the crowd and sang. He had something to celebrate: he'd moved one more place up the table. Tough luck on Duncan. Pity it hadn't happened to O'Neill, he thought, then it would have been two places . . . Kellaway nudged him. "Heard the new diet joke?" he asked.

"No."

"How to lose ten ugly pounds at a stroke: volunteer to be O'Neill's observer." Kellaway giggled. "Get it?"

Paxton turned and went out. He took his binoculars from O'Neill's bedside and walked to the far end of the aerodrome where there was an oak tree he could climb. It was dusk, and he watched the starshells and flares and coloured rockets to the east. Sometimes, when he was lucky, he saw the actual flash of guns. It was magical and beautiful, thrilling and manly. It made him feel cleaner and stronger.

Chapter 14

Breakfast before a dawn patrol was always hard-boiled eggs and tea. Nobody liked the eggs but they were better than nothing. After an hour of O'Neill's aerobatics Paxton's stomach held nothing and his mind was full of murder.

Tim Piggott's briefing had needed very few words; it was obvious to Paxton that everyone knew the drill. Dawn patrols were freelance affairs: the British artillery was still in bed, so there were no shoots to cover, and the light wasn't good enough for photo-reconnaissance. Hornet squadron was going over to show the flag, to remind fritz how inferior he was. O'Neill's words to Paxton were even briefer. "Puke on your boots," he said, "not on me."

They were a mile up and two miles over when he began throwing the FE about. At first he swung in and out of a series of tight bends as if swerving past obstacles, wings tipped almost to the vertical. Paxton quite enjoyed that. O'Neill levelled out. Paxton turned to look at him and as he did, O'Neill stuffed the nose down hard and Paxton whacked his face against the back of the cockpit. He was still struggling to get back in his seat when the dive abruptly bottomed out and became a climb. His breakfast began to come loose. O'Neill stalled at the top and Paxton braced himself as the FE toppled sideways and threatened to fall on its back. A frighteningly long sideslip grew into another dive. The rush of air tore at Paxton's bloody face. His goggles had been knocked upwards and the gale made him weep. He never saw how the dive ended; all he saw was a small cloud dead ahead that was rotating rapidly, clockwise. Then the machine smashed into the cloud and bounced like a rubber ball and came out into sunshine with the Earth hanging sideways from the sky and Paxton hanging desperately in his straps while boiled eggs and tea fought to get out of his mouth. After that O'Neill began attempting some quite ambitious stunts.

The adjutant doubled as intelligence officer. When they landed he took their report. "Nothing much," O'Neill said. "One stroppy little Fokker tried to jump us. He wasn't very good. Soon got fed up."

Brazier looked at Paxton. "Did you damage him?"

"No." He peeled a bit of dried vomit off his chin. "No, he was always behind us, wasn't he?"

"Not always."

"And it wasn't a Fokker, it was an Albatros. Two Albatroses."

Brazier crossed out what he'd written.

"Fokker," O'Neill said. "One Fokker."

"Make up your ruddy minds."

"I observed two Albatroses," Paxton said, "and I should know because I'm the observer."

Brazier grunted, and wrote some more. "Where's that black ink you said you were going to get me?"

Paxton had completely forgotten about it. "They were sold out," he said. The adjutant sniffed disbelief. "Everyone's been buying it," Paxton said. "The stuff the Army issues is like gnat's piss."

The afternoon patrol was similar but worse. Paxton lost his lunch, bruised his elbows and knees and bloodied his nose. O'Neill told Brazier the German archie had been bad, so he'd dodged about a bit. "Anything to add?" Brazier asked. Paxton shook his head. The archie had been quite light but he hadn't the strength to get into an argument. Instead he stared at the thick growth of hair sprouting from the adjutant's nostrils. How ugly. How insanitary.

O'Neill whistled his aimless, dreary whistle as they walked to their billet. Eventually Paxton recognised the tune through the wreckage: it was *Jesu Joy of Man's Desiring*. Once, Paxton had told Kellaway that it was his favourite piece of music. That was why O'Neill was murdering it, of course.

"I say, you do look grim," Kellaway remarked. "Pale, too."

"I offered to lend him my rouge," O'Neill said, flat as mud, "but he's very fussy about these things."

Paxton had a bath and slept for an hour. When he awoke the others had gone. He went outside. The air smelt marvellously fresh, as if he had convalesced for a week. What he wanted above all was tea, hot sweet tea. The mess would have people in it. He went instead to the Orderly Room. Corporal Lacey had a Mozart piano concerto on the gramophone. He reached to turn it off but Paxton shook his head and sat down. Lacey got on with his work. Mozart got on with his genius. The piano duelled brilliantly and courteously with the orchestra and won a fair fight. Silence. Paxton sighed and pointed to the kettle. Lacey made tea. Next door the clerk-typists began pecking.

"I hear you met Mrs. Kent Haffner," Lacey said. "A very spirited young lady."

"That seems like a month ago." Paxton warmed his hands on the half-pint mug. He could feel the tea reviving him. "How do you know her?"

Lacey smiled. "Just chance. I understand you have another uncle who owns a company that makes gramophone records. Why don't you write to him? Jazz, ragtime, songs from the London shows."

"Cigars aren't good enough?"

"Not always. With a supply of records I could get two cows and fifty hens. Fresh milk and eggs for the mess."

Paxton looked at him. Lacey's feet were on his desk and his hands were linked behind his head. "I can't help thinking you should be an officer," Paxton said.

"I probably should. I don't want to be an officer. I've never wanted to be an officer. War seems to me to be a very silly affair. I can't see the glory in killing people, still less in being killed."

"But you joined the Army."

"Well, I decided I'd better do what I wanted to do before somebody else ordered me to do what I disliked intensely. You see, I never believed that this would be a short war. It was obvious when war broke out that everyone wanted it and was thoroughly pleased with it. They weren't going to let go of it in a hurry. On the other hand, if it did last a long time, I might get conscripted and sent to stick bayonets in Germans, or, even worse, made to lead other men with bayonets. So I took a course in shorthand and typing. Then I joined up. A man who can type fast and accurately and do shorthand is like gold in the Army. Ask the adjutant. Such a man is *never* going to be put in the trenches. Nor is he ever going to be pushed into a commission. So here I am, utterly indispensable. What more can a man do for his country?"

Paxton got up and went to the door. He threw the dregs of his tea onto the grass. "He can die," he said.

"Oh, anyone can die. It takes no great skill to die. No skill at all, in fact. Thoroughly unqualified people do it all the time. Personally, I reckon that dying has been highly overrated. I blame the newspapers."

Paxton returned his mug. "Thanks for the tea," he said. "No thanks for the philosophy."

Hornet Squadron was pleased with itself that night. During the afternoon, Plug Gerrish had found a Halberstadt two-seater and stalked it for twenty minutes until he crept under its tail and Ross, his observer, killed the pilot with a burst of only seven bullets. This was the squadron's first confirmed kill since Milne's ramming (which didn't really count) and it was regarded as a change of luck. Then Goss and Stubbs had come across a German balloon stuck high in the sky. It must have had trouble down below, a jammed winch or something, because they were able to fly right up to it. At first the archie was furious but when the two German observers took to their parachutes the risk of harming their own men silenced the guns long enough to let Stubbs pump tracer and incendiary into the big bag, which burned like a beacon. So it was a happy day. Dinner in the mess was loud with triumph. The air criss-crossed with flying bread.

A reaction set in when they moved to the anteroom for coffee. It had been a long time since the hour before dawn when most had been shaken awake by their batmen. Some, including Cleve-Cutler, wandered off to bed. Foster went for a walk. Others slumped in armchairs or sofas and watched

209

Goss and Ogilvy play ping-pong. The gramophone played loud ragtime until Charlie Essex took off a sock and stuffed it into the speaker. "You chaps haven't got the brains to do that," he said. "But of course I was at Cambridge."

"What else did you learn there?" the adjutant asked.

"Oh . . . Let's see. Two pints one quart, four quarts one gallon, and after that you're too plastered to climb into college so it doesn't matter."

"That's all? Didn't they teach you anything else?"

"Um . . . I learned how to do the polka. Well, nearly."

"Heroic," Brazier murmured.

Paxton was dozing in a corner, but the word stirred his memory. After a moment his memory reported its findings. "I say," he said to Dando. "What's heroic surgery?"

Dando blinked. "Extraordinary question," he said. "Well, when normal measures have failed to save the patient, the surgeon may take extreme measures – I mean, do things he would normally consider too violent, too dangerous – as a kind of a last-ditch attempt to save the patient's life. That's known as heroic surgery."

"Multiple amputation?"

"Yes, that's the sort of thing. Why d'you ask?"

"Chap I met the other day was very keen on heroic surgery. Said the record for chopping off all four limbs is just over twelve minutes but he reckoned he could do it in eight minutes dead." Paxton was about to mention the axe and then thought better of it.

"My goodness." Dando made his eyes big and wide. "Eight minutes, you say . . . That's more than heroic. That's herculean."

Gus Mayo stirred and yawned. "Bit tough on the patient, isn't it? I mean . . . What if he didn't want them all cut off?"

"Then he should have said so at the start," Charlie Essex told him. "Now he hasn't got a leg to stand on."

Some laughed, some groaned. Mayo got up and began beating Essex with a cushion. Essex fought back. His chair fell over. The scuffle went on until they were both too tired to fight and lay side by side in a pool of feathers. Goss came by, searching for a lost ping-pong ball, and they tripped him up, so he hit them. The scuffle began again. Ogilvy got tired of waiting for Goss to come back and he left the table. "When it comes to heroic surgery we've got the champion right here," he said. "Haven't we, adj?"

Brazier took his pipe from his mouth, looked into the bowl, put his pipe back, and waited.

"I got another letter from my chum in the trenches," Ogilvy said. "The adj used to be his CO. Billy Winters, adj. Remember him?"

Brazier nodded. "Reliable fellow. A bit wild, but he led his company well."

"And you remember Ashby?"

In the same voice Brazier said: "I shot Ashby. He didn't lead his company so well, and I had to shoot him."

The scuffling had stopped.

"What did you shoot him with?"

"A rifle. He was forty yards away. The Service revolver is useless at that range and I couldn't wait until he got closer. I took the nearest rifle and shot Ashby through the chest. Through the heart. I'm sure he never knew what hit him. The others did, though."

Everyone was very awake now. Brazier picked a shred of tobacco from his thigh and let it fall in an ashtray.

"I take it there was a panic," Ogilvy said.

"There was indeed a panic."

"And you were then a colonel."

"I was then a colonel and my regiment took part in an attack, a most important part, and the attack miscarried and the enemy counter-attacked. There was fierce fighting, very fierce fighting indeed. Ashby's men fought with the bayonet and the rifle-butt. Many men died but the line was held. Then the German artillery bombarded Ashby's position. The enemy attacked again. Ashby got up and ran. His men ran too, until I shot him and told them to go back and fight. They went back and fought and again we held the line."

There was silence while they absorbed this information.

"Billy says the attack was a flop," Ogilvy said.

"The attack failed, because the enemy brought up their heavy mortars. You were in the trenches, weren't you? Perhaps you experienced *minnenwerfers* yourself?"

"Only once. That was enough. Frightful brutes."

"A forty-two-inch shell makes a big explosion. We had no answer. We withdrew."

"What does Billy say next?" Dando asked Ogilvy.

"Billy says there was hell to pay and when the dust had settled the colonel was a major."

"Two things," Brazier said. "First: Captain Ashby was the son of a baron. Only the third son, but his blood was blue. Second, I had not shot him quietly. On the contrary, I made sure everyone heard my ultimatum. I shouted, very loud: *Ashby, stop. Go back or I'll kill you.* That, after all, was the whole point of shooting him: to influence the others. I suppose Divisional HQ thought I should have shot someone less eminent and done it more discreetly." Brazier re-lit his pipe.

Mayo said: "Or perhaps they thought you shouldn't have shot anyone at all."

Brazier fanned the air to dissipate a cloud of blue smoke and looked at Mayo as if he were a child who had unexpectedly wandered into an adult conversation. "Oh, somebody had to be shot. It was just a matter of how and when."

Paxton tried to make sense of that, and failed.

"According to Billy you got shunted off to a different division," Ogilvy said.

"There was some expectation that I would get myself killed leading a rather more ambitious attack. My men were given the task of capturing an enemy strongpoint. It was terribly well defended. We got very close to it – at a cost, of course – and then a German machine-gun pinned everyone down in a string of shell-holes. I knew we could knock out this gun if we all charged at once but nobody would move. I tried to buck them up but they were all afraid. The longer we waited, the more time the enemy had to organise a counter-attack. So I told my men that they had a choice. They could advance and risk being killed by the Hun, or lie there and be utterly sure that I would shoot them. Then I gave the order to advance. Nobody moved. I shot one man with my Service revolver, a private named Yelland. Scarcely anyone moved, so I shot another private. His name was Haslam. After that they all went over the top in a rush, me with them, and we took that German machine-gun in no time."

"At a cost, of course," Dando said.

"Of course."

"Including your rank. Down from major to captain. Why? You shot nobody eminent, and you did it discreetly."

Brazier stood up, and ducked to avoid a hanging lamp. "Yelland died, Haslam didn't. He made a great fuss and there was an inquiry. After all, it's a serious matter when officers go around shooting their men in the back. I think I'll turn in. Good night."

When Mayo was quite sure that Brazier had gone, he said: "Fancy shooting a chap in the back."

"What should he have done?" Ogilvy asked. "Rolled him over and shot him in the front?"

"You know what I mean."

"No I don't. I'm damned if I do."

Charlie Essex pulled his sock out of the gramophone. "Thank God we don't have to shoot anybody in our job."

"You don't?" said Dando, startled.

"No. Only aeroplanes."

"With men in them."

"Well, that's their silly fault. Who wants a game of ping-pong?"

"Ball's bust," Goss announced.

"I'll play," Paxton said. "I've got a new ball."

"Come on then, Pax," Essex said. It was the first time anyone in the squadron had been slightly friendly to Paxton. He suddenly felt accepted.

O'Neill came across an invisible, lumpy seam in the weather just above eight thousand feet. Two airstreams of differing speeds jostled each other, creating a layer of turbulence. He let the FE bounce up through it and when he reached calm air he tipped the nose down and let the FE bounce down through it. Then he climbed very gradually. The FE bucked and plunged and shuddered for a long time. Paxton kept his mouth shut and tried to forget his sore, bruised rump. The patrol was more than half over and his lunch was still in his stomach. This was progress. He tried to ignore the smell of whalegrease, smeared on his face to keep out the battering cold air, but every now and then a breath of whalegrease mingled with the aftertaste of stew and threatened disaster.

213

The FE bucketed through another lumpy patch. He tightened his jaws and thought of Sherborne.

Then O'Neill was climbing and the air was smooth. Paxton raised his goggles and blinked hard to clear the tears. O'Neill's fist banged the top of his helmet and Paxton searched the sky where O'Neill pointed.

It took him ten seconds to find a speck the size of a pinhead, high to the right, and then he blinked and lost it. The sky was baby-blue, softened by a screen of cirrus two miles above them. He found the speck again. It was bigger and fuzzier, and falling; falling fast. Quite soon he could see the wings, razor-thin lines on either side of the tiny blob that must be the engine and propeller. The FE was booming and vibrating: O'Neill had opened the throttle wide. Paxton swung the Lewis to the right and tested it: only a brief stutter: he was going to need the rest of the drum. The blob was growing. It was a biplane, blue or purple, yellow wheels, and it was diving at a speed that made Paxton feel the FE was standing still. O'Neill shouted something but whatever it was it was lost. Paxton's brain was so calm that he felt tranquil yet his body throbbed with excitement. The enemy plane was magnifying at an astonishing rate and he knew with absolute certainty that he could destroy it. Tracer pulsed from its nose, searching for him, missing; the range was too great; he did not fire back. The Hun blossomed in his sights, still firing, and he waited and made sure and then squeezed the trigger as O'Neill flung the FE onto its right wingtips and sheared away from the enemy. Before Paxton could stop himself he had fired at the empty sky. O'Neill hauled the FE into a tight circle. By then the enemy – an Albatros – was half a mile away, a dwindling dot.

Usually, when they got back to Pepriac, Paxton handed over the Lewis to the armourer and got away from O'Neill as quickly as possible. This time he waited.

O'Neill talked briefly with his fitter and rigger and then headed for the pilots' hut. Paxton blocked his way. "If you don't want a gunner, leave the gun behind," Paxton said. "Leave the ammunition behind. Save weight."

"You had your chance."

"What? What chance? Precisely when I opened fire, you turned sharp right."

"Because I couldn't wait any longer."

"Wait for what? Until then, that Hun wasn't in range."

"No? *We* were in *his* range."

"Rubbish. He opened fire when he was miles away."

"You know bugger-all about air gunnery."

"I know that the bigger the target, the better your chances. And just when that Hun got big enough for me to hit him you lost the target."

"I made damn sure *he* lost *his* target, that's what I did."

"You ruined my shot."

"You were too constipated to fire."

It was hot and they were sweating. O'Neill shed his flying jacket. Paxton said, savagely: "If you're such an expert, why don't you do the damned gunnery, and I'll *guarantee* to get *you* close enough, *and* keep you there."

O'Neill laughed at him.

They got out of their flying kit and Paxton wiped off the whalegrease. Brazier heard their report; Paxton contributed little. They walked to the billet in silence. Again and again Paxton kept seeing in his mind that beautiful purple-blue yellow-wheeled Albatros enlarging perfectly in his sights, and being snatched from him just as he squeezed the trigger. It was robbery. He'd been swindled. "You did it deliberately, didn't you?" he said.

O'Neill yawned. He was stretched out on his bed.

"Of course you did," Paxton said. He walked around the room, kicking a waste basket. "I should have guessed. You don't like me, you're certainly not going to give me a chance to pot a Hun, are you?" He booted the basket over O'Neill's bed and glared at him.

"I don't give a stuff about you," O'Neill said.

"Well, you'd better start bloody learning, my fine Australian friend." Paxton found the basket and gave it another boot, aiming at O'Neill's head and almost hitting it. "Because our job up there is killing Huns, in case you didn't know."

"I've killed more Huns than you've had wet dreams."

"Next time we meet one, I want him. I want you to get

me near him and stay there while I kill him. That's your job. You're just the blasted driver. You drive. I'll kill. Understand?"

"You had your chance, chum. You muffed it."

"Peter King and James Duncan never met," the padre said, "yet now they lie side by side, as brothers. For, as the poet said, he today that sheds his blood with me, shall be my brother."

There had been a sharp storm half an hour before the funeral and everything in the churchyard dripped. The bodies had been lowered into an inch of water. The air smelt clean and cold, as if it had never been used before.

"One day, when this dreadful conflict is over, some passer-by may pause here and wonder just what King and Duncan achieved. The answer is that they died in a just and decent cause, and that by their deaths they helped to win a splendid victory for freedom and for honour. I need not remind you of their gallantry. Those who go forth to do battle in the skies possess a special courage. They display a golden chivalry that shines in the gloom of war like a torch of inspiration." He said something about the supreme sacrifice and the triumph of right, and then rounded it off as usual.

Frank Foster walked back to camp with him.

"Well done, padre."

"Thank you, Frank. I think Jimmy would have liked it."

"Jimmy wouldn't have understood half of it. He was one of the stupidest men I ever met."

"Surely not."

"Oh, don't worry. Not your fault. He was born thick. Just as well, perhaps. It pays to be thick in our job. Once you start thinking about it you're heading for a crack-up."

"You can come to me at any time, you know."

"I know. I don't belong to your club, padre. I've been upstairs often enough and, believe me, there's no sign of a bloke with a beard and a box full of thunderbolts. So will you do me a favour? If and when I go west, and you get called upon to propose the toast, leave out all the God stuff, will you?"

The padre hesitated. "I'm by way of being in the God business, you know."

"Well, I'm not and it's my funeral. I don't want any of that high-minded stuff about dying in a just cause, either. Freedom and justice and honour and whatnot. You can forget all that."

"If you say so, old chap."

"What I don't want above all is any waffle about democracy."

"No democracy. I see."

"Democracy never did me any good, and if I survive this nonsense I shall inherit the family title and a large slice of England and I shall have earned it ten times over, so democracy can keep its sticky fingers off me."

"You have grown bitter, Frank."

"I've grown honest, chum."

"But surely there are qualities to admire? Courage, chivalry, truth? Shouldn't we recognise them?"

"All right: tell the truth. Tell all the truth. Tell everyone how courageous our late comrade was and also how frightened he was. And lonely. Even in a two-seater. You've no idea how lonely and frightened you can feel up there. Just you in several hundred cubic miles of sky, and then all of a sudden here comes the Hun trying to kill you. Nothing personal about it. I'm sure the Hun is the soul of chivalry, as long as it doesn't get in the way of putting a few bullets in your stomach or your head or your lungs, anywhere as long as the blood comes out in a rush. By all means, you go ahead and recognise the admirable qualities of truth and chivalry. Tell us the truth about chivalry. I'd like to know what it is, because I've never seen it in action. If it means that one sportsman waves his hat and lets the other man fire first, that's not chivalry. That's suicide. That's idiocy. So leave it out, will you?"

The padre jumped nimbly across a set of puddles. "You make my task extremely difficult. I suppose I can safely mention the fact of your death?"

"As long as you don't call it the supreme sacrifice."

The padre threw up his hands. "What greater sacrifice could there be?"

"It's not a bally sacrifice at all! Use your imagination, padre. D'you honestly think poor little King *gave* his life?

D'you think Jimmy Duncan had any choice? D'you think *any* of us would die if we could wangle some way around it? You make the supreme sacrifice sound like the noblest, cleverest, bravest thing a man could do. That's rubbish. When we get killed it's because we got it wrong. Or blind chance. Archie. Nothing clever about that."

"No indeed." The padre put a long, heavy arm around Foster's shoulders. "You've emptied my stock, Frank. Why don't you tell me what I ought to say?"

"Just say . . Just say: 'He wasn't a bad sort, paid his debts, told a few good jokes, and took five wickets for 39 runs in the match against Harrow.' That's enough. In fact it's too much. Cut out the bit about the jokes. They weren't all that good "

Chapter 15

Rainstorms blundered in from the west more and more frequently. A canvas hangar was blown down and all flying was cancelled. A lot of poker got played and the gramophone never stopped. Lacey fixed up the cinema projector and showed some Charlie Chaplin films, which were enormously popular. Boy Binns drew dozens of cartoon portraits, which were no better than his usual efforts. "That's libellous," Spud Ogilvy said when Boy showed him a sketch. "You've made me look like Charlie Essex." Boy held the sketch at arm's length and closed one eye. "I think this *is* Charlie," he said. "I got them mixed up. *That* one is you."

"No, it's not. It looks horrible. That's another picture of Charlie."

Boy took it over to the light. "Maybe this one is Gus Mayo," he said. "I drew Gus when he was smiling."

"Whoever it is, someone just kicked him in the goolies. Why don't you put names on the damn things?"

"I'm an artist," Boy said, "not a writer."

As a flight commander, Foster was entitled to his own room. During a lull between cloudbursts he moved out of his room and into a bell tent, far from the officers' quarters. He took the dog Brutus with him, and a clarinet that Corporal Lacey had swapped for some of Paxton's cigars. Foster couldn't play the clarinet but he tried. Brutus sat beside him and howled. Their wretched duet drifted across the camp, fading and reviving as the wind gusted and fell away.

Spud Ogilvy and Charlie Essex went to visit him.

"What's the idea, Frank?" Essex asked.

"That's a good question. It's a very good question. What the blazes are we all doing here? I mean, what's the point of it all? Any suggestions?"

Ogilvy hesitated, but Essex was bouncing on the camp bed, testing its comfort. "Obvious, I should have thought," Ogilvy said. "We're here to win the war, aren't we?"

"Is that all?" Foster took his clarinet away from Essex, who had begun playing with it. "If that's all, then I can do it easily. I can end this war with one little bullet. It's simply a matter of killing the right man."

Essex said: "And who's that?"

"I'll find him, don't you worry." Foster was standing in the door of the tent, his arms folded, looking through the rain at the billets. "He's not far away. If I can find him I can kill him."

"And that will end the war?" Ogilvy asked.

"Instantly and for ever." Foster turned and lifted his revolver from a nail in the tent-pole. "I always keep it loaded, because you never know when your chance may come. True?"

Ogilvy shrugged. "Charlie's brought a fruit cake his aunt sent him. Shall we eat it?"

"Certainly." Foster hung up his revolver. For the rest of their visit he was perfectly normal and charming.

Paxton mooched about the camp. He was more popular now it was known that he and Lacey had organised the flicks, but he didn't much feel like mixing with people. He met the adjutant and sheltered under his giant golf umbrella. "This is going to sound pretty silly, adj," he said, "but why don't we have a swimming pool? I can easily lay on a bunch of Chinks to dig one." The adjutant told him to go ahead, as long as the pool was well down-wind of the camp, to keep the mosquitoes away. So that settled that. Rain rattled on the umbrella. The windsock stood out horizontally.

"I was in the anteroom the other night," Paxton said. "In my opinion you should have been decorated, not demoted."

"Funny you should say that. I wasn't the only officer who had to do a bit of shooting. There was a captain in my battalion who stopped a panic with his revolver. I wrote a commendation afterwards. I wrote: 'By his presence of mind and resolve he shot a lieutenant and a private of his company, thus preventing the spread of panic and ensuring that the line was held.' It was a brave act and he certainly deserved a decoration. I believe my commendation was burned. Let me know exactly where you want to put that swimming pool, won't you?"

Paxton drew a Lewis gun and two drums of tracer ammunition from the armourers' hut and carried them to the firing range. The wind was so strong that he had to lean against it; even so, some of the gusts made him stagger. That was good. The stronger the better. He placed the gun two hundred yards from the butts, and fired off the ammunition in brief bursts of five or six rounds, watching each time to see how the wind made the tracer bend. The further it went the more it bent. That made sense. He did some guessing and some simple arithmetic and decided that, firing a Lewis sideways from an FE doing eighty miles an hour, at an enemy attacking head on, you should aim off by one length for each one hundred yards' range. More or less.

Worth getting wet for.

The storm exhausted itself the following morning, leaving behind a trail of battered cloud. By afternoon most of Hornet Squadron was flying (a couple of planes had been knocked about by the wind) and nearly everyone made some sort of contact with the enemy. Gerrish and Ross claimed to have driven down a Pfalz monoplane, or it might have been a Fokker; anyway it was giving off a lot of smoke when last seen. Cleve-Cutler, flying with Boy Binns, had a long scrap with a Rumpler two-seater until they both ran out of ammunition; Binns said he hit the German gunner, maybe killed him. Others chased a variety of Huns but lost them. As usual the balloons were heavily defended; nobody got near one. Tim Piggott's engine conked out over the Lines but he managed to glide to a field and land between the shell-holes. O'Neill's FE came back with three inches missing from one wingtip. "Too much cloud," he told Brazier. "This Hun suddenly popped out and gave me a burst and popped back."

"Indubitably." Paxton nodded briskly.

Brazier looked at him, but Paxton had finished. Brazier made a note.

O'Neill said: "I saw a Hun about a mile away, Halberstadt I think, but I couldn't catch it."

"Indubitably." Paxton nodded briskly. This time they both looked at him but he had nothing to add. Brazier made another note.

"Cruised around for a bit," O'Neill said. "Saw a Hun much higher than me, Albatros maybe, couldn't get up to him."

"Indubitably." Paxton nodded briskly.

"Sounds like the Hun's come out to play at last," Brazier remarked.

"One wonders," Paxton said.

"Then a bit later, I saw a Hun below me," O'Neill said. "Looked too much like a decoy. Left it alone."

"Indubitably." Paxton nodded briskly.

"And besides I was getting low on fuel."

Paxton said nothing. Brazier looked at him. "Forgotten your lines?" he asked.

"Oh, indubitably," Paxton said, and nodded slowly.

"I take it you didn't open fire," Brazier said.

"No risk of that," Paxton said. He gave the adjutant a sly smile and took O'Neill's arm. "Come along, old chap," he said. "I'll get you a nice cup of cocoa."

O'Neill shook him off. "Not much archie," he told Brazier. "Cloud was too thick."

"Indubitably," Paxton said.

They were halfway back to the billet when Paxton noticed that O'Neill was not whistling. Paxton began whistling a tearaway version of *Jesu, Joy of Man's Desiring*. To his surprise O'Neill joined in. He whistled a different part of the melody and did it as badly as ever. Thus they were both whistling, after a fashion, as they entered the hut.

Kellaway was writing a letter. "Isn't it great?" he said. "Dando just told me I can fly again. He says my head's in pukka shape. At least I think it was Dando." He frowned.

"You'll enjoy flying," Paxton said. "It's so relaxing. I've nearly finished reading *Treasure Island*."

"He was so relaxed he nearly finished breathing," O'Neill said.

"Every time I looked up there was a different Hun," Paxton told Kellaway. "First I saw a big blue one, but he didn't fancy the colour. Then I saw a red one, but it was the wrong shape. Then I saw a very pretty speckled one, but it must have been going in the wrong direction or something. Anyhow, it didn't suit him. He's hard to please. Fussy."

"It *was* Dando," Kellaway said. "I wrote his name down."

O'Neill was cleaning his nails with a penknife. "He thinks the Huns line up to be shot down. He's a fairy in a fairy tale."

"Very, very fussy," Paxton said. "He must have been spoiled rotten when he was a kid, don't you think?"

"There's a rumour going around about a Russian squadron just landed at St. Omer," Kellaway said. "D'you believe it?"

"Indubitably," Paxton said.

"Keep that up and I'll give you my fist to suck," O'Neill said. He took his towel and went out.

"What's wrong with him?" Kellaway asked.

"He's got the runs. He was certainly running hard today."

"They must be Russians because they smell of vodka," Kellaway said. "That's what I heard. D'you think they'll come here?"

"Only if they want to be bored to death."

Next day the weather was perfect and all flying orders were cancelled. Instead, Colonel Bliss came down from Brigade HQ to speak to the squadron.

The battle for Verdun, he said, was fizzling out. Frankly, it was a shambles down there, more bodies than either side could count. The French urgently wanted a British attack, pronto, to take the remaining pressure off Verdun before the frog troops started to mutiny.

So the Royal Flying Corps had two new jobs. We had to keep the German Air Force pinned down behind their own Lines so they couldn't snoop on our preparations. This squadron (and many others) could expect to fly a lot of Deep Offensive Patrols in future – five, ten, fifteen miles beyond the trenches. We were going to show the Hun who was boss.

Bliss saw some long faces in his audience, and he hurried on. The other job, he said, was trench-strafing. When the British infantry went over the top, the Flying Corps would go with them, harrying the Hun from his hole. Obviously this called for expert low-level flying, so the Corps Commander had had a dummy stretch of Hun trenches dug, with plenty of smoke and bangs to make everything thoroughly realistic. Hornet Squadron would practise there this afternoon.

Bliss offered his congratulations on recent kills, and Cleve-Cutler led him away to his office for a drink.

"Fifteen sodding miles," Goss said. "That's deeply offensive all right."

"It's too far," Mayo said.

"It's safer than being over the Front," Piggott told them. "Much less archie."

"It's halfway to bloody Berlin! What if something goes wrong?"

"Don't worry," Goss said. "The wind will blow you the rest of the way." That brought laughter, but it was brief and nervous. The prevailing west wind was no joke. Almost every patrol over the enemy lines ended up having to labour home into a headwind. Hun patrols, on the other hand, got blown home. It was a swindle.

"I don't know what you're bitching about," Gerrish said. "You might as well complain about falling into twenty feet of water instead of ten feet, or five. You get just as wet, either way."

"Come off it, Plug," Mayo said. "Fifteen miles with a dicky engine? Losing height? Huns taking turns to polish you off? That's a long trudge, that is. No thanks."

"Orders is orders," Ogilvy said.

"I can't count up to fifteen," Mayo said.

"That's funny, I can't get up to ten," Goss said.

"I meant ten," Mayo said. "Come to think of it, I meant five."

Gerrish was not amused. He said: "The last squadron I was in, we had a pilot who didn't go where he was sent. Next time, his flight commander flew behind him with his finger on the trigger."

"The adj would approve of that," Ogilvy said.

Paxton said: "Did he pull the trigger?"

Gerrish turned and stared. "None of your damned business," he said.

Paxton stared back. Gerrish's anger had made him angry, and he enjoyed the sensation. "Just trying to improve my mind," he said.

"I went to Cambridge, you know," Charlie Essex said. "I can count up to five with one hand tied behind my back."

They played cricket until lunch, and then killed time with cards and newspapers, waiting for orders. At three o'clock the trench-strafing exercise was cancelled. "It seems that some bright spark thought it would be a good idea if the trench were under actual artillery fire while strafing took place," Cleve-Cutler told them. "Two aeroplanes got badly damaged by shrapnel or blast, and one got blown to bits, before they decided it was a bit too realistic."

"How can they be so stupid?" Piggott demanded.

"Centuries of practice, old boy," Cleve-Cutler said.

The adjutant disapproved of Foster's bell-tent and of the noises that came from it, and he told Cleve-Cutler so. "I don't care what school he went to," Brazier said, "he's not entitled to behave like a gypsy. The men won't respect him for it. No respect means no discipline."

"He's still a very good flight commander. That hasn't changed."

"Something's changed. I remember once I had a chap in Madras who suddenly dyed his hair green and said his mother was the Queen of Sheba. Thoroughly competent officer, but he had to go."

Cleve-Cutler shook his head. "Pilots are different. In my last squadron we had a brilliant pilot, but when he wasn't flying he was the most feckless brat you could imagine. His idea of fun was to go for a walk and throw stones at people."

"A British *officer*?" Brazier was deeply offended.

"So you see I don't care if Frank dyes his hair sky-blue-pink. He won't get the sack from me. I need him too much."

*

Before long the dog Brutus chewed up Captain Foster's clarinet. Corporal Lacey managed to find a secondhand valve trombone, and Foster was in the doorway of his tent, working on *The Eton Boating Song*, when he saw the Canadian, Stubbs, out for a stroll, and called him in for a drink.

They sat on the camp bed and sipped whisky from tin mugs.

"Do you really like France?" Foster asked. "Don't you find it awfully dull after Canada?"

"Actually I'm an American," Stubbs said. "I only joined the Canadian Army because it was a quick way to get into the RFC, but don't tell anyone."

"America." Foster dipped a finger in his whisky and sucked it. "America. I'd love to be an American. No ties. Free to go anywhere, do anything."

"I never lived anywhere except Grand Rapids, Michigan."

"Grand Rapids. That sounds exciting."

"I guess it is if you like making furniture." Stubbs rubbed Brutus with his foot. "Would you like a job making furniture?"

"Not . . . all day, no."

"In Grand Rapids they make furniture all year." Brutus squirmed away from Stubbs' foot and began chewing the trombone.

"Look here," Foster said. All of a sudden he sounded tense and nervous. "I'm going to ask the most enormous favour." He gave Stubbs the full force of his smile.

"Okay. Try me."

"Well . . . the last time I went home on leave I did a damn silly thing. I met a girl, took her out, shows, dinners, dancing, all that nonsense."

"Lucky you."

"Yes, you might think so, I suppose. Trouble is, I sort of . . . well, fell in love. Can't get her out of my mind." Foster was frowning heavily. "Absolute bloody disaster, of course."

"Why? Doesn't she like you?"

"Oh, yes." Foster gripped his tin mug so hard that his fingertips went white. "Yes, I'm pretty sure she was quite fond of me."

"Sounds like a nice combination, then."

"No. No, it's quite hopeless. I'm afraid there's absolutely no future in it."

"I don't see why. Just—"

"No future at all, believe me. I've thought about it a great deal and it's all over, I can't go on like this, it's unfair to her. the only possible thing is to end it now, dead."

Stubbs was briefly silenced by this burst of feeling. Then he said: "So what's this big favour you want me to do?"

Foster sighed. "She keeps writing. I can't forget her as long as she keeps writing, so I've decided the best thing for both of us would be if I arranged my demise."

"Your demise. You mean your death?"

Foster nodded.

"Nothing but the best for the British aristocracy," Stubbs said. "Okay, how d'you want to demise? With or without lilies?"

"I'd like you to write a letter, telling her that I was killed in action. It's got to be definite and final. No half measures."

Stubbs gave it some thought. "I could tell her I saw you get shot down. And crash."

"Better say I was riddled with enemy bullets."

"Listen, I can have you blown up in mid-air. No extra cost."

"A flamer. Make it a flamer."

Stubbs looked away. He finished his whisky, sip by sip. "Not a flamer," he said. "I'll say the rest, but not a flamer."

Foster gave him pen and paper. "I'd do it myself," he said, "but she knows my handwriting."

"Okay," Stubbs said. "What's her name?"

"Jenny," Foster said. "Her name is Jenny."

Stubbs began to write. In a corner of the tent, Brutus was testing his teeth on the horn of the trombone. "Don't tell anyone else about this, will you?" Foster said.

By 10 a.m. the day was as grey as a ghost. O'Neill flew a random pattern above a BE2c that was spotting for a shoot. About a thousand feet above him, the overcast spread from horizon to horizon. It looked like the biggest tarpaulin in the western world.

Paxton had begun this patrol eagerly. Now, after forty minutes, he was so bored that he was scratching his initials on the inside of the nacelle. The German archie was a bore. It was always in the wrong place or at the wrong height. The shoot was a bore. As soon as the guns found one target they switched to another. The German air force was a bore because it wasn't to be seen. And then, suddenly, it was. A Fokker monoplane came out of the east. Paxton sat up as if he'd been stung.

The Fokker was at about the same height as the BE2c and was heading for it. O'Neill had seen the Fokker too; he dipped a wing so as to get a better view. Paxton fired a test burst. If they went down now they could catch the Hun when he was still a mile from the BE2c.

O'Neill did not go down. He circled, and after a while he climbed. Paxton couldn't believe it. He turned and stared at O'Neill but all he got was blank goggles. Below, the Fokker was chasing the British plane across the Lines. Shellfire from both sides, black and white, littered the sky. Paxton slumped and swore. The FE levelled out and O'Neill cruised around for half an hour. Then they went home. O'Neill told Brazier there was nothing worth reporting.

Lunch was cold bully-beef, boiled potatoes and salad. O'Neill ate his meal quickly and went out. Paxton stayed in the mess.

"Hey!" Kellaway said. He was reading a week-old *Daily Mail*. "Lord Kitchener's dead!" He was amazed. Nobody else was.

"General Gordon's not feeling too good, either," Goss said. "And Napoleon's quite poorly, so I'm told, while Alexander the Great . . ."

"Yes but . . . I mean, he was a field-marshal." Kellaway was dismayed by their indifference.

"Who shot him?" Foster asked.

"I don't think anyone did."

"Too bad. A good opportunity missed." Foster lost interest.

Kellaway turned to Stubbs. "Do you know Lord Kitchener's dead?" he asked.

"No, but you sing it, and I'll pick up the tune as we go along," Stubbs said brightly. There was a weary chorus of groans and hisses. "That's considered a pretty damn good joke back in Grand Rapids," he protested.

"Says here he was drowned," Kellaway said glumly.

"How's your swimming pool coming on?" Goss asked Paxton.

"Oh, they've made a start." The others looked interested, so he explained: "I've got a couple of dozen Chinkies digging a hole in the next field. Borrowed 'em from a labour battalion. Dig like beavers." The prospect of having a pool was exciting, and he answered a lot of questions. Success felt good.

O'Neill was on his bed, asleep. Paxton kicked the bed. "What didn't you like this time?" he asked. "The colour of his eyes, or the way he parted his hair?"

O'Neill took a long time to wake up.

"We had that bloody Hun on a plate," Paxton said. "It was a damned gift from God, that bloody Hun." He was so worked-up that he couldn't get the words out fast enough: they tripped and stumbled. "But you didn't want it! One look down, and up you went! So the poor bloody Quirk got chased home while we chased rainbows!"

"You didn't see the Albatros," O'Neill said flatly.

"I didn't see any Albatros, nor any golden eagle, nor—"

"Why not? You're the observer." O'Neill rubbed his face as if trying to push it back into shape.

"I observed the Fokker. One Hun's enough for me."

"Arse-hole. Our job was to guard the Quirk."

"Which got jumped by the Fokker."

"Balls. They saw it coming, they quit, they knew it couldn't catch them, and it didn't."

"But *we* could have caught it! I could have cut the blasted thing in half!"

"You never saw the Albatros." O'Neill had taken Paxton's eau-de-cologne from his shelf and was splashing it on his neck and face. "It was in and out of that cloud like a whore who's lost her handbag."

"Help yourself, it's free," Paxton said.

"Thanks." O'Neill took a mouthful, rinsed his teeth and spat out of a window. "Back home we make better booze than this out of dead dingoes . . . That Albatros wanted our Quirk."

"So you say."

"And he was fast enough to catch the Quirk. But I knew he was up there, and he knew that I knew, and we both knew he wasn't going to risk it while I was in the way."

"I don't believe it."

O'Neill raised one knee and broke wind. "God save the King," he said. "Indubitably."

In the afternoon they were listed for a Deep Offensive Patrol. The air was still and dull as they walked from the pilots' hut to the FE. The inevitable flurry of flies tried to get a taste of their sweating heads.

"I can't hit the Hun if you never get near him," Paxton said. O'Neill said nothing. "We've got nothing to protect this afternoon except ourselves," Paxton said. "If we see a Hun, are you going to let me fight him?"

"Depends. Depends how many there are, how high, and how late in the patrol."

"You mean how desperately you want to get home for tea and cake?"

Their fitter swung the propeller. The Beardmore coughed and spat, banged and coughed, and grudgingly decided there was nothing else for it and so settled down to work. O'Neill slowly built the revs, and the roar broadened and deepened to a bellow, while black exhaust smoke got sucked into the propeller disc and sliced into nothingness. The wheels leaned hard on their chocks, and everything shook like a wet dog on a cold day. Paxton sat in the front cockpit and tried to focus on the dancing flies. He knew it couldn't be done but it was something to do. O'Neill slowly brought the revs down. The chocks were dragged clear. The FE rolled. The flies gave up the chase. Paxton stared at the rushing grass until it became a blur. He had a sudden moment of panic when he thought he'd left his chocolate behind, but it was in his pocket after all. By then they were flying.

O'Neill went through the overcast and into a new world where the cloud was as white and smooth as linen and the sky had the huge, friendly blueness that gave heaven a good name. Paxton blinked with approval a few times and then got down to the business of hunting Huns.

230

O'Neill took them up so high that cold began to seep like a stain through the flying gear, and Paxton couldn't believe he had ever been hot and sweaty. He loosened his straps and moved about, working his body as he searched. After an hour he was tired and all they had seen was a couple of British Nieuports and a Vickers Gun Bus. Paxton waved as they passed and hoped they would go away.

He no longer heard the engine-roar and the wind-rush. The FE seemed not to be moving. It hung in space, occasionally leaning one way or the other. He had eaten his chocolate. He was chilled and he had cramp in his right buttock. The whole silly afternoon was a wash-out. He was glad when O'Neill turned towards the sun and began to lose height. That way lay steaming hot baths and drinks before dinner. The FE stopped its gentle dive and began climbing, hard. Paxton, irritated, looked around and saw O'Neill pointing to the left and high, almost vertically.

It had to be an enemy machine. Only an enemy would be falling so far, so fast. Paxton fumbled for his binoculars and before he got them out he knew it was too late to use them. Already he could make out details: a biplane, sleeker than most, glossy purple, with a snout-like exhaust poking straight up. O'Neill had turned to face it, but his climb was so much flatter than the enemy's dive that Paxton had to crouch to get it in his sights. He tested the Lewis, saw a round of tracer fall away, remembered that he was firing *upwards*, must allow for that. Now the Hun seemed to be accelerating, quite startlingly: Paxton had the impression of adjusting the view through binoculars and making it rush closer. He saw prop-disc, undercarriage, tailplane. When he could see the wing-struts he would open fire. He saw the struts and fired, and his tracer passed tracer jetting from the nose of the Hun, and he edged his fire down and saw it washing and wandering all around the Hun while a magnificently destructive banging hammered in his ears, and he was remotely aware of the enemy tracer flickering past, missing him, harmless, and the target was big, unmissable, perfect and suddenly it was snatched from view because the FE had been flung aside. "*You bastard!*" he shouted. "*Gutless bastard!*" He dropped the Lewis and snatched a flare pistol from its clip, swung around to face O'Neill and fell off his seat when the FE banked even more steeply. Paxton fired. He was half-sprawled in a corner of the cockpit, left arm hooked around his seat. The flare was red, a hot brick-red, and it raged across O'Neill's cockpit and streaked between the struts of the left wing like a slice of a furnace. O'Neill threw up an arm: too late: it had missed him. But Paxton tasted joy. The red blaze of the flare matched his rage at O'Neill for cheating him of his kill. The FE heaved itself from one bank to the other. Paxton tumbled with it, got his boots against the side, stood, hurled the pistol at O'Neill, missed by a yard. O'Neill didn't even duck. He was pointing dead ahead. The FE levelled out and Paxton saw the Hun, half a mile away, turning to attack. He fell over his feet getting to the Lewis.

Big black crosses outlined in white, on deep purple shimmering to silky green: the enemy looked as pretty as a butterfly. It made its turn and became a sharp silhouette. This was going to be a simple, head-on attack, both machines at the same height. He just had time to rip off the half-empty drum and bang on a full one. Flame was flickering in the nose of the Hun like impossibly rapid Morse. Paxton aimed, squeezed, revelled in the battering, stammering racket. The enemy propeller-disc shattered in a whirl of fragments and he lowered his aim as the Hun lost speed and sank. He could see the pilot's head. Strikes sparkled around it. Everything magnified as if the plane were being inflated and then it exploded and was gone.

O'Neill hauled the FE up to escape the whirling debris. By the time he had circled, there was only a fading smudge of black smoke and a handful of bits of aeroplane already well on their way down. Paxton leaned out and watched them until they hit the cloud. *It really is like bursting a balloon*, he thought. *Just like bursting a balloon*.

Cleve-Cutler and Tim Piggott were watching the last of the afternoon patrols return. They saw O'Neill and Paxton land. They saw them get out, and they saw O'Neill kick Paxton and Paxton punch O'Neill and both men go down in a wild tangle. By the time they had strolled over to the fight it had lost almost all momentum through sheer exhaustion. "Give these gentlemen my compliments," Cleve-Cutler said to the fitter, "and ask them to meet me in my office as soon as they can bear to be separated."

Cleve-Cutler sat behind his desk, looking even jauntier than usual. Piggott leaned against the door. Paxton and O'Neill stood as far apart as possible. They were still in flying kit. Paxton's face was white where his goggles had been and black around the mouth and chin from the blow-back of the Lewis. O'Neill's face was rubbed green with grass-stain.

"I don't care who starts," Cleve-Cutler said.

"Fucking maniac tried to kill me," O'Neill said. "Tried to kill himself too. I don't mind *that*, he can kill himself any time he likes, I'll hold his coat." All his Australian accent had vanished.

"How, when and where?"

"Right in the middle of a scrap with a Halberstadt. Two seconds after the Hun finished having a go at us, this fucking maniac turned round and had a go at me. With a flare pistol. Just missed me, just missed the propeller, just missed setting fire to the wing, just missed doing the Hun's job for him."

"Missed?" Piggott said. "How could he miss? He was only three feet away from you."

"He was crashing about like a drunk in a knocking-shop. So was the bus, come to that."

Cleve-Cutler asked: "Why did he fire the flare pistol at you?"

O'Neill threw his gauntlets on the floor. "He didn't like the way I flew the aeroplane," he said.

"Oh!" Paxton said. Cleve-Cutler looked. Paxton gazed back, and then let his gaze fall and his shoulders slump. "Sorry, sir. I shouldn't interrupt."

"Too late now." Cleve-Cutler waved him on.

"Well, sir . . . I mean, he doesn't half tell a lot of whoppers."

"Such as."

"Well, I never did any such thing."

Cleve-Cutler turned to O'Neill. "The accused declares that he did not utter the words alleged."

"No, no, no," Paxton said fast, "I mean I never fired any flare pistol at anyone."

"You . . . lying little *bastard*!" O'Neill heaved himself forward but Piggott jumped between the two men and checked him. "He tried to shoot me!" he shouted. "He wanted to put that bloody flare straight through me!" The mask had gone. O'Neill was furious and it showed.

"I don't think that's a very good idea," Paxton said. He licked his upper lip, which was split and bleeding. "I don't think observers should go around shooting their pilots, not in the sky anyway. You need someone to drive you home, don't you?"

Cleve-Cutler looked at Piggott. "What would you say, Tim?"

"It's always been the generally accepted idea."

"He's a fucking maniac," O'Neill growled. "He wants to kill everyone."

Paxton cocked his head, as if he had heard a distant voice. "Not *everyone*, surely. The odd Hun, perhaps." He began to smile at O'Neill and hurt his split lip. "Ow!" he said. "Mustn't do that."

"Well, you got one Hun today," Cleve-Cutler said.

"Yes, thanks to O'Neill. He got close enough for me to apply the finishing touches. He did all the hard work."

"You prick," O'Neill said. "You piss-poor lump of shit."

"I sense here a difference of opinion," Cleve-Cutler said.

"Hey!" Piggott said. "I've got an idea. Why don't we take a look at the pistol? Then we can see if it's been fired or not."

"I lost it," Paxton said. "Awfully sorry."

"Lost it? How the hell did you come to lose it?"

"Dropped it over the side. I took it out to make sure it was loaded and suddenly the plane sort of went over sideways and before I knew it . . . Goodbye pistol." He grimaced. "Didn't want to mention it. I mean, a chap feels such a juggins."

Piggott sniffed. "Well, you'll have to pay for it, that's all."

"Bollocks," O'Neill grunted. "All bollocks."

"What about the way O'Neill flies the aeroplane?" Cleve-Cutler asked.

"I think he's jolly brave," said Paxton. "When the Hun's coming at us he holds the plane absolutely straight and level so I can get the best possible shot. I'm frightfully lucky to have a pilot like that."

Cleve-Cutler nodded to himself, slowly and at length. "Buzz off, both," he said. They went out.

"Well," Piggott said. He scratched his head.

"Couldn't have put it better myself," Cleve-Cutler said.

"D'you think he tried to shoot him?"

"I'm sure he did. Have you ever seen Frank in such a bate? Eyes like headlamps."

"Then he was right. Paxton's crazy."

Cleve-Cutler tugged at his left ear. "Um," he said. "Ah. Well, now. He was crazy *then*, up there, for a little while. He's not crazy *now*, is he?"

"No, but he's a bloody liar, isn't he?"

Cleve-Cutler laughed and laughed. "That was damn good, wasn't it? I must say I enjoyed that. He's pure animal, is our Paxton. Half blood-lust and half low cunning, all wrapped up in the old school tie." The thought made him laugh again. "What a shocker. I wish I had more like him."

Paxton and O'Neill kept well apart on the way to the pilots' hut. As they were getting changed, O'Neill said: "You're not a sodding juggins. You're a halfwit. All you had to do was say that flare pistol got lost through enemy action, and they'd have given you another one, free."

"It's something called honesty," Paxton said. "You wouldn't understand."

They said nothing until they met the adjutant to report on the patrol. O'Neill gave a fairly detailed account of the fight; he identified the enemy as a Halberstadt D II single-seater, one gun synchronised to fire through the propeller arc. The way it disintegrated in the second attack, just blew apart, made him believe that its fuel tanks were punctured and an incendiary bullet touched a stream of vapour. Good pilot. Determined.

"Anything to add?" Brazier asked Paxton.

"Only to say what a pleasure and a delight O'Neill's company has been, and how I look forward—" O'Neill punched him on the side of the head, a slog of a blow that hurt the hand as much as the head. Brazier cried, "I say, there! Now come along!" Paxton swung a fist wildly and blindly and hit

O'Neill in the stomach. Then they were whacking and slamming at each other, usually missing, until Brazier grabbed them by the collars and dragged them apart. He hoisted them onto their toes and gave them a good shake. It was an astonishing feat of strength. Paxton's teeth were rattling, and O'Neill's hands were flopping as if his wrists were broken. "Now listen here!" Brazier shouted. He gave them a good flourish to gain their attention, and blood sprayed from O'Neill's nose. "That sort of thing's not on! You're not at home now. I'll have no brutality in this camp. Cut it out or I'll take on the pair of you and beat you to a bloody pulp." He tossed them aside.

O'Neill went to the mess for a drink. Paxton went to his billet and got cleaned up. Then he went to see Piggott. On his way there, three people congratulated him on his kill. He asked Piggott's permission to go into Amiens for a couple of hours. "Yes, yes, by all means, go, for Christ's sake get out before you start another fight," Piggott said. On his way to borrow a motorcycle, Paxton was congratulated by four more people. Several others waved as he rode out of camp. He never knew he had so many friends.

Chapter 16

There was nobody on the lake, and the tennis courts were empty. The grounds were empty, too. The further he rode up the drive the emptier everything looked. It was a drab, lifeless evening and when he glimpsed a corner of the house it seemed big and unfriendly. What if Mr Kent Haffner met him? He lost his nerve and turned back and rode fast to the entrance gates. The old man who had opened them to let him in emerged from the lodge and opened them to let him out. Paxton sat on the bike with his feet on the gravel and counted the pounding heartbeats. What was he afraid of? A middle-aged American diplomat? *We reposing especial Trust and Confidence in your Loyalty, Courage and good Conduct . . .* So what the dickens *was* he afraid of? He revved the engine. It backfired and the old man jumped. He was afraid of meeting Judy, of course. Afraid she might not like him this time. How feeble! He turned the bike again and roared back up the drive.

His heart was still thumping and thudding when a maid showed him into the library. He felt slightly giddy, and when he saw Judy Kent Haffner wrestling with another young officer he felt ill. They were sitting on a sofa and they were flushed and breathless with laughter. "You're a cheat and a stinker," she said, gasping, and pushed the man away. "David's going to thrash you. Aren't you, David?"

"Within an inch of his life." Paxton was impressed by his voice: he sounded calm and easy. They had been playing backgammon. It was all just fun. He ordered up a smile and walked across the room as if he walked across rooms every day. She stood and tossed her hair back and kissed him on the lips. It came as a shock. He never knew girls tasted so good. "Goodness, you're all dusty! Anne-Marie . . ." The maid was still there. "Show Mr. Paxton to the Chinese bathroom."

When he came back, looking pink and smelling of jasmine, the other man had gone. She took both his hands and led him onto the terrace. "You saved me from a dreadful fate," she said. "I was getting whopped, absolutely *whopped*. Now tell me, how is the war going? You'll stay for dinner, you *must*, otherwise I shall be miserably lonely and probably shoot myself between the fish and the meat, which is a very painful place to get shot, and where the hell have you *been* all this time?"

"Fighting the foe."

Still holding his hands, she took a step back and studied him. At first he went slightly red but then he asked himself what he had to be ashamed of? Nothing. All his mother's friends said he was goodlooking. So he turned no more than slightly red and he looked straight back at her. It was a wonderfully enjoyable experience.

"Do you still have your marvellous machine-gun?" she asked.

"Yes, of course."

"And am I going to find out how long it is?"

"No. Military secret."

"You're my hero."

They walked to the rose garden, where the air was heavy with scent. "You know, we ought to be able to *eat* roses," she said. "Look at that one: pure rich cream. And here's one like the flesh of a peach."

"I heard about a breed of wild deer that eats roses non-stop. Just the flowers."

"Clever animal."

"My aunt doesn't think so. She breeds roses."

"Silly woman! I'd love to be a deer."

"Would you? Can you jump?"

She picked a lemon-yellow rose and twirled it. "I jumped for my living," she said. "You can get a free show, if you like."

She took him into the house, to a small ballroom, empty of furniture. "Be a sweety and put something on the gramophone."

He wound the machine and was startled to see her kick off her shoes and pull her dress over her head. She was wearing the tightest bathing-costume he had ever seen. He had never known that girls' legs were so long and so beautiful. "Golly!" he said. "You look absolutely . . ." He took a huge breath.

"Yes, well, ballet dancers are supposed to look absolutely and that's what I was before I got married. You never saw one of these before? Leotard." She was bending and stretching. "I like to practise every day. Come on: music, music!"

He put on a record: Bizet's *Carmen*. She was right, she could jump. And she flexed like rubber. He kept changing records and learning things he had never suspected about the way women were shaped, until suddenly she stopped dancing and sat in the middle of the room, gasping for breath. "Why does everything beautiful," she asked, "hurt so much? Don't try to answer. Come and talk while I bathe."

He followed her to yet another bathroom, where she went behind a screen of smoked glass. Paxton sat in a cane chair and watched her blurred shape while he talked about life at Pepriac. He had never before been in the same room with an utterly, totally naked woman, and when he thought about it he got peculiar aches just behind his ears, so he tried not to think. That was impossible. Why does everything beautiful hurt so much? At last she came out, wearing a towelling robe. "Want a bath?" she said.

"Um . . . Not at the moment, thanks."

"I'll scrub your back."

Now he knew he was being teased. "I have a batman who does that for me," he said.

Dinner was excellent. Baked stuffed mushrooms, buttered whitebait, tournedos Rossini, strawberries with kirsch. Lots of wine. They talked about trivialities until she ate her last strawberry and said "Tell me about the war."

He drank more wine while he thought what he ought to say. "Don't think," she said, "just say what you feel."

It was a challenge. "All right. I wouldn't say this to anyone else, especially not the other chaps, because they'd—"

"Stop explaining, David. Just tell me."

"Yes. Very well. Um . . . Well, I think it's the most

wonderful thing I've ever seen. Exciting, and colourful, and and . . . beautiful. That's the only word, beautiful."

"How can it be colourful? Everyone's in khaki."

"Yes, but there are dozens of different regiments. D'you know the most wonderful sight of all, for me? A battalion of infantry on the march. There's something about the drums, and the crunch of the boots. I get quite a lump in the throat. And when it gets dark the Front is lit up like a firework display! Flares of all colours, and starshells . We can see them from the aerodrome. And hear the guns."

He was so happy that he made her smile. "I wish I could see it," she said. "I've got a little cine-camera . Is there really going to be a battle? People keep talking about a Big Push."

He nodded. "There's going to be the most glorious scrap, and we're going to hit Master Fritz for six, you watch."

"And you're going to be in it?"

"I must be the luckiest man alive. I'm in the right place, at the right time, on the right side! Can you beat it?"

Coffee came, and brandy. "You haven't said anything about flying," she said. "But I can see you've been in action." She meant his split lip.

"That? Oh, that's nothing." Now that he had to tell her about his kill he felt awkward, although it was the main reason for his visit. "We were up on patrol this afternoon," he said, taking a deep look into his coffee-cup, "and I had a spot of luck. Shot down a Halberstadt." He glanced up, shyly.

She stood and came over and put a finger under his chin to tip it up and kissed him on the lips. "Bully for you," she said, and stroked his cheek.

"Actually . . ." Paxton took her hand. "You said you'd teach me to dance if I got another kill."

They went to the ballroom. She put a slow waltz on the gramophone. "Don't try to think," she said as they held each other. "Just let your body follow mine." Paxton had taken a couple of dancing lessons during the school holidays so he knew a bit about the waltz, but dancing with Judy was a far more exciting experience. For one thing she held him much closer than his partners had, and she would often rest her cheek against his chin.

When the fourth record spun to an end they stopped and she said: "You're perfect. Get another kill and I'll teach you something else."

"Try and stop me," he said. It wasn't a very clever remark, so he kissed her. It was meant to be a quick, thank-you sort of kiss but she let it grow into much more than that. Unprecedented ideas drifted into his head, until she pushed him away. "Mr. Haffner is due home any time," she said. "But come again, won't you?"

The old man at the lodge had the gates open for him. Paxton gave him some money and chugged into the night. A rich, full day, he thought.

A week passed, a bad week for Hornet Squadron.

A man called Macarthur, a new boy, a replacement pilot, stalled on take-off. He got to a hundred feet, over-revved the engine and lost it. Then he did what he had repeatedly been told not to do: he tried to turn and land on the 'drome, instead of gliding forward and crash-landing wherever he could. So the FE fell on its back like a load of old furniture pushed over a cliff. More work for the padre.

Then a quite experienced crew – two months and one kill – was lost over the German Lines. Their names were Surridge and Nash, so they were called Sausage and Mash. They were at eight thousand feet, setting out on a Deep Offensive Patrol, when the first shell of the first pattern of German archie struck the engine and exploded with enough violence to destroy a house. Surridge knew nothing of it: before any message could reach his brain his body had been shattered, wrecked, blown to bits. Nash was somewhat protected from the blast by Surridge's body. He got flung through the plywood nacelle and broke most of his bones. For a few seconds his eyes did their job and recorded the whirling nightmare. Then his body twisted one way and his head jerked the other, and he broke his neck. Thirty-five seconds later his body landed in a patch of nettles and buried itself three feet deep. Nobody saw it. Nobody found it. A month later the nettles had covered the scar in the earth.

Macarthur was a newcomer but Sausage and Mash were regular fixtures in the squadron. Or so everyone had thought.

Their loss – reported by several infantry units in the trenches – hit Pepriac hard. Nobody took archie terribly seriously; it was easy to dodge when you saw where it was. The frightening thing was that first shot. You couldn't dodge that, because you didn't know where it would be. Of course what happened to Sausage and Mash was sheer luck. Some bloody Hun battery commander had aimed at a fast-moving target a mile and a half up and hit it first shot. It was appalling, lousy luck. It might never happen again. But it showed it *could* happen. That was what was frightening.

Cleve-Cutler smelled doom and despair and mixed up an especially stimulating batch of Hornet's Sting. When everyone had a pint of the stuff bubbling in his gut Cleve-Cutler organised a knock-out battle with soda-syphons, each Flight attacking the other two. The anteroom was awash and the squadron was soaked when they went into the mess for dinner. Dinner was sausage and mash. Everyone thought that was hilariously funny. Most of it got thrown. Afterwards there was another battle with soda-syphons to wash the food off. You could hear the racket from Pepriac churchyard. Surridge and Nash had been seen off in style. They were rarely mentioned after that. Which is not to say that everyone forgot them, or their way of going.

Next morning it rained before breakfast and then the sun came out. The grass glittered. Gerrish and Ross were in their FE with the engine thundering, ready to taxi out and take off, when a pigeon flew into the propeller. Blood and guts and feathers everywhere. Gerrish switched off.

While his crew cleaned off the mess and examined the prop for chips or cracks and checked for any other damage, Gerrish got out and talked to Foster, who had been watching. Ross felt warm and comfortable with the sun on his face. He was too hungover for violent exercise. He stayed where he was.

"Ugly brute, isn't it?" Foster said. He meant the FE. "Doesn't look much like a bird. Looks more like the old lady who lived in a shoe and was frightfully prolific. With wings on."

Gerrish took off his sheepskin coat and sat on it. "Someone told me that Jerry calls it 'the flying packingcase'. I expect that sounds better in German. Or worse. Bloody ugly lingo, German."

Foster sat behind Gerrish and leaned against him. The aerodrome was quiet; no engines were being run. From the next field came the faint gabble of Chinese as the labour gang squabbled about something. "I don't suppose you've had a lot to do with women, Plug," Foster said.

"No? Why not?"

"Because of your extreme ugliness, old chap."

"If it didn't mean getting up I'd bash your face in. Then women wouldn't have a lot to do with *you*."

"Too late, alas. One poor creature has decided that she cannot live without me."

Gerrish grunted. "I've got a tailor like that. Keeps writing me grovelling bloody letters. Tell her to go to hell."

Foster sighed. "Actually, I told her *I'd* gone to hell."

"So you have. Pigging it in that wigwam with that bloody dog and playing the concerto for the back passage on the trombone all night. I mean to say, dash it all, Frank."

"She thinks I snuffed it. You see, I arranged for her to hear that I'd been shot down. And now *she's* snuffed it."

"What d'you mean? Dead?"

"So I hear, Plug." Foster blew his nose, and Gerrish felt the vibrations. "Message from a mutual friend. Jenny's snuffed it."

Gerrish released his breath, puffing out his lips. "That's going a bit far, that is," he said.

"My fault. People in our line of business shouldn't fall in love. It's not fair on anyone." There was a faint tremor in Foster's voice. "Too late now, alas."

"Definitely snuffed it, has she? I mean . . ."

"Blew her brains out, old boy. Don't tell anyone, will you?"

"Must have used a very small revolver, that's all I can say." When there was silence he said: "Sorry, Frank. I didn't mean that."

A series of bangs erupted inside the FE and Ross began screaming.

Ross had grown bored. He knew the story about Paxton, O'Neill and the flare pistol – the whole squadron knew it – and he started wondering how accurate the thing was as a weapon. He unclipped his own flare pistol, knowing it was unloaded, and tested the trigger action, squeezing harder until it fired and it *was* loaded and the flare roared out like dragonsbreath. It ricocheted around the inside of the cockpit and hit a drum of Lewis ammo. Ross was dazed and dazzled. The flare rammed itself in the drum and, burning furiously, sent it skittering about the floor. Bullets detonated. Three hit Ross in the leg, one went through his left arm, another entered his thigh.

Everyone fell flat. Ross went on screaming until the firing stopped, and then he began swearing. Later, when Dando had taken him to hospital, twenty-seven bullet-holes were found in the nacelle.

"They say these things always go in threes," Foster said. "I wonder what's next."

"We've had three," Gerrish pointed out. "Macarthur, then Sausage and Mash, and now this."

"Macarthur . . . I forgot about Macarthur. Or maybe nobody told me. Did he crash?"

"He snuffed it, like your lady-friend. At least Ross hasn't snuffed it. What a bloody fool, though."

For Paxton the worst part of the week was his failure to add another kill to his score, or even to claim that he'd damaged a Hun. He was moving steadily up the table in the mess, which was fine, and most people had come to accept him, especially now the camp had fresh milk and eggs every day from the cow and hens that Lacey had acquired. It was amazing what Lacey could get in exchange for good cigars or new records: a billiards table, a case of Cooper's Oxford marmalade, a crate of soft toilet paper, rugs for the billets, carpet for the mess, fresh fruit galore including bananas, which were Cleve-Cutler's favourite. Paxton received his share of the kudos for making all this possible. Pepriac developed a reputation for being the camp with everything; certainly its gramophone had plenty of the latest records, and the gramophone was the beating heart of every RFC mess.

That stuff was all very nice but it wasn't blood. The enemy was in the sky but he wasn't in the mood. At the end of the week O'Neill had got close enough to an aeroplane to force a skirmish on only three occasions. Always the enemy held off, backed away, stayed out of range. In a dozen patrols Paxton fired just one burst, and then the range was enormous. The other plane immediately turned and dived to the east.

"Looked like a Roland," O'Neill told Brazier. "He ran away."

"How could you tell?" Paxton asked. "Your eyes were too wet to see anything."

"The great mouth speaks," O'Neill said sourly.

"He's sorry for the Hun," Paxton told Brazier. "Goes all weepy when one appears."

"Any complaints, see your Flight Commander," Brazier said. "I just do the paperwork."

They bickered all the way to their billet.

"Of course the stupid Hun got away," Paxton said. "You gave up."

"Right, I did."

"That's my wild colonial boy. First prize in the backwards dash."

"I gave up because I didn't want to have tea in a prisoner-of-war camp. Don't you ever look at your watch?"

"Constantly. It's so boring up there I can't wait—"

"Shut your trap, fartface. We had enough fuel to get back, *or* chase that Roland and have a scrap. Not both. Simple enough?"

"Oh, indubitably."

"Trouble with you English is once you've stirred your tea you've strained your brain for the rest of the day."

They argued in and out of the bathhouse and all the way to the mess anteroom.

"If I were driving we'd chase the sods until we jolly well caught one," Paxton said.

"If you were driving we'd stall on take-off."

Paxton drank some whisky-soda. He was getting to like the taste. The gramophone played *Ragtime Cowboy Joe*. "Hey, Kelly," he said, and threw a cushion at Kellaway. "What's the difference between an Australian and a dead kangaroo?"

Kellaway chewed on a corner of the cushion. "Give up," he said.

"Right first time. The Australian gives up." Paxton was delighted, and tittered into his drink.

"Don't get too excited," O'Neill warned. "You'll wet yourself again."

Mayo stopped playing ping-pong to say: "I've got an uncle in Australia and he's never seen a kangaroo. He says it's all rabbits. Bloody rabbits everywhere." He served.

"One escaped," Paxton said. "O'Neill's a bunny."

"It's running down your leg," O'Neill said. He was beginning to sound edgy.

"Oh dear. Bunny doesn't like being called Bunny. Do you, Bunny?"

Goss put down his newspaper. "Is that chap annoying you?" He got up and tipped Paxton out of his chair. "You leave my friend Bunny alone! He can't help it if he's got big ears. Can you, Bunny?"

Paxton lay on the carpet and wrinkled his nose at O'Neill. For once, O'Neill had no answer except to turn away. From then on he was known as Bunny. He did not find it amusing. That night, as Paxton was brushing his teeth, O'Neill paused beside him and said: "You're the great comedian, aren't you? All right, we'll see how funny you find it next time we're in a scrap. You'll think our fucking FE's on tramlines, and so will Fritz." Paxton spat, and looked up, and wrinkled his nose.

A large pilot called Jumbo James, in 'B' Flight, had a bright idea. He got it when he was talking to a chum who was with an anti-aircraft battery defending a British balloon site. He thought it over, and told Plug Gerrish.

"There's one place the archie tries not to fire," he said. "That's directly above the balloon, in case any of their red-hot shrapnel falls on the damn thing and busts it. So I reckon a chap might be able to come in high and dive straight down and pop it."

"He might. What then?"

"Well, assuming the observers have taken to their parachutes, like intelligent men, what you do is circle around them as tight as you can. The archie can't hit *you* without hitting *them*. Then you scoot home. Clever wheeze, isn't it?"

Gerrish told the CO. "It's a lousy idea," Cleve-Cutler said, grinning fiercely. Gerrish asked why. "I don't know why," Cleve-Cutler said. "I just hate bloody balloons, I suppose."

"But you asked everyone to try and think of—"

"I know, I know. Does Jumbo want to test his idea? All right. I suppose I'd better come and watch."

There was no lack of German balloons to attack. They were up every day, and higher than ever. Jumbo James made his attempt one bright morning when he hoped he could hide his FE in a convoy of chunky clouds sailing from west to east, not too high. Gerrish and Cleve-Cutler took off at the same time.

Perhaps it really was a good idea, or perhaps the ground defence was half-asleep. Jumbo fell out of a cloud in a near vertical dive. No archie. Five hundred feet above the balloon he had to pull out or risk tearing the wings off. No archie but the balloon was going down. He climbed until he stalled and slid sideways into a spiralling descent, steeply banked to give his observer a good view of the balloon. The Lewis was loaded with incendiary bullets and tracer, five to one. Still no archie.

To Cleve-Cutler it looked like a fly buzzing over a toffee-apple. The FE had that long-legged, nosey look of a greedy insect; the balloon was brown and plump. Yellow sparks journeyed from one to the other, but the gasbag seemed to absorb them. Still no archie. No parachutes, either.

The observer was reloading. Jumbo was close enough to see how the network of ropes crimped and squeezed the balloon. It was descending faster than ever. He kept chasing but he felt no great enthusiasm for destroying it: the thing was too huge and helpless to hate. A flame as big as a marigold showed itself halfway up the balloon. It split and each part set off in a golden race to reach the other side, a race that was never won because the entire balloon turned itself into an open furnace.

Jumbo felt a blast of heat as he sheered away. There was archie everywhere he looked. It was as if someone was trying to fill the sky with black blots. This wasn't right. He looked for parachutes but all he saw was the blazing wreck of the balloon with its basket tumbling below it. This wasn't right at all. The FE hit a patch of shattered air and staggered over the smoky ruins. Coloured tracer came reaching up like party streamers. One streamer flicked a wing and the joystick kicked in Jumbo's hand. The wing sank and the ground tipped up and nothing he could do would change it. This was all wrong. Jumbo was strong, very strong, and angry. He whacked and wrenched the joystick until it came away in his hands. He was still looking at it when a grass field raced up and smashed into him.

O'Neill and Paxton returned from another wearying and completely dud patrol. O'Neill washed before lunch, and when he went back to the billet Paxton was rummaging through O'Neill's chest of drawers. "Where d'you keep your clean socks, Bunny?" he asked, still searching.

"I don't keep them. Bastards like you steal them."

"Not steal. Exchange. I always leave a dirty pair . . . Hullo, what's this?" He came away with a pair of clean socks. "Anything of mine you want, Bunny, just help yourself. My trunk is never locked."

O'Neill sat on his bed, and yawned. "I could break your arm," he said. "That would be nice."

"Nearly forgot. You had a letter from home." Paxton sent it skimming across the room. "Auntie Doris got arrested for interfering with a kangaroo, very nasty, and brother Bill's got another boil on his backside, very painful."

"Keep taking the prunes," O'Neill said as he began reading the letter, "and for Christ's sake stay downwind. Even the flies have moved out since you arrived."

Kellaway came in. "Heard about Jumbo?" he asked. Paxton nodded. "He owed me fifteen francs," Kellaway said.

Not looking up, O'Neill said: "Then you'd better bloody hurry, hadn't you?" It took Kellaway a few seconds to work out what he meant. He hurried out.

O'Neill grunted, and put his letter away. He watched Paxton brush his hair. "Jimmy Gordon was a lousy gunner," he said. Paxton stopped brushing and looked. O'Neill had never spoken to him like that before. The words were as flat as ever but they were the beginning of something, not the end. "Oh, yes?" he said.

"Jimmy couldn't think ahead. You get a Hun diving at you. Say he's in front and a bit to the right. Coming down at two o'clock, say. No good aiming straight at him is it?"

"No. You've got to aim at where he's going to be in the time it takes the bullets to reach him. He's diving, so you aim ahead of him."

O'Neill waited for more, and shook his head. "We're dead," he said.

Paxton stared. He could see that Hun; he could hear the hammering Lewis, follow the streaming tracer. "Aim a bit to his left, of course. To allow for our own speed. I mean, that's bound to push the bullets to the right."

"We're still dead."

Paxton finished brushing his hair. "Maybe the gun jammed," he said lightly, and wished he hadn't.

"He's high, we're low, you're firing uphill. What about gravity?"

"Oh yes. Bullet-drop. Aim high to allow for bullet-drop. I took that for granted." He picked up his cap and twirled it on his finger. "Coming to lunch?"

O'Neill didn't move. "It only takes one bullet, you know," he said. "You won't even know it hit you."

"True." Paxton's voice sounded thin. "Very true," he said more confidently.

"You want a steady gun-platform. I can do it. I can fly straight and level. That's perfect for you. It's also perfect for the Hun. You miss him, and he'll definitely kill us."

Paxton cleared his throat. He could think of nothing to say.

"Now that Ross has gone, Gus Mayo's the best gunner in the squadron," O'Neill said. "For Christ's sake go and talk to him"

"Right," Paxton said.

Next day Frank Foster and Gus Mayo saw a trail of smoke at six thousand feet. It was being made by a Fokker monoplane with terrible engine trouble. The Fokker tried to dive to safety when it saw them but its wings got the shakes and it had to pull out. Foster cruised underneath it and Mayo shot it down. "You wouldn't believe so much smoke could come out of such a little plane," Mayo told Brazier. It was no great triumph. Certainly no cause for serving Hornet's Sting.

Dando was awoken at three in the morning by the howling of an animal. It rose and fell with a regularity that would have been musical but for the desperation behind it.

Rain was drifting, making a soft, fine mist. Dando put on his boots and tunic and took an umbrella and a flashlight. He traced the sound to Captain Foster's tent where the dog Brutus was making an unhappy noise. But the howling was coming from Foster, who was having a nightmare. His face glistened like wet marble, and his eyelids flickered non-stop.

Dando shook him awake and the howling died in a gasp of terror. Foster's eyes were as clear and empty as a child's. Dando kept talking, repeating their names, making reassuring noises while he lit a hurricane lamp. Foster's head was drenched and his pyjamas were soaked. "I'm coming back," Dando said. "Don't get up."

He roused Foster's batman. They got Foster out of bed, stripped off the drenched pyjamas and towelled him dry. All the time he stood, shoulders slumped and knees wavering, with his mouth open and his eyes half-shut, and said nothing. Dando got fresh pyjamas on him while the batman changed his bedding. He was asleep before they got him into bed. Dando checked his pulse: it was bumping along like a cart on a stony lane. The batman had found half a bottle of rum. They each had a tot, and Dando gave Brutus a mouthful in a saucer for good luck.

At breakfast it was obvious to Dando that Foster remembered nothing of the night; he was good-humoured and seemed refreshed. Dando found an opportunity to tell Cleve-Cutler. "So what, old boy?" the CO said. "Half the squadron has nightmares. I have nightmares. Don't you have nightmares?"

"No, sir."

"Something wrong with you, then. Sometimes I wake up in the small hours and this camp sounds like Christians versus Lions. All quite normal."

However, at lunchtime Foster bought Dando a drink and took him aside. "Was it you made Brutus squiffy?" he asked.

"Guilty."

"Don't do it again, old boy. You probably don't know this, but there have been attempts to poison the poor hound." Foster looked squarely into Dando's eyes.

"Why would anyone do that?"

"I'm surprised you find it necessary to ask."

"Well, I'm a newcomer here, remember."

Foster took a long look around the room. It was noisy and cheerful as it filled up for lunch. "You can tell them this from me. If they want to kill Brutus they'll have to kill me first."

Dando signalled for more drinks. "Do you have any particular person in mind?" he asked.

"Second-lieutenant Paxton," Foster said. "I've been watching him. He enjoys killing. Well, I'll enjoy killing him. I say, Paxton!" he called, and beckoned.

"I honestly don't believe he means you any harm," Dando said.

"Look here, Paxton," Foster said, amiably, "you've got a reputation as something of a ladykiller. What?"

"Oh, not half. Why?"

"Somebody killed my girl in London. She cut her throat. Wondered if it was you."

"Not me, old chap."

"On your honour?" Now that it was obvious that Foster was mocking him, Paxton's only reply was an uncomfortable smile. "No honour, you see. Paxton doesn't really belong in this squadron," Foster told Dando. "He's a common tradesman. A merchant of death to home and industry." And he winked. Dando noted the brittle glitter in his eyes, and wondered how much of it was drink.

In another part of the room, Gerrish was telling Tim Piggott: "I worked out where Jumbo's idea went wrong. He was going to use the balloon crew as his shield while they parachuted down. But he was more or less directly *above* the balloon when he was shooting at it, so I reckon his bullets went straight through it and killed the crew in the basket, so they never had a chance to parachute. See?"

"Maybe there never was a crew," Piggott said. "Maybe the basket was empty."

"A decoy? Bit expensive, isn't it?"

"Dunno. Look what they got: one FE, Jumbo, his observer. Or maybe it was just a test flight. Testing the balloon."

Gerrish kicked a chair. "The old man said it was a lousy idea."

"Got your replacements yet?"

"Arrived this morning. Pilot's thirteen, observer's twelve. Shout loudly and they burst into tears."

Chapter 17

Somewhere a dam had burst. It was a huge dam, stuffed with thunder, and in its rush to escape, the thunder rolled over itself and made a double thunder, and then the double thunder exploded with a roar, and the roar swelled until the air was swamped with noise. Fifteen miles away, lying on O'Neill's bed, Paxton thought the hut would collapse under the weight of noise. A pane of glass fell from a trembling window and shattered. He rolled off the bed just as O'Neill came in. "You've been signing my name on your mess chits, you prick," O'Neill said, pitching his voice to penetrate the roar.

"Well, you've been signing mine on yours, you turd. What the hell is *that*?"

"Guns. They go bang. Didn't you know?" He began rummaging in Paxton's trunk. "I wish you wouldn't have so much starch put in your shirts . . . Is this my bottle of rum?"

"I expect so." Paxton was in the doorway, looking to the east. He expected to see a distant sign of such a colossal roar, but there was nothing. A few panicking pigeons clattered overhead. "Is this the Big Push?"

"Christ knows. Is this my toothbrush?"

"I expect so."

"Jesus . . . Can't you get your own?"

"I did. You took it. How long will this last?"

O'Neill removed a bunch of coloured photographs from Paxton's hand. "I wish to buggery you wouldn't breathe on my naked ladies," he grumbled. "And go and stink in your own pit."

"It's wonderful," Paxton said. "Just listen. It's superb. Isn't it superb?"

"Get your bonnet on," O'Neill said. "Let's go and get some breakfast."

They took off half an hour later, to cover a Quirk on a photographic patrol. All the squadron was in the air. Paxton was eager to see what the bombardment looked like but when they crossed the Front it was obscured by a drifting fog of smoke from the guns, and the enemy trenches were completely lost under a cloud of grey-brown dust, which occasionally gave birth to shapely puffballs when the heavy howitzers caused an unusual amount of damage. The barrage drowned out the FE's engine. There was so much din that Paxton heard nothing. He thought he might have gone deaf, so he undid his flying helmet and peeled back a flap. His ears hurt. It was like being in the middle of a mob of angry blacksmiths He did up his helmet, fast. Behind the British Lines, gun-flashes made a flickering stream of red and yellow that wandered to the north and faded into their own smoke. Paxton turned his head. Another stream wandered south, as bright as fireflies. *Those guns have fired a thousand shells while I watched them*, he thought. *How magnificent! How stunning!*

They rendezvoused with their Quirk and took care of it while it paraded up and down, infuriating the archie. If O'Neill held his course and height for thirty seconds the archie had a go at him, too. But this was not their day. The Quirk got its pictures and went home. O'Neill still had fuel. He climbed and searched further to the east.

There was nothing much to see: the odd speck, hopelessly remote and going away; the odd line of cloud, and not much of that. O'Neill decided to make a certain cloud his turning-point. It turned out to be big and sprawling, with a massive overhang that almost formed a cave. The shadow of the FE got there first by half a second and went flitting across the face of the cloud until he caught up with it and they charged into the near-cave and came out the other side as an Albatros came flying in. For an instant O'Neill's stomach clenched as hard as stone because he knew their wings must hit. They flicked past each other. He slumped, forgot how to breathe, and recovered to find his arms and legs automatically stuffing the controls into a corner so as to drag the FE into a tight turn before the Albatros came back and cut it to pieces.

Paxton found it very entertaining. It was like sitting in the cinema, with unexpected pictures suddenly appearing and disappearing. The FE banked, and that was like sitting in a fairground ride, swinging in a circle that pressed you into your seat. Enormous fun. The tail of the Albatros crept into his vision. He screwed his head around. It was a dove-grey two-seater. The observer had the rear cockpit, and a cutaway in the top wing gave him a wide field of fire. Paxton saw him swing his gun, release a squirt of fire, and raise his head to check results. Missed by a mile.

That short stutter of bullets roused Paxton. He shoved himself forward and swung the Lewis to the side. Hopeless: with the FE in such a steep bank he was aiming at the ground. He sat on the cockpit floor and aimed as high as possible. Still too low. A ten-round burst went nowhere near the Albatros. He shouted at O'Neill and shook the Lewis. O'Neill saw, but he held the FE in this tail-chasing turn, the wings almost vertical. O'Neill had his own problems.

The Albatros carried a machine gun in its nose, synchronised to fire through the prop. At least he was pretty sure it did. The FE had a nose gun. First plane to get behind the other would score. So each pilot hauled his machine into the tightest of circles. With the planes banked on their wingtips, each observer was trying to fire above his head and it couldn't be done. The gun fittings made it impossible. O'Neill could flatten his turn and give Paxton a shot, but only at the cost of slackening the circle and letting the Albatros catch him.

So round and round they went.

Paxton got back on his seat. He wondered if he could unfix the Lewis and fire it from his shoulder. Unlikely. He took out his Service revolver and blazed away at the enemy, hanging perpetually opposite him. He might have been firing blanks for all the difference it made.

O'Neill worried about fuel. He worried about it so much that he failed to notice a stubby little German biplane arrive overhead. It flew up and down, apparently intrigued by the scene below. Paxton saw it, and pointed. There was nothing O'Neill could do except curse, so he cursed. After a while he lost sight of it. There was nothing he could do about that, either.

The stubby Hun had vanished because he had decided to interfere. Perhaps he thought the Albatros needed rescuing. More likely he thought the FE was easy meat. His plan of attack was simple. He would approach, straight and level, until the FE, tipped on its side and presenting a large target, flew into his sights.

This happened and he opened fire and that was that. Half his bullets missed, two or three splashed against the case of the Beardmore, and several holed the nacelle or the canvas wings. These last bullets kept going, of course, and a cluster of them found the tailplane of the Albatros, whose pilot abruptly found his machine threshing about and trying to fly crabwise. The tail-chase was over. Paxton saw the Albatros wandering into his sights and he gave it a burst. O'Neill saw a collision dead ahead and kicked the FE until it reversed its turn and sheered off. The next time he saw the Albatros it was far below and diving hard. The stubby little Hun had disappeared. *Very wise*, O'Neill thought. *Forget it ever happened*. He flew home, carefully, counting the bullet-holes. He could see fifteen. The mechanics later found another twelve.

"Bloody lucky," O'Neill said.

"Piss off, Bunny." Paxton showed him the heel of his left flying boot, shot through and flapping loose. "Bloody Huns can't shoot straight."

O'Neill tried to undo a button but he couldn't make his fingers work. "You don't take it seriously, do you?" he said. "It's all just a game, isn't it?"

"As long as we win, Bunny." Paxton wrinkled his nose and undid the button for him. "Who cares? Just listen to those guns!"

The opening barrage had lasted an hour and ten minutes. It subsided to a perpetual thunder. For weeks the London papers had been predicting a big new offensive. Well, everyone knew now where it would be. The mood at Pepriac was optimistic. The Hun was taking a tremendous battering, the sun was out and the Chinks had finished digging the swimming pool.

Most of the squadron strolled over to look. It was a very big hole, brimful of water from a diverted stream. "Bet you haven't got anything like that back in Grand Rapids," Mayo said to Stubbs.

"Awesome is the word for it," Stubbs said. "Truly awesome."

"No, I think wet is the word," Ogilvy said. "Where's Charlie? He was at Cambridge."

Essex tossed in a small stone. "Liquid," he said. There was a round of applause. "Or maybe fluid," he added.

Mayo said: "I think Pax should declare it open. After all, it was his idea."

"Who, me?" Paxton said.

"Brilliant." Mayo pushed him in. Stubbs pushed Mayo in. After that everyone got pushed in until only Charlie Essex was left. They all got out and chased him and caught him and threw him in. He couldn't swim, and it was a few moments before Spud Ogilvy remembered this, so they had to fish him out and hold him head-down to empty him. But it was an excellent pool and there was no need to wear trunks. Paxton felt the hot sun on his wet skin and looked about him at the leaping, splashing bodies. *Comradeship*, he thought. *That's what this war is all about.*

"Nothing was happening," Tim Piggott said. "That's the funny thing. We were in the middle of a patrol, no Huns, no nothing. And I got this sudden overwhelming impulse."

"Well . . . perhaps not *quite* overwhelming," the padre said. "Otherwise you wouldn't be here now, would you?"

"If I hadn't been strapped in I wouldn't be here now. I tell you, padre, the urge to climb out of the cockpit and walk away was enormous. Irresistible. All right, *nearly* irresistible."

"This may seem a silly question," the padre said, "but where did you think you were going?"

"Nowhere. Just . . . away, I suppose. Away."

They were sitting in the padre's room. The guns rumbled like a passing train that never passed.

"I would suggest a spot of leave, but . . ."

"I've already *had* a spot of leave. Hated it. Ended up in London, getting drunk. Came back a day early."

The padre chewed on his lower lip for such a long time that Piggott grew worried that he might draw blood.

"I promised myself I'd stop doing this," the padre said, "but evidently my will is weak. Take the Bible, shut your eyes, let it fall open wherever it will, place your finger on the page, see what verse you get."

"Rather like using a pin to find a winner." Piggott followed instructions and opened his eyes. "Ecclesiastes, nine, verse ten. 'Whatsoever thy hand findeth to do, do it with thy might, for there is no work, nor device, nor knowledge, nor wisdom, in the grave, whither thou goest.'"

"I say! That's pretty snappy, isn't it?"

Piggott read it again, silently. "Life is better than death," he said. "That's what it boils down to."

"Yes indeed. And personally I find it very encouraging. I must admit I was beginning to despair . . . But what's your opinion?"

"If it wins, I'll back it," Piggott said.

Someone had changed the soap in the Chinese bathroom. Now it had a delicate scent of lemons. The towels were crisp and thick, and had snarling red dragons woven into them.

Evidently she was giving a party. The terrace and the rooms opening onto it were full of talk, laughter, music. Paxton guessed there were fifty officers, all young, and half as many nurses, all pretty. You could drink champagne, or champagne. Everyone was drinking champagne. Chinese lanterns hung all around the terrace and never mind the blackout.

He wanted her with an urgency like hunger but he wanted her to himself. So he strolled around the edge of the crowd and kept away from her. He hadn't been invited and she didn't know he had arrived. Once or twice he had a very odd sensation: as if he were outside himself, overhead, watching himself stroll around. He had a drink and the sensation went away. He knew he wasn't drunk. Maybe he was sick with wanting. Certainly there were moments when he could have killed all these people, just swept them away so that nobody was between him and her.

He drank a bit and smiled a lot. People chatted to him, or he to them. It was amazingly easy to talk to strangers: you just said the first thing that entered your head and before you could finish, they interrupted with something they wanted to tell you, and it was all balls so who cared? And all the time he kept away from her.

A car appeared below the terrace. One group left, and then they were all going. They made a lot of noise, and suddenly the only noise was the last car going down the drive.

He sat on the terrace wall, in the shadow between two lanterns. "Hullo," she said from the house.

"Hullo yourself."

"If you're a real burglar, come inside and start burglaring."

He got down and went inside. Now that he could get a close look at it, her dress – green silky stuff, so thin you could sort of see through it – was even more startling than he'd thought. It didn't cover much, and what bits it covered seemed to be obvious whenever she moved. Half of him was scared of touching it and the other half wanted to give it a little tug to make it fall off. "What a rotten party," he said.

"Oh, a real stinker."

"I hated it."

"Fine. Next time I shan't invite you."

"Again."

"Certainly, again. I knew you wouldn't like it. And I was right, wasn't I?"

"You're always bloody right," he said gloomily. "Everything about you is completely and utterly bloody right. That's what I can't stand about you. In fact I—"

"Oh, shut up." She kissed him on the mouth, and this time it was much better. He knew where his nose went, and what to do with his tongue. He even had some success with his hands. When she tipped her head back and looked at him she said: "This must be your birthday."

"Why?"

"All of a sudden you've grown up."

He felt both pleased and embarrassed, so he said: "I've come for another dancing lesson."

"Another kill?" She was delighted. It wasn't flattery; he could see the sparkle in her eyes, feel the sudden hug.

"Another kill." It wasn't true, but who cared? "Devil of a scrap, against two of the blighters." Anyway, it *might* be true, maybe the Albatros crashed, it was certainly shot-up.

"And how's that big strong machine-gun of yours?" She put her cheek against his and whispered: "Still going bang-bang-bang?"

"None of your business," he whispered.

"Don't worry. I'll winkle that secret out of you."

They danced. The music was very slow, and she was more interested in kissing than in dancing. "You're the loveliest killer I danced with all night," she said. He thought about that remark all the way back to Pepriac.

The bombardment had lasted all day and all night. When dawn came it took away the pulse of light that had danced along the eastern skyline, but the rolling thunder went on. "Get used to it," Cleve-Cutler told his flight commanders when he called a meeting after breakfast. "I don't know any secrets but the general impression at Wing and Brigade is that this is just the beginning."

Piggott said: "If we're going after the Boche artillery we must have hit every gun they've got twice over by now."

"It's not that easy," Gerrish said. "I bet the Hun pulled his artillery back as soon as he saw what we were up to."

"So what's this? A summer sale? Clearing out old stock?"

"We're after their wire," Cleve-Cutler said, as breezy as a master of foxhounds. "Troops can get past shellfire but they can't climb over barbed wire. So we're blowing it to blazes."

"Then what?" Gerrish asked.

"Then we capture their first-line trenches, of course."

"There won't *be* any first-line trenches left to take, if we go on chucking shells at them like this."

"Then we take their second-line trenches. That suit you?"

"Or failing that, the outskirts of Berlin," Piggott said.

"Funny you should say that," Foster said. "Last time we had a Big Push, we captured about half a mile. Assuming we have two Pushes a year, I calculate we'll reach Berlin no later than—"

"Save it, Frank. I have news," Cleve-Cutler said. "We're getting a better FE." That made them sit up. "It's the FE2d. What happened to the FE2c God knows, they probably murdered a few test pilots with it before they realised the wings were on back-to-front. Anyway, this version is supposed to be bigger and stronger and faster and climbs higher and for all I know it makes Welsh rabbit and tells your weight and fortune if you put a penny in a slot . . ." He was dishing out fat envelopes to each man. "It's all in there. Go off and read it and brief your blokes. We're supposed to get these new machines today. I'd like a word with Frank."

As the other two went out, the steady booming of the guns sharply increased to a colossal, hammering roar. Piggott looked at his watch. "Same time as yesterday," he said. "Nice to work with people with such tidy habits, isn't it?"

Cleve-Cutler let them get well away, and said: "Dando told me he had a rather curious conversation with you."

"Curious?" Foster fanned himself with the envelope. "Well, Dando's rather a curious sort of fellow, isn't he?"

"Is he? I thought he was a typical doctor."

"Typical bloodsucker, if you ask me. D'you know what he had the nerve to do? He had the nerve to wake me up in the middle of the night and ask me how many flamers I'd got. For two pins . . ." Suddenly Foster was so furious that he couldn't get the words out. He glared at the CO. His lips kept tightening and slackening, and he swallowed again and again. "For two pins I'd smash his head in," he said.

"You didn't, though."

"The man's a leech. A damned leech." Foster looked at his hands, and then stuffed them in his pockets. "He'd better not try it again, that's all."

"Why was it so important to him? Damn it all, the middle of the night . . ."

Foster had control of himself again. He could even smile a little. "Perhaps Dando is losing his wits," he said. Cleve-Cutler gave his roguish grin full throttle, and Foster went away happy.

Ferry pilots delivered the new FE2ds, stayed for lunch and flew out the old machines.

All the crews went out to look at the first arrival. The tricycle undercarriage had gone but otherwise its basic design was much the same. It sounded far more powerful. The engine had been vastly improved: now it generated 250 horsepower and turned a four-bladed propeller. That meant just about everything was better: shorter take-offs, a faster rate-of-climb, higher ceiling, greater speed, better stunting. The pilots were happy and the observers were delighted when they heard that the new model carried three Lewis guns. One was mounted on the nose as usual and another was installed just in front of the pilot so that the barrel poked over his observer's right shoulder; this was a fixed gun, which meant the pilot aimed the whole aeroplane when he fired it. The third gun was even more remarkable. A metal post rose just behind the observer's seat, tall enough to clear the upper wing. "This must be what they call the 'pillar mounting',", Piggott said. "Apparently you attach the Lewis to the top. That's what the book of words says."

"Bloody long way up," Boy Binns said. "Do they supply a piece of string to tie to the trigger?"

"You have to stand on your seat," the ferry pilot explained. There was a moment's silence. It was such an absurd idea; everyone was waiting for the rest of the joke. But he was serious. They all laughed. "Get me a couple of guns and I'll show you," he said. "Why two?" Piggott asked. "You'll see," he said.

Two Lewis guns were brought. One was fixed to the pillar mounting, the other to the nose. As usual the balance of the guns left them pointing upwards. The ferry pilot heaved himself into the front cockpit. "Actually the seat's too low," he said, "but if you stand on the arms . . ." He climbed onto them and swung the Lewis on the pillar so that he was aiming past the tail. "As you can see, I've got to lean back or I can't work the gun," he said, "which is why my backside is perched on the drum of the other Lewis. What it comes down to is you've got to sit on the front Lewis in order to use the top one." He swayed from side to side, pretending to fire.

Mayo said: "What it comes down to is you've only got your boots inside the cockpit."

"Has anybody ever actually done this?" Gerrish asked. "I mean, in action?"

"Doubt it." The ferry pilot climbed down

"You'll never get me up there," Stubbs said. "I've got no head for heights."

"You'd have to be a real athlete to do all that," Mayo said. "I mean, it's not easy with the bus on the ground, let alone whizzing along at eighty or ninety."

"Make that a hundred," the ferry pilot said.

Cleve-Cutler had kept in the background. Now he said: "Well, you don't have to do it if you'd rather get shot-up by a Hun on your tail."

"Personally I think it's a spiffing idea," Paxton said. "Of course the driver will have to keep the bus straight and level, won't he? But then, that's what bus drivers are paid to do." He wrinkled his nose.

"What d'you say, Bunny?" Piggott asked.

"I say the pillar's not long enough," O'Neill said. "I say make it twenty feet long and give the silly bugger a rope ladder and a packet of sandwiches and he can stay up there all day."

The pattern of the previous day's bombardment was repeated: stupendously heavy pounding for about an hour and then a steady thunder, so constant that people forgot it. The ground crews had work to do, checking and adapting the new machines, testing the engines, painting numbers on the rudders. The officers went swimming.

Boy Binns chucked a bucket of water at Paxton, so he dived into the pool and cruised underwater until his outstretched fingers touched the other side. He came up to see Corporal Lacey looking down at him.

"Circumcision is clearly a hallmark of the British middle class," Lacey said. "I make the vote fourteen to three in favour of the amendment, with one member indecisive."

Paxton climbed out. "What about you?"

"Oh, quite, quite conventional. As an infant I shut my eyes and thought of England, or at least the Home Counties, while the surgeon's knife made the supreme sacrifice. So I suppose you could say I did my bit for my country. Not a very big bit, but—"

"Look here," Paxton said, "I really don't care, so if that's all you came to tell me . . ."

"I wondered if you'd mind witnessing Rufus Milne's will."

Paxton dried his hands on a towel, took the document, and glanced through it before he fully understood what Lacey had said. "How on earth can I witness his will? The man's dead. There's no signature here. He hasn't signed it."

"A detail. To be added later."

Paxton turned a page. "One thousand pounds to the Golden Sunset Donkey Sanctuary, Taunton, Somerset," he said.

"Milne was very fond of donkeys."

"I don't believe it."

"A generous gesture. It will be much appreciated."

"You've faked this, haven't you? It's all a cheat."

"Nothing of the sort. It's all perfectly valid. I spent two years in the family law office, you know." He took the will back. "My mother's sister, Maud, set up the Golden Sunset Donkey Sanctuary. She does splendid work, but funding is an endless headache . . . Oh well, if you won't witness it I shall have to find someone else."

"You'll never get away with this."

"I always have. Toby Chivers, for instance, left five thousand to the Leeds and District Society for Unmarried Mothers. That's my cousin Harriet's main interest in life."

"I think I'll turn you over to the police."

"In that case I shan't tell you about the equipment for the tennis courts that I've just got hold of."

"Ah." Paxton was quite good at tennis. It would be nice to be squadron tennis champion. "Nets and stuff, eh? We ought to find a nice level bit of grass."

"I've found one. Perfectly level, no slope, but it's got a few bumps."

"We need a roller, then."

"We need a company of infantry. There's a battalion in camp behind the church who seem very keen on drill. Why don't you ask some of them to come and march up and down on our tennis court? Take a box of cigars with you."

"All right." Paxton looked at Lacey and shared in the warm glow of the Public School Spirit. "Hell's bells, what the devil, give me your pen," he said, and witnessed the will. "It can't be illegal," he said, "because I'm not actually witnessing anything, am I?"

"You know, it's time you put your own affairs in order." Lacey said. "I'll draft something for you to look at."

Chapter 18

Before the day was out, all the new aeroplanes were in the air. Everyone liked them. The German air force was up in strength and there was much skirmishing. Cleve-Cutler, three miles over the Lines, came across an elderly Rumpler two-seater that seemed to have lost something, it was wandering about so vaguely. He searched above, and eventually saw a tiny scuff in the sky, so small it could have been wiped away with a flick of a cloth. He left the Rumpler and spiralled up, climbing steeper and faster than the old FE could have managed, until the scuff grew wings, pale-blue and translucent. It was an Albatros. Just above it was another.

They came down to meet him and then seemed to change their minds and parted, one to the left and one to the right. Cleve-Cutler admired these simple tactics. Whichever plane he challenged, he would expose his tail to the other. He turned his back on them both and flew away. They chased for a mile and gave up. He circled, and climbed a little, and watched them watching him. He had plenty of fuel. Far below, through gaps in the cloud, he saw the Allied barrage, a wandering trail of brilliant sparks. It looked quite pretty. Like an expensive Christmas decoration.

At about the same time, ten miles to the north, Ogilvy and Essex found a splendid target.

The two FEs had been patrolling separately when each saw a blob coming out of the east. It grew to be three Aviatiks in arrowhead formation over a fourth machine, which Ogilvy identified through binoculars as a Roland CII. It was on reconnaissance duty. He could see the black box of the camera clamped to the outside of the observer's cockpit.

The FEs attacked at the same time from opposite sides but by then the formation had broken. It was very smoothly done. One Aviatik climbed, the other two turned to face the attacks, and the Roland dived towards the nearest cloud. There followed one of those hectic scraps that the pilots, if they survived, could never properly describe to Brazier because all they remembered was a flurry of images: planes that seemed to be sporting like swallows at one moment and charging head-first into a suicide pact the next; bright blurs of tracer, bending to chase a target; a swooping shadow; blood surging as the plane banked; the magnificent, exuberant hammering of guns; the panic of trying to look three ways at once and nearly colliding and screaming abuse and firing and missing; dragging the FE round in a turn so tight you think you can see your own tail; and thank God the air is empty behind. So you climb and hurt your neck by looking everywhere for everyone, but everyone has gone. The scrap lasted two minutes, maybe. How could the sky be crammed with fighting one moment and empty the next? When they landed, Ogilvy and Essex asked each other: "Where did you get to?" It wasn't important. They'd got back, and now the scrap seemed like tremendous fun. It was only later, when one or other of them woke, far too soon, in the dreary stone-grey half-light before dawn, that terror got a bit of its own back.

Stubbs, flying with Goss, was probably the first to use the new pillar-mounted gun.

Before take-off they had agreed to try to lure an enemy machine onto their tail. Goss would fly fairly slowly and not too high, and Stubbs would be ready to unstrap himself and stand on his seat. After that, Goss would have to fly straight and level until Stubbs got down from his perch.

They crossed the Lines and wandered about, above cloud where the archie was blind. There was no lack of Huns but they were all too high or too low or too busy going elsewhere. After about twenty minutes an Albatros came wheeling in, out of range, nose gun blazing; as soon as Stubbs opened fire it curled away and dived for home. A novice, Goss decided. He also decided that this particular experiment wasn't going to work. He opened the throttle and eased back on the stick to gain some height and automatically scanned the sky. With the corner of his eye he caught a glimpse of something drifting behind him; when he turned his head the glimpse had gone.

Stubbs moved fast. His legs were braced against the shove of the slipstream, his rump pressed against the front Lewis, and the Hun wasn't even in range: just a silhouette, slim as a child's kite. Stubbs waited. He enjoyed the luxury of not having the rushing air squeezing his face, and suddenly realised there were other advantages in firing backwards. The FE's speed would actually *help* his bullets. So the Hun was in range after all. He fired off half a drum, marvelling at the way he just missed propeller and tail, and saw his tracer washing all over the enemy. That was all he saw. He blinked, and it was gone. No hope of giving chase. Stubbs climbed down, giving Goss a beefy grin.

After that the patrol was an anticlimax. Goss saw two distant scraps but they dissolved before he arrived. He became impatient; he wanted to try out his new fixed forward-firing Lewis.

The FE was a pleasure to dive. It cut through the thin curtain of archie like a locomotive through mist. Goss felt total confidence in the big Beardmore. From the way the wires and struts sang, he knew this was going to be a joyride. The rising countryside was spread out for his delight: he could choose what he wanted. He chose a field that was a town of tents and strafed it like a small mechanical storm, rising and dipping again and again to bring his gun to bear. Stubbs shot at anything that moved. It was all so easy. They heard bugles sounding the alarm, and saw men with their mouths open. Then the FE was gone, and Stubbs was busy reloading both guns. Goss found a column of infantry on the march and they shot it up too. Just point the bus and pull the trigger. You couldn't miss. Rifle-fire chased him as he climbed high and went through the archie again, and flew home.

Cleve-Cutler had watched and waited a very long time. He was watching the decoy Rumpler, still pottering about down below, as well as the two Albatroses, who were loitering half a mile away. It would be foolish, he thought, to take on two of the enemy's best fighters; but if he hung about long enough, anything might happen. Aircraft in various markings passed. All had their own business to attend to. None of this was very exciting. Far away, somebody's business ended in a bright bead of flame strung on a long black thread of smoke. Now *that* must have been exciting.

A Gun Bus appeared, saw the Rumpler and changed course. The escort let it get close but not too close before they each dropped a wing and slid into a dive. Cleve-Cutler went down with them. It was an odd feeling, looking down on the decoy and the dummy, pressing your lips together against the rush of air trying to open them, feeling the controls stiffen as the speed built, knowing that in a few seconds these five machines would be mixed up in a wild tangle. The Gun Bus had seen what was coming and had turned away. Bad move. When attacked, always turn and face. Too late now.

One Albatros fell on the Gun Bus while the other tried to cut across Cleve-Cutler's path and scare him off. Nothing worked. For a chaotic instant half a dozen streams of machine-gun fire crossed each other. Almost everyone missed. The Gun Bus decided, too late again, to keep turning and face the attack, and it wallowed in the wash of the first Albatros. The second Albatros got hit by some shots from the Rumpler that were meant for the FE, pulled out of its dive and began to make smoke. The Gun Bus, still wallowing, took a snap shot at the Rumpler and nearly hit the FE. Cleve-Cutler's observer swore in fury and fired and nearly hit the Gun Bus. The Gun Bus put its nose down and fled. The damaged Albatros was leaving, escorted by its partner. That left the FE and the Rumpler, which was departing with all speed. Cleve-Cutler chased it and closed for the kill. His observer's Lewis jammed after two shots; his own fixed Lewis jammed after ten. The whole thing was a balls-up. The Rumpler's gunner was good and getting better with practice. Cleve-Cutler quit for the day.

O'Neill and Paxton were one of the last crews to take off. Everywhere they went they found German aeroplanes high above, willing to fight. The fight was always short: the Hun dived, fired, and kept going. O'Neill always turned to face the attacker and twice he held the FE rock-solid while Paxton did the shooting. Other times he kicked the rudder across as hard as he could when the enemy gunfire began pecking at their wings. As soon as he levelled out, Paxton would jump up and stand on his seat, eager to shoot down the Hun he thought was following them. O'Neill swore, and punched his legs to get him down. Until he came down O'Neill couldn't manoeuvre. Usually Paxton got down quickly, but on one occasion he kicked at O'Neill to stop him punching. O'Neill, totally blind to what was happening behind, could only wait. And worry.

Paxton hung onto the Lewis with his right hand and stooped until their heads were close together. "When I do this," he shouted, and waggled his left hand, "climb!" He straightened before O'Neill could answer.

The FE flew on. Clouds steadily readjusted their positions. O'Neill studied the view between Paxton's legs and hoped that he was not wandering into an area lousy with Huns. Paxton opened fire, a series of short bursts and then a long one, sounding to O'Neill exactly like a small boy trailing a stick along some railings. Paxton's left hand waggled vigorously. O'Neill climbed, shouting "I hope you sodding well know . . ." Paxton fired, a very long burst that emptied the drum. He jumped down, thoroughly delighted with himself, and leaned over the pilot's windscreen. "*Got him!*" he shouted. He tugged O'Neill's nose. O'Neill lashed out with his fist and knocked Paxton into his cockpit. The Hun, when O'Neill found it, was so far below them that it almost blurred with the landscape. He knew it was there because it had left a long smear of smoke. Which could mean something, or nothing.

Drill was just drill to the Royal Flying Corps: a means of moving groups of men from here to there without losing any of them. To the battalion in camp behind Pepriac church, drill was an expression of the soul of the regiment. When invited to send a company to march up and down on part of the aerodrome, they put on a display of drill so crisp and confident that in the end all the squadron came out to watch. The troops were Yorkshiremen, and somewhere the company commander had found enough white roses for each man to wear one in his cap.

Cleve-Cutler, Dando and Brazier stood together, watching an about-turn on the march which flattened a dozen small molehills. "Makes you feel proud, doesn't it?" Brazier said.

"Personally, no," Dando said. "There are twenty-six bones in the human foot, including the ankle, and why the British Army has to perform its drill in a manner calculated to dislocate the lot of them, I can't imagine."

"Prussians are worse," Brazier said. "Reinforced concrete parade grounds in Prussia."

"These men seem to enjoy it," Cleve-Cutler said. "Just look at them. Proud as peacocks."

"I don't have your intimate knowledge of the human foot," Brazier said, "but I think I can safely tell you that our troops will *march* across No-Man's-Land with their heads high, and in line abreast. So this is very good training."

"You're talking about *after* the victory."

The adjutant shook his head.

"Well, come on, adj, tell us the secret," Dando said. "I thought No-Man's-Land was where you held your head high and Jerry blew it off."

"Jerry won't be there. This bombardment will continue for the rest of the week."

"*All week?*" Cleve-Cutler said. "You mean non-stop, day and night? It's not possible. Have we really got the shells?"

"Wait and see. When our men go over the top, there won't be a German soldier left alive in their first-line trenches. We shall simply walk forward and occupy them. I have this on good authority." Brazier stuck an empty pipe in his mouth as if to signify that that ended the matter.

The infantry halted, right-turned, presented arms. Dando thought about asking the adjutant if this too was in practice for crossing No-Man's-Land but decided against it.

"By the way, I had a word with Frank Foster," the CO told Dando. "He said he thinks you're dotty."

"Yes, I know. He came and apologised for that. He was very calm and civilised about it. Apparently he's been under a lot of strain concerning a personal matter."

"Family problems?"

"I'm not sure I ought to discuss it."

"If he's told you, he's told half the squadron," Brazier said. "It's about his lady-friend in England, isn't it?"

"Yes. It seems someone wrote and told him she had died, rather violently. That's why he got so upset. Now he's heard it was all a mistake, she's really alive and well."

"Good," said Cleve-Cutler. "So that's all right."

Dando grunted. "I hope so. He certainly tried hard enough to make me think so."

"If you're worried about Foster's state of mind," the adjutant said, "you could always send him to see a doctor called Jackson. That's who my general sent me to see after I shot young Ashby. Jackson's the Army's top man on heads, I understand."

"How did you get on with him?"

"Useless. The man's mentally defective."

"As a matter of interest," Dando said, "how could you tell?"

"Simple. He wanted to talk about panic. How could one recognise panic? So I picked up the poker and chased him round his desk for a couple of minutes. He knew all about panic. Didn't thank me for it, though. Got very angry, screamed, made no sense. Touch of insanity somewhere in the family, I shouldn't wonder."

"Forget Jackson," Cleve-Cutler told Dando.

"And forget Foster?"

"He's happy flying and killing Huns. And besides, I'm not about to go looking for a new flight commander just when the Big Push is starting."

O'Neill and Paxton returned from patrol as the drill display was ending. Paxton walked over in his flying gear to thank the captain commanding the company and to offer him a drink. "Did you have any luck up there?" the captain asked.

"I think we may have winged an Albatros. Mind you, that sort of thing cuts both ways." He showed him the flapping heel on his flying boot.

"My stars! That was close."

"Rotten shot. The Huns can't shoot for toffee."

The captain asked him what the bombardment looked like.

"Oh, wonderful," Paxton said. "Finest thing you every saw. Master Fritz has got a nasty headache, if he's still alive. Frankly, I don't see how he can be. I mean, nothing's left. You can tell your chaps they'll have a walkover."

The troops were given a good meal and a bottle of beer each, and were then marched back to camp.

Only a few crews were flying after lunch. Some officers were at the pool; some sat in deckchairs and watched Corporal Lacey supervise the putting-up of the tennis nets. Nobody noticed the rumble of the barrage any more. It was like living near a waterfall.

Stubbs was reading a letter. "Holy cow!" he said. "My kid sister's gone and got married."

Charlie Essex yawned. "Pregnant, I assume," he said.

Stubbs read on. "Yes, as a matter of fact, she was."

Essex woke up with a start. "Oh, I say, old chap . . ." he had gone red in the face, as if someone had slapped him. "Please forgive me. I'm most frightfully sorry."

"Forget it." Stubbs turned a page. "Uncle Henry's farm is doing well. Crop prices are up. He hopes the war goes on for ever."

"He's in for a rapid disappointment," Paxton declared.

Goss discarded his newspaper. "I do wish the Russian generals didn't have such spiky names. I keep biting my tongue . . . What was Charlie apologising about?"

"Nothing," Stubbs said. "Forget it."

O'Neill told Goss: "Charlie made a mistake, and Stubby's sister's going to have a baby."

"Charlie wouldn't do a thing like that," Ogilvy said. "Charlie and I were at Eton together, for heaven's sake."

"Collins!" Essex shouted. "Soda water!"

"Charlie has an alibi," Goss said to Stubbs; but Stubbs was talking to Paxton. "You reckon it'll be all over pretty soon, do you?" he said.

"Certainly. We've got them licked at sea, haven't we? Take that scrap at Jutland! The German battle fleet had to run away home like a whipped cur!"

"Never apologise when you've got an alibi," O'Neill told Essex. "It's nothing to be ashamed of."

"And we've got them licked in the air. That's obvious."

"I had an alibi once," Mayo said, "but Dando gave me some ointment to rub on it."

"And in a few days we'll lick them on the land. The infantry will do their stuff and the cavalry will go through the Hun like a dose of salts. You watch."

"Look here, Charlie," Goss said, "you don't want to live in Grand Rapids. Give Private Collins a shilling and he'll marry the girl, won't you, Collins?"

"No, sir."

"Collins is trying to haggle," Goss warned. "Don't go above half-a-crown."

Essex took a soda-water syphon from the tray that Collins was carrying. He walked over to Goss and sprayed him. Goss lay back. He shut his eyes and opened his mouth and gratefully accepted the jet of soda water. Essex walked around him, spraying hard. The dog Brutus raced around them, barking and trying to bite the water.

"You're really enjoying this war, aren't you?" Stubbs said.

"I'm glad we're winning," Paxton told him.

"I bet you're glad you're not in the trenches, too," said Ogilvy. "Up to the armpits in mud and fighting the rats for your rations."

"I don't see any mud. Everyone tells me the Front is as dry as a bone around here."

"Next time," Goss said as Essex's syphon ran dry, "be so good as to add a slice of lemon and the odd ice cube."

"Anyway," Paxton said, impatient at the way Stubbs kept looking at him, "there's more to it than *winning*. I mean to say, look what we're fighting for. Land of hope and glory, and all that sort of thing."

Foster, who had seemed to be sleeping, cleared his throat. "That's why we're here, is it? I thought it was something to do with Belgium."

"Yes, and whose fault was that?" Paxton demanded.

"One thing they taught us at Cambridge," Essex said. "Belgium did not invade Germany. I remember making a note of that."

"It started in Serbia, not Belgium," O'Neill said. "Christ Almighty, you lot are pig-ignorant."

"And whose fault was *that*?" Paxton insisted.

"The Austrians," Mayo said. "I think."

"Serbians fired first," Goss said. Soda-water dripped from his ears.

"Austrians are no good," Essex said. "Austrians yodel."

"So would you if you had to wear leather knickers," O'Neill said.

"Very clever," Paxton told him. "Well, I know what I'm fighting for, even if you don't." He began searching his tunic pockets.

"There's someone sitting in your cockpit, Pax," Mayo said.

"Carpenter, probably," Paxton said, still searching. "Plugging bullet-holes."

"No. I've been watching. This chap seems to be hiding."

Paxton found the paper he was looking for, turned and studied the FE, a hundred yards away. "I don't see anyone."

"Well, you wouldn't, would you?" Mayo said. Paxton stared at him, trying to guess the joke. "Please yourself," Mayo said.

"I don't know about you," Paxton said to Stubbs, giving him the paper, "but this is why I'm here. It's something my cousin sent me, last year. He copped it a month later. This didn't mean much to me then, but it does now. I'm going to stretch my legs." He walked towards the FE.

Stubbs read the paper and passed it to Goss. "I guess I've got the wrong accent for this," he said.

Goss read it aloud, clearly and evenly.

July, 1914–1915

A year ago, at Henley –
   A year ago, at Lord's –
The rival crews; the cricket Blues;
   – They dreamt that life affords
No keener joy than contest,
   No sweeter sound than cheers;
Far, far away they fling to-day –
   Life's mimic hopes and fears.

To-day they play the Great Game.
   To-day they play the man:
In every sort and kind of sport,
   – Whene'er they rowed and ran –
They learnt it, all unknowing,
   The secret of the game,

That what you do for team or crew
   Or country's just the same.

And where the shells burst round them,
   And bullets whistle past,
And every yard with wire is barred
   The men are dropping fast,
Ripe grows the fruit of training
   So little thought upon,
The steady eye, the heartening cry,
   "Stick to it, boys! Come on!"

And yet, in trench and dug-out,
   When darkness floods the sky,
These lads, at rest, in sudden jest
   Recall with half a sigh
The joys wherein their senses
   Were bound with silken cords
A year ago, at Henley,
   A year ago, at Lord's!

"It's all about you, Frank," Ogilvy said. "You're the only one here who wears silk underwear."

"What d'you make of it, Frank?" Goss asked. He handed him the paper.

"Sorry," Foster said. "I'm afraid I wasn't listening . . . Is this Paxton's? Just another death warrant, I expect. Not important." He screwed it up and threw it for Brutus to chase.

If the squadron carpenter was hiding in the front cockpit, he was sobbing and sniffling like a child.

Paxton paused to listen. The rim of the cockpit was higher than his head, so he couldn't see in. Was it sobbing or was it whining? Maybe the dog Brutus had got stuck in there.

He put one foot in the observer's stirrup and hauled himself up. A very young soldier lay curled in the bottom of the cockpit, shaking with sobs. He had wept so much that now he was too weary to make a lot of noise. His head rested on his upper arm; the rest of that arm fell across his face. His knees were almost up to his chest, and his chest jerked occasionally. He was wearing his best uniform. It looked to be a size too big for him.

He didn't see Paxton until Paxton leaned over to get a view of his face. Then the arm fell away and Paxton knew him at once. Even through that wretched tear-sodden expression he knew him. It was Private Watkins, the young man who had mended his motorbike. "My goodness!" he said. "What the devil are you doing here, old chap?"

Watkins straightened up and blinked at Paxton. For a few moments his lungs were working so hard that he couldn't get a word out. Paxton gave him a handkerchief. There was snot on Watkins' upper lip, and Paxton couldn't stand the sight of snot. Other people's snot, that is; he was quite interested in his own. "Take your time, old boy," he said. "Nothing to be afraid of. You're perfectly safe here."

Watkins cleaned up his face and gradually stopped gasping. "You promised you'd take me up in your aeroplane," he said. His voice was croaky and thin.

"Did I really?" But Paxton remembered very well; there was no denying it. "You're absolutely right. So I did."

"I want to go now."

Paxton almost laughed and then was glad he hadn't. Watkins was looking up at him like a hungry orphan who's just walked ten miles to ask for a crust. Nothing was funny to Watkins any more. "I'm afraid it's rather difficult just now," Paxton said. "What with the Push coming up and, you know, all that—"

"I want you to fly me to England."

Paxton felt he could reasonably smile at that. He swung his legs inside and sat on the cockpit edge. "You don't really want to go to England, do you?" he said.

"No, I want to go to fuckin' Australia where they'll never fuckin' catch me but if I can get to England maybe I can stow away on a fuckin' boat or something." His elbows were propped on his knees, and Paxton's handkerchief was pressed hard against his cheek. Paxton tried to remember how old he'd said he was. Eighteen? Seventeen? He looked about fourteen. He looked as if he could do with a damn good meal, too. "I've thought it all out," Watkins said flatly. "Bleedin' France is no good, I don't parley-voo an' I got no francs, fuckin' police are everywhere, they'd catch me like they caught poor old Dodds, an' shoot me too, so you got to take me to England, I got a fuckin' chance if I can get there."

"Look here, I'm sure you've got this all wrong," Paxton said.

"Could we be there in time for tea? Is it really fast, your aeroplane?"

"Let me try to explain," Paxton said.

"I'd give any bloody thing to be home in time for tea. Any bloody thing." He was chewing on his knuckles. "They had to shoot Dodds twice. Firing party fucked it up. Bastard officer had to finish the poor bugger with his revolver. We all heard it." He looked at Paxton, accusingly, appealingly. "That's never bloody right, is it?"

"I don't know. What had he done?" When Watkins looked away, Paxton asked: "Did he desert? Was that it?" Watkins nodded. "Well, you know as well as I do," Paxton said, "desertion's a very serious crime. Was Dodds a particular friend of yours?"

"He wasn't in my mob. I just happened to know him." Watkins yawned. "You said you'd fly me to England. You promised." He wasn't pleading; merely reminding.

"I'm afraid we've got our wires crossed, old chap. I never said anything about England. Besides, have you any idea how far it is from here? It's a jolly long way, and much further to Yorkshire. This bus won't fly for ever, you know. One's got to land and refuel several times."

"I'll pay you for the petrol."

"No, no, that's not the point—"

"I've got the money at home. Cash."

Paxton sighed. This was becoming very difficult.

"Two pounds, I've got saved. Will it be more than two pounds, the petrol?"

He really was a handsome lad and Paxton would happily have paid more than two pounds to see him smile, but it was time to be firm. "It's quite impossible for you to fly to England," he said, "because for one thing you'd be deserting and for another thing my machine is going up on patrol very soon. Incidentally, how did you know this was my machine?"

"You got out of it and came over and talked to our Captain Jameson."

"Ah. So you were one of the drill unit? Excellent performance, by the way. Congratulations. Now look here, old sport:

you don't want to go back to England. Damn it all, you're a volunteer! You're one of Kitchener's Army!"

"So what?" Watkins said, with the bleak fatalism of a child. "What's the sodding difference? They brought in fuckin' conscription months ago, didn't they? Bastards would've got me, one way or the other."

"But you don't want to miss the show!" Paxton urged. "I mean, this is the grand finale! Don't you want to join in the fun?"

"Fun." Watkins rested his head on his arm again. "Fun."

"Yes, certainly, fun! You'll be able to tell your grandchildren: 'I went over the top at the Somme and we walked all the way to the Hun front line and we captured the lot!' It'll be a cakewalk."

"You believe all that bollocks, do you?"

"Listen to the guns."

"Fuck the guns. I hate fuckin' guns. I've been in an attack an' I know what it's like an' it's not like what you saw us do that day I mended your motorbike. That's a fuckin' fairytale, that is. It's not like that in a real attack."

"Indeed? What's the difference?"

Watkins turned his head and looked at him, a long, wide-eyed look that seemed so candid and trusting that Paxton was quite flattered until he realised that Watkins was looking straight through him. Eventually he said: "I used to be a gardener's boy." *So did Dick*, Paxton thought, *what a coincidence*. "One day I was cuttin' the grass, pushin' the lawnmower, up an' down, up an' down, an' I saw this spider in the grass, just in front of me, runnin' like a bastard to get away an' before I could stop the lawnmower I'd run over the bugger. I thought at the time: poor little sod, chopped up by a fuckin' great lawnmower, never stood a chance. Well, that's what it's like when you go over the top. You're like a spider under a lawnmower."

"Come on." Paxton reached down to help him but Watkins would not move. "I'll give you a lift back to your camp on my trusty motorbike."

"Too late. I'm overdue. Absent without leave. I'm fucked."

"No you're not. I'll make up an excuse for you. I'll tell them I needed you to help me do something."

"What have we here?" said Brazier. His head and chest appeared above the cockpit, and instantly Watkins scrambled to his feet, hatless, face smudged, eyes frightened, and looking as guilty as a murderer.

"It's quite all right, adj," Paxton began.

"You don't belong here," Brazier said, using that bright, confident tone that every soldier knows means he's in trouble to the armpits so there's no point in trying to dodge it. "I don't know your face, do I?"

Paxton said: "Honestly, adj, I can—"

"What a filthy, tatty, shabby apology for a private soldier you are." Brazier reached out with his cane and flicked a tunic button. "Do your buttons up, lad. And put your headgear on. And *stand to attention when addressed by an officer!*"

Watkins stopped fumbling with the button and searching for his cap, and jumped to attention. Paxton was amazed by the transformation Brazier had achieved. Watkins now looked as if steel rods had been inserted in his small body. His shoulders were forced back, his chest stuck out, his chin was tucked down and his head was quivering with the strain of holding himself so erect. "Name, rank, number," Brazier snapped.

Paxton climbed down from the aeroplane while Watkins chanted his reply. He knew there was no point in talking to the adjutant. The Army had taken over; you couldn't talk to the Army. He walked away and sat on the grass. He could hear Brazier asking about permission, and intentions, and absence from duty. If Watkins answered he spoke very quietly. Paxton lay on his back and counted the clouds. Brazier shouted: *"Duty NCO!"* in a voice that could have knocked the flies off the cookhouse roof. When Paxton stood up, Brazier and Watkins were standing beside the FE and the Duty NCO was doubling across the field towards them. Paxton gave up. He strolled back to the deckchairs. Most of them were empty. It was nearly time to get dressed and go on patrol.

"Who was he?" Goss asked.

"Nobody."

"You had a long chat with him. For a nobody."

"He was a lost dog, if you must know. And now I suppose they'll send him to the dogs' home." The Duty NCO was quick-marching Watkins towards the guardroom.

"Here's your toilet-paper," O'Neill said. He held out the sheet of poetry.

"Oh, fuck off," Paxton said.

Goss and O'Neill looked at each other. "I don't know where he picks up these words," Goss said. "Not from me, I'm sure."

"He's been playing with those nasty boys in the street," O'Neill said. "Just look at his fingernails!"

"For God's sake let's get upstairs," Paxton said. "I'm sick of being down here."

Chapter 19

The adjutant's information had been right. The barrage went on, night and day, thundering perpetually and erupting into an hour of colossal, concentrated devastation every morning. It was said that the British guns stood wheel to wheel for twenty miles, that the hillocks of empty shellcases stood fifty feet high, that hordes of rats – maddened by the battering detonations – were fleeing from the Front, even that the bombardment could be heard by people living on the south coast of England. This last claim was true: men coming back from leave confirmed it; in fact some said the gunfire could be heard in London, when the wind was right.

So nobody had any doubt where the Big Push would be. The only question was when.

Meanwhile, Hornet Squadron was being worked increasingly hard: three patrols a day became normal, four not unusual. Inevitably, men died and machines crashed. Kills were claimed by Gerrish and Piggott and O'Neill (or by their observers) and a dozen crews said, more or less confidently, that the enemy plane had abandoned the fight in a steep and smoking dive. But three FE2ds were missing, one from each flight, and the ground crews were working through the night, every night, patching the battle damage and servicing the overstrained engines and occasionally washing the blood out of the cockpits. Boy Binns had his right arm almost shot off and Dando finished the job with a pair of scissors, kneeling in the wreckage of the observer's cockpit in the middle of the field while his medics dragged the pilot clear and cut away his flying coat in order to find the bullet-holes. Dando got Binns onto a stretcher just as the wreckage caught fire with a rush that singed their hands and eyebrows. Binns' arm got a quick cremation. Both casualties were in the squadron ambulance within minutes, and they got excellent surgical treatment within half an hour; there were casualty clearing stations everywhere, full of keen young doctors with nobody to save. The pilot died, perversely, while they were stitching up his chest and stomach. Shock, they said. Massive trauma and postoperative shock. Classic case of Moran's Disease. The body got moran it could take.

Boy Binns survived. He had hardly any blood but somehow he survived. He felt rotten, he looked rotten and he developed pneumonia a month later, which killed him. That wasn't what Cleve-Cutler wrote to his parents, of course. If they had to grieve, they might as well grieve over a more glorious death than pneumonia. Boy Binns went down gallantly, outnumbered but fighting pluckily to the end. Or some such. Cleve-Cutler knew what to say. He had written many letters before he wrote that one.

A curious thing happen to Paxton on the fifth day of the barrage. After their third and last patrol, at about seven in the evening, he went with O'Neill to report to the adjutant on what had happened up there and he couldn't remember anything about it. "You mean you've lost your memory?" the adjutant said. They were in his office, out of the rain.

"No, no, of course not. I can remember yesterday, but today's patrols are a blank. Isn't that funny?"

"Come on, then," O'Neill said. "What happened yesterday?"

"Um . . . Well . . . Nothing happened yesterday, did it?"

"You two got a flamer yesterday," Brazier said. "At least, that's what's in my notes."

"Hey, that's good," Paxton said. "That's *very* good, isn't it? My sainted aunt! A flamer! That's tremendous."

"Don't drench your drawers, Pax, because we didn't get one today," O'Neill said. "In fact we got bugger-all on that last patrol except a chunk of red-hot archie through the wing."

Brazier made a note.

"I seem to remember today was damn good fun," Paxton said.

"You frightened a couple of Aviatiks, I suppose. Put down that he frightened a couple of Aviatiks, adj. And put down that he terrified me as usual."

"Really?" Paxton said. "How?"

"I'm going to have a bath." O'Neill went out.

"What on earth did he mean?" Paxton asked.

Brazier shuffled his notes together and put them away. "Bunny's looking tired," he said.

"Is he? I hadn't noticed." Paxton licked his lips and tasted the salty chemicals left by the blowback of the Lewis. It was a taste he enjoyed. "Dunno what he's got to be tired about. All he does is drive the bus. I'm the one who does the hard work. Not that I'm complaining, adj. Bloody good fun."

"So you say. From what you can remember. How about Private Watkins? Can you remember him?"

Paxton laughed. "The spider in the lawnmower . . ." Brazier raised his eyebrows. "Never mind, adj. Too complicated to explain. Yes, I remember Watkins, poor little chap. I thought you were a bit hard on him, to be frank. I mean, why not—"

"Why not kiss it better and give him sixpence for sweets? Because that's not how battles are won."

"Oh, come on! Watkins isn't going to win a battle for anyone, ever. He's—"

"He's tried to desert three times already, so his company commander told me. He'll never win a battle, you're right there, but he could easily help to lose it. You let one man get away because he doesn't feel like fighting and the rot spreads through his platoon, his company, his battalion. They go into battle but they won't stand and fight. They run, just as Watkins ran. They abandon their comrades on the flanks and leave them exposed to the enemy. Far better to shoot one man now than lose a thousand when the line fails."

"Good God," Paxton said, all humour gone, "he's not going to be shot, is he?"

"If I had my way, yes. I'd parade the battalion in a hollow square, I'd march Private Watkins in, I'd read the charge and the penalty and I'd have him shot, which would save a lot of decent men's lives later on. But it's not up to me, and I don't know what they'll do with him."

Paxton had strolled over to a window. "Pity about the rain," he said. "Just as we got the tennis courts finished."

"If you don't want to be thrown through that window," Brazier said, "you'd better leave by the door."

Paxton left by the door. Lacey was in the Orderly Room, unpacking gramophone records. "Watkins is quite safe for the moment," he said. "He was sentenced to death as a matter of form, but in view of the imminent battle it seemed superfluous, so they've done the usual thing and given him a chance to redeem his crime . . . I know it's a matter of taste, but I wouldn't have thought Watkins was your type."

Paxton frowned. "I don't know what you mean."

"Well . . ." Lacey blew some straw off a record. "He's quite pretty, I suppose, but *sullen*. And I'm sure he's never owned a toothbrush in his life. No ambition there. And you are ambitious, aren't you?"

Paxton thought about that. It made him uncomfortable, so he asked: "What was all that about redeeming his crime?"

"Don't you know? I assumed everyone knew. They'll give Watkins the most dangerous job in the first wave. That will give him the greatest chance to demonstrate enough bravery and devotion to duty and similar abstract nouns to wipe out his offence."

"Oh," Paxton said. "I hadn't heard of that."

"Oh yes. You'd be surprised what an incentive to heroism crime can be. Young Watkins will emerge with the VC. You watch."

Cleve-Cutler took Piggott out of a game of poker and led him to the end of the bar, where Foster was standing. "I think you ought to hear this, Tim," he said. "Just wait a sec while I get Dando." He went away.

"I had a king-flush," Piggott said.

Foster smiled sadly. "Think yourself lucky," he said. "Archie Ryan had gangrene."

It took a moment for Piggott to remember Ryan and what had happened to him. "That's damn bad luck. I liked Archie."

"People shouldn't play around with guns."

Piggott was silenced by this remark. Cleve-Cutler came back with Dando and Gerrish. "Frank's invented a new way to win the war," he said. "Fire away, Frank."

"You are, I'm sure, familiar with the works of Samuel Taylor Coleridge," Foster said. He flashed a keen, conspiratorial grin at each man.

"No," Gerrish said.

"Probably a writer," Cleve-Cutler said. "Chaps with three names are usually writers, aren't they?"

Foster raised a forefinger. "Water, water everywhere, nor any drop to drink."

"Oh yes," Dando said. "Coleridge. *Rime of the Ancient Mariner*. I had to learn great chunks of it at school. He shot a bird, didn't he? Shot the wrong bird and brought bad luck to the ship."

"Exactly," Foster said. "And the same thing's happened to us. Why have we had all this bad luck? Damn decent chaps, all gone west, one after another? I'll tell you why. *Somebody in this squadron has shot down an Albatros with a crossbow.*" He raised his eyebrows and looked hard, checking to be sure they understood.

"Come off it, Frank," Piggott said. "Who would want to attack a Hun with a crossbow? It's absurd. Where on earth would anyone *get* a crossbow?"

"Harrods," Foster said.

"Listen," Gerrish said, "do you know this for a fact? I mean, who is this idiot?"

Foster suddenly became quite passionate. "I know for a fact that decent chaps keep going west day after day," he said, "and *somebody's* got to be responsible. Don't you agree?" His head was trembling with anger.

"I still don't see the point," Cleve-Cutler said. "Why pot an Albatros with a crossbow?"

"To *humiliate* the enemy, of course," Foster said. It was so obvious to him that he could only look pityingly at the CO. "Any fool can see that. But while he's been humiliating the Hun, this chap has been bringing the squadron all this shocking bad luck. No doubt he means well. But it's got to stop."

They stood in silence. All except Foster looked awkward and uncomfortable. Foster looked angry and determined. "Don't worry," he said. "I'll track him down. I'll get him, and that will bring this war to a sudden end, believe you me." He took his umbrella and went out.

"I realise we've discussed this before," Dando said to Cleve-Cutler, "but how much longer can you let him go on like this?"

"Just as long as his Flight keeps on knocking down Huns," the CO said. "It's as simple as that. If we kicked out all the loonies in the RFC, we'd be down to single figures in a fortnight."

Dando nodded towards the other two, who were arguing about how best to shoot down an Albatros with a crossbow. They were getting quite excited. "Want my job?" Cleve-Cutler said to Dando. "The pay's not much but the prospects are lousy."

A string of limousines lined the drive. They were black, shiny, serious cars that never got driven for fun. You had to have whiskers and a pince-nez and a stomach you could eat your dinner off before you were allowed in the back of one of those cars. Paxton rode past, sneering at them and their owners, and parked his motorbike in the stable yard.

A maid met him at the main entrance, showed him to a small reception room and went away. He stood at the window and watched the rain. It looked finer and silkier than the rain at Pepriac. For the rich, even the weather watched its manners.

After five minutes a very old wolfhound wandered in, looked him over, decided he wasn't worth knowing, and wandered away.

After another five minutes the maid came back with a card. All it said was *Shan't be long.* He knew the writing.

Another maid brought a tray of sandwiches and a bottle of claret. Also the London papers.

It was dusk before she came in. "Thank God, a human being at last!" she said and kissed him, a full, unhurried kiss with both arms around his neck. "Is that horseradish sauce I taste?" she asked.

"More likely cordite. I get it off the Lewis gun."

"Yummy. It suits you."

"Is something important going on here?"

"Formal, yes. Important, no. Fortunately, they've reached the cognac, so I slid out. Come on, David, let's go for a swim. Bring the wine."

They walked down to the lake, hand in hand, under a giant golf umbrella. The claret was stuffed in his tunic pocket. The rain was more like mist; he felt as if he were in a secret, enclosed world, a place where he was no longer in control. So he relaxed entirely and let things happen to him.

The boathouse was black except for the open end, which showed the misty lake like a picture in a book. "I can't find any coat-hooks," he said.

"Hang your stuff on the floor. That's what it's for. Oh God . . . That water is going to be so wonderful. You can't imagine how sticky I feel. Those creaky old men have been rolling their eyeballs over me all evening. Are you ready?"

Paxton found himself trembling, although it was not cold. He took a huge breath, so big that a couple of joints creaked, and he stretched. Her hand found his and she led him onto a diving board, broad enough for two. "This is new," he said. Their weight made it bounce excitingly. His toes felt the end of the board. Still he had not been brave enough to look at her. Her arms, very cool and strong, went around him and as they kissed, strange new contours pressed against him. Her feet stepped onto his and her hands drifted down his back until they held his buttocks. Judy knew best. He did the same to her. His eyes were shut; his brain was flooded with pleasure; he had surrendered all control of his senses, including the sense of balance. They toppled together. There was a fraction of a second when he knew he was falling and another fraction of a second when he enjoyed it, and then the lake exploded in a burst of cold, bracing foam that pulled them apart.

They raced each other to the little island, and she won.

"Okay," she said. They were lying side by side on the smooth boulder, and he was gasping for breath. "What's new with the war?"

He told her about the barrage, heard here as a ceaseless

grumble, about its sparkle by day and its colour by night. "Honestly, I think it's the prettiest thing I've ever seen," he said. "Present company excepted, of course." He was finally looking at her. There was no moon, but his imagination filled in the gaps. "And we've got a marvellous new bus, just the job for trench-strafing." She wanted to know what strafing was. "You find some Hun infantry," he said, "and you fly as low as you can and you shoot them up. Or shoot them down. Wonderful sport. Jolly dangerous, of course, because they tend to get peeved when you knock 'em down, so they fire back."

"What happens? When you knock them down, I mean. What does it look like?"

Paxton laughed. "Not like what you see on the pictures, I can tell you that! They do all sorts of gymnastics. Some spin around, some do cartwheels, some seem to run backwards! Very comical, it is. Sometimes I laugh so much I can't shoot straight."

Judy hooked her little finger with his. "I wish I were a man," she said.

"Mind you, it's damned hard work. Especially now we've got this new bus that flies so much higher. You see, the air gets thin at ten or twelve thousand and it's bloody tiring, jumping from one gun to another." Suddenly his memory cleared. Suddenly he remembered the flamer. "I made a hell of a good kill yesterday," he said.

She got up and sat astride him, and held his hands so that his arms were raised. "Tell, tell," she said.

"It was a Fokker two-seater. We were miles high. He must have come out of the sun – they do that if they can – because first thing we knew, his tracer was buzzing past. It really does buzz, just like a lot of hornets chasing you. He was behind us but we've got a really spiffing new gun that fires backwards, over the tail, so I peppered him good and hard with that." Her fingers tightened. "Then somehow *we* got behind *him* and I used the nose gun. We were so close I could see the Hun gunner, he looked very surprised. Then he tumbled back and his gun pointed up in the sky, so I knew I'd killed him." Now her grip was almost painful. "The Fokker tried to dive but he wasn't fast enough. I fired the rest of the drum into the pilot and of course the pilot sits on the fuel tanks so I hit those too and all of a sudden, *whoosh*!" Her nails were digging into his flesh. "The flames are so bright, all yellow and red. and they burst out so suddenly, it's not like something burning, it's more like an enormous flower in the sky. Beautiful. Unbelievably beautiful."

He could feel great tension in her arms and thighs, squeezing and pressing. Abruptly she relaxed and fell on top of him, biting and pinching, not enough to hurt but enough to make him wrestle. At first he tried to win. Then he discovered it was more fun to lose. The fun was becoming serious when she made them both roll into the water, which was too deep for wrestling.

There were towels in the boathouse. They dried each other, which was fun of a different kind, and finished off the claret. "You haven't asked me how big my machine-gun is," he said.

"I don't need to," she said.

Chapter 20

In the air, Douglas Goss had never suffered so much as a scratch. It was always on the ground that things fell on him or collapsed under him, and he was usually limping, or nursing an arm, or wearing a strip of plaster. None of this made any difference to Goss's skill as a pilot, but sometimes he worried about the danger of having some innate physical weakness. He kept a close watch on all parts of his body, including his head. "I think I'm going bald," he told Dando.

"Not impossible." Dando sat him in a chair and ruffled his hair. "Looks perfectly adequate to me."

"Really? You should see my hairbrush. Dreadful sight. The thing is . . ." Goss smoothed his hair. "Well, you see, I'm the only son in the family so everyone expects me to keep the line going, and I read somewhere that baldness can also mean problems with the plumbing. You know, impotence and all that."

"There's absolutely no evidence that I know of."

Goss nodded and frowned. "D'you think I could have an X-ray?" he asked.

"Maybe," Dando said. "It depends which part of the problem you want X-rayed."

Goss nodded again, and hunched his shoulders. "Bloody tricky, isn't it?"

"Why don't you think it over, Dougie? There's no rush. These things take years to come about. See me when you get back from patrol. I'll change that plaster on your elbow, too."

Flying Orders for the day were that there were no orders except to fly and to harass the enemy. Goss and Stubbs took that to mean ground-strafing, which had the great merit of being terrific fun and of not requiring them to spend two hours beyond the Lines: as soon as they had used up their ammunition they could honourably fly home. The sun was up. It looked like a good day to grab half an hour at the pool between patrols.

A new pilot, called Black, asked Goss if he might follow and generally hang about to see how ground-strafing was done. "Be my guest, old chap," Goss said. "Make yourself conspicuous. If they're shooting at you they won't be shooting at me."

Goss had a nasty moment while he was above the Trenches. The FE got violently buffeted. There was no archie; the wind was light; for a horrible moment he thought a main spar had snapped and thrown the plane out of control. Then it bounced against another buffet and he felt ashamed of his own stupidity. The turbulence was caused by shell-bumps. He had forgotten about the eternal barrage and he was low enough to be caught in the shove of air displaced by the bigger shells. Which meant they had nearly hit him. What a bloody silly way to die, blown up by your own artillery! He climbed hard. Even so, he actually saw a shell, one of the huge projectiles flung by the great howitzers, as it poised for a second at the top of its arc. Stubbs saw it too, and kissed it goodbye.

Goss flew well beyond the German trench-system before he turned. He knew he was unlikely to find any worthwhile target near where the shells were falling, and he had decided to leave infantry camps alone. With so much strafing taking place the Hun was bound to be protecting them. What he wanted was a nice little unit on the march, a couple of hundred men crossing a field or going up a lane, with their rifles slung and no heavy machine guns nearby. That would be perfect.

There was the usual casual traffic wandering about the sky, the usual sporadic archie, a couple of minor scraps too far away to matter. Goss raised a glove to Black, and tipped the FE into a dive. Black waved back, and began circling.

Goss expected a lot of ground fire to start coming up at him, and it did. Much of it was coming from his right, so he swung to his left and ran away from it. The big Beardmore was roaring like several lions and the FE seemed perfectly balanced. It was just like driving a big racing car down a very long, steep hill.

Stubbs pointed to a road but Goss had seen a small river and he chose that because it meant he could get below the surrounding land and then, with any luck, pop up and surprise someone. He raced just above the water and tried not to think about telephone wires. Naked men stopped washing and stood up, or ran, or sometimes jumped into the river They were not important enough to shoot; and besides, Goss felt squeamish about shooting naked men. A bridge appeared, and then rows of poplars, forcing Goss to turn away. He chased his shadow across a little field, jumped the fence and found what he wanted waiting in a much bigger field. A company of infantry, standing waiting to be killed.

Perhaps they were tired; perhaps they were new to the Front; perhaps they were badly led. They were certainly surprised. Stubbs swung his Lewis like a scythe and shot fifteen or twenty men before they moved. Goss gave the FE a little rudder so that he could aim his own fixed Lewis into the scattering mass, and as he kept firing he could see the line of his bullets advancing as fast as the FE, knocking over soldiers as if they were all tripping on the same unseen obstacle. He flew too low at the end and actually hit a couple of men with his undercarriage. Stubbs saw this, and howled with delight. "No bloody road sense!" Goss shouted.

By the time he had turned and come back, Stubbs had changed the drums and the field was dotted with running men. Goss chased them and Stubbs shot them. He missed a very tall man in a distinctive helmet, who stopped and shook his fist, so Goss came back and chased him until Stubbs cut him down. Rifle fire was beginning to fizz past the FE. A few holes spotted the wings like raindrops. Goss was unworried; panicky troops were rotten shots; it would have to be a very lucky bullet indeed that did any real harm. And so it was. A very lucky bullet struck the engine and smashed the crankshaft. The engine stopped dead. Goss had just enough height to clear the fence and land in the next field.

Stubbs jumped out, Goss fell out. Stubbs had the flare pistol and he shot an incendiary flare into a fuel tank. They ran away from the slaughter.

Black knew that Goss had crashed when he saw flames and he went straight down to investigate. His observer spotted Goss and Stubbs stumbling and lumbering across a field of young corn. Fifty or sixty German soldiers were chasing them. Black opened his throttle wide and came in from the flank, both guns chattering. That stopped the chase, but only briefly. Black made six attacks in all before he ran out of ammunition. Then he could only circle and watch the troops catch the airmen. The bayonets went in with great vigour.

Cleve-Cutler was waiting on the aerodrome when Foster came back from patrol. "Goss and Stubbs," Cleve-Cutler said. "I wanted to be the one to tell you, because I know what pals you and Dougie were."

Foster chewed his lip and glanced from side to side, as if he were assessing the value of the information he had been given.

"Stubbs, eh?" he said. "He was a flamer, wasn't he?"

"No, as a matter of fact he wasn't."

Foster nodded, several times. "I knew he was a flamer," he said.

"I've just told you he wasn't."

"I think I know better," Foster said. He spoke gently and courteously, and gave the CO a mild, reassuring smile. "You see, I killed him. Stubbs wrote a letter to someone saying that I'd gone west, I was a flamer. I asked him to write it. And this is the result." He tossed his goggles in the air and caught them. "Oh dear. Dear oh dear oh dear."

"Stubbs wrote a letter," Cleve-Cutler said. "Have you still got it?"

"Jenny got it. But of course Jenny's dead too She hanged herself, poor creature."

"Go and get cleaned up, Frank. I'll buy you a drink."

Foster didn't get cleaned up. He went to the padre's room. "Got a knotty problem for you," he said. "How does one recognise the Word of God when one hears it?"

"I don't think I've been asked that one before. Let me think . . . Normally, the question doesn't arise, I suppose. God makes it abundantly clear who's speaking."

Foster made a grimace.

"No, that's not very adequate, is it?" the padre said. "May one ask: do you suspect that you might have been on the receiving end?"

"God knows. All I know is I've been getting some very strange messages lately."

"Such as?"

Foster picked a cricket ball out of a chair and sat down. "I'm afraid the first message was that I shouldn't tell you or any of the others."

"Ah." The padre buffed his crucifix on the sleeve of his cassock. "Well, I can only say that He knows best, of course, but it's most unlike God not to operate through the normal channels. Could it be that transmission was garbled, perhaps?"

Foster shook his head.

"My guess is," said the padre, "that you are somewhat reluctant to proceed. Otherwise we wouldn't be having this discussion." Foster nodded. "I've been in the same dilemma," the padre said, "and more than once I've found it very helpful to let God reconsider His decision. 'Look here, God,' I've said, 'if that's really what You want me to do I'll do it, but frankly, speaking as man to God, I think You ought to sleep on it.' And next day He's changed His mind." The padre stopped because it was clear that Foster wasn't listening.

"You heard about Stubbs?"

"Yes. A sad loss. Such a likeable—"

"It's a forgery. He wasn't a flamer at all. The whole thing was a joke. You watch, he'll be back in time for dinner, large as life and twice as ugly." Foster stood up.

"I feel I haven't been much help," the padre said. "Look here: before you go, just pick a verse at random in the Bible. It sometimes helps."

Foster opened the Bible and let his finger fall. "Proverbs 25, verse 33. 'Yet a little sleep, a little slumber, a little folding of the hands to sleep'."

"Not very thrilling. Want to try again?"

"It's the Word of God," Foster said. "It must mean something."

Kellaway walked into the billet and said: "Goss and Stubbs have—"

"We heard," Paxton said. "Too bad. Shut up, Bunny's got the shakes, I'm trying to cure him and we've only got half an hour."

Kellaway watched. They were standing by the table. O'Neill hugged himself, making his biceps bulge, and then relaxed. "Take a breath," Paxton said. O'Neill took a breath and reached for a nearly-full glass of red wine. Just before he touched it he pulled his hand back and turned away in disgust. "It's not going to bloody work," he said.

"Imagine it's a block of wood. Just pick it up. Forget the wine."

O'Neill tried again. He gripped the glass, released it, gripped it differently, raised it. "Bloody good!" Paxton said. O'Neill got the glass halfway to his mouth and his wrist started to tremble. Wine slopped. "Oh, *bollocks*," he said, and put the glass down.

"Try using your other hand," Kellaway suggested.

"Try using your other head," O'Neill snarled.

"Maybe if you kept your elbow tucked in tight," Paxton said. He demonstrated. The glass went up and down smoothly. O'Neill tried it and spilled very little. "Makes me feel crippled," he said.

"Trouble is you're pissed," Kellaway said.

"Trouble is I'm *not* pissed."

"Well, get pissed and then you'll be okay."

"How can I get pissed when I keep spilling the stuff?"

Paxton drank the wine. "You've got the Australian Disease, old chap. No known cure except death, which I can arrange although it's very expensive."

"Why not?" O'Neill said. "You nearly arranged it once today already."

"I hit the Hun, didn't I? He hardly touched us. You've got to have faith, Bunny."

A batman knocked and came in. "Captain Foster presents his compliments," he said, "and would Lieutenant Paxton do him the honour of joining him in his tent."

"Me?" Paxton said. "How odd."

"I expect he wants you to turn the pages of his music for him," Kellaway said.

Foster poured another inch of whisky into Paxton's tin mug and spilt half an inch over his hand. "I'm telling you all this," he said, "because I was like you once, and I wish someone had told me. If someone had told me all about women, poor old Stubbs wouldn't have been a flamer. Women aren't all they're cracked up to be. Flamers aren't all they're cracked up to be. And that's not all. I'm not all I'm cracked up to be, and it's taken me a hell of a long time to discover *that*. Hell of a long time. And I'll tell you another thing I've learned. Time isn't all it's cracked up to be. Time isn't worth a damn. You can take that from me. It comes and it goes, and you can't do anything about it. See?" He pointed to an alarm clock, loudly ticking on his chest of drawers. "Five seconds just came and went. That's five seconds of your life you'll never have again, Paxton. Never mind. Life isn't all it's cracked up to be. D'you know how many Huns I've killed? Forty-two thousand eight hundred and fifteen. I've got their names here somewhere. Names aren't all they're cracked up to be. Take mine. Next stop, a peerage. Who wants to be a bloody silly peer? House of Lords isn't all it's cracked up to be, not by a long chalk. Full of Old bloody Etonians. Eton isn't all it's cracked up to be. Full of thugs and skunks. Half of them are in the boneyard, I expect. Killed in action. Killing isn't all it's cracked up to be. I should know, I've killed a few. Killed Stubbs this morning." He sipped his whisky.

"I honestly don't see how it could have been your fault," said Paxton. He was getting a bit bored with Foster.

"All it takes is a gun. It doesn't take courage. You think you're brave, but courage isn't all it's cracked up to be. I know you. You're not brave, because you're never afraid. I'm afraid. I've been afraid for months. I was afraid James Yeo might get killed. I liked James, I *loved* James. Love isn't all it's cracked up to be. Didn't save James, did it? Didn't make a blind bit of difference to the war, either. Bloody war. It just goes on and on and on. Listen to it. War's not what it's cracked up to be. Any bloody fool can go to war. The trick is to get out of it. I wish somebody had told me that years ago." He pulled open a drawer and took out his Service revolver. "Fucking flies," he said, and fired three thunderous rounds at the flies circling inside the tent. Brutus bolted. Paxton had fallen off his chair and dropped his whisky. Foster looked at the smoking gun. "Nothing's what it's cracked up to be," he said, and put the muzzle to his head and fired again.

Four gunshots were nothing unusual on Pepriac aerodrome. The place was rackety with small explosions all day long: trucks backfiring, motorbikes being kick-started, aero engines being tested. FEs were always landing, taxying, revving up, taking off. The armourers fired Lewis guns into a great heap of sand, and above all the barrage made its constant din. Nobody noticed the four gunshots except O'Neill, who was sitting on the grass looking at his shaky right hand and waiting for Paxton to come back so they could go on patrol.

He found Paxton sprawled beside his overturned chair, staring at the body. "Oh, Christ," O'Neill said wearily. "Now why did the silly bugger go and do that?"

Paxton tried to stand, but his legs wanted to have nothing to do with it and he fell heavily on his rump. O'Neill gave him both hands and helped him up. "He said . . ." Paxton began, but even the words felt thick and clumsy and unwilling to be spoken. He took a good grip of the tent pole and looked into O'Neill's face. As long as he looked at O'Neill he could avoid seeing Foster and the flies buzzing around his head.

"What did he say?" O'Neill asked. Brutus had come back and was licking the spilt whisky.

"He said that . . . um . . . nothing's what it's cracked up to be," Paxton said. "And he wanted me to know that."

"Let's get out. *Fuck off!*" O'Neill aimed a kick at Brutus, who had begun sniffing Foster's head. The dog bolted again.

Paxton put his arm around O'Neill's shoulders and stumbled out of the tent. "Fidler!" O'Neill shouted. "Fidler, you bastard!" Paxton began to cry. "That's the stuff," O'Neill muttered, "have a damn good weep, let it all out. *Fidler!*" He steered Paxton towards their billet. "*Fidler!*"

Fidler arrived. O'Neill gave orders: fetch the adjutant, fetch Dando, fetch the Duty NCO. Fidler went. Paxton stopped crying. He felt sick, and said so. O'Neill held him while he threw up. "That's the stuff," O'Neill said. "Let it all out." Paxton, hands on wobbly knees, blinked at the grass, spattered with his vomit.

By the time they reached the billet, Brazier and Dando had reached the tent. "You want to get that lousy taste out of your mouth," O'Neill said. He poured two glasses of wine and gave Paxton one. O'Neill's hand did not tremble. "Beats me, too," he said. They drank.

After a while the adjutant came in and asked some questions. As Paxton answered, the whole incident in the tent seemed to recede until it was as if he were describing something that had happened to somebody else; something he had seen in the pictures, perhaps. He felt much better. Dando came in and listened. Brazier reached the end of his questions and stood, head down, hands in pockets, thinking.

"Look," Paxton said, "if that's all you need, it's time we got off. On patrol."

Dando checked his pulse, and thumbed an eyelid up so that he could study the eye. "Do this," he said, and stretched out his hand. Paxton did it. His hand might have been cast in bronze. "Off you go," Dando said.

Cleve-Cutler was flying when Foster killed himself. The adjutant met him with the news as soon as he landed. "Three gone and it's only lunchtime," the CO said. "I don't feel much like lunch."

"I've sent a couple of men over to the churchyard with spades. A funeral this evening might be advisable."

"It was damn near four, or five. Come and look at this." He showed the adjutant the FE's instrument panel, shattered by a slash of bullets. He showed him where the bullets had hacked a ragged hole in the nose of the nacelle. "Should have gone through Gus Mayo," he said, "but Gus was standing on his seat, using the top gun." They climbed down. "So. A funeral for one, this evening. Agreed. What's the rush?"

"Tomorrow will be a very busy day," Brazier said.

*

When the last patrol touched down at 8 p.m. there had been a couple of forced landings; one kill, perhaps two; and many frights and lucky escapes. But the score of dead was still only three.

Cleve-Cutler called a meeting in his office: adjutant, padre, surviving flight commanders, Dando, Paxton, Essex, Ogilvy. "I don't want to put Frank in his grave without knowing the facts," he said. "I want to know, and then forget. I want to bury the poor blighter and bury his story too. Let's start with the letter. Did Stubbs actually write a letter saying Frank was dead?"

"Yes, he did," the adjutant said.

"Bloody daft thing to do. So when Stubbs snuffed it, Frank went off the deep end. Right?"

"Yes and no. Stubbs wasn't the only one who wrote that sort of letter for him. Ogilvy wrote one."

"It was all balls," Ogilvy said. "He kept on about it. I did it to keep him happy, and it didn't work. He started on Charlie next."

The CO looked at Essex. Essex shrugged.

The adjutant was looking at his notes. "Ogilvy, Essex, Mayo, Binns, Goss and several others, all wrote letters for him. I found them in his tent. They were never sent."

Cleve-Cutler shook his head. "I'm not equipped for this sort of thing."

"At least we know he wasn't responsible for his girlfriend's death," the padre said. "Her suicide, I mean."

"Frank never had a girlfriend," Ogilvy said.

Dando said: "That makes sense. Explains not sending the letters."

"How d'you know?" Piggott asked Ogilvy. "Maybe he had someone you never knew about."

"Women terrified him," Ogilvy said. Piggott sniffed. "Listen, we spent our last leave together," Ogilvy told him "Went to the races and got drunk. Every day I knew Frank better than anyone. We were at Eton, after all, you know. He wouldn't let a woman get anywhere near him, ever."

"So as I see it," Cleve-Cutler said, "he shot himself because Stubbs wrote a letter he never sent to a woman he never knew, who never killed herself. And Stubbs went west."

"If it hadn't been Stubbs it would have been somebody else," Dando said. "He needed a reason."

"I think there was another reason," Charlie Essex said. The words came out in a rush, but then he was silent. He looked weary and grim.

"Come on then, cough it up," Cleve-Cutler said.

"He wasn't writing to a woman at all, real or imaginary. I should have worked it out long ago, he made it pretty obvious, poor bugger." Essex rubbed his eyes. "Jenny isn't Jenny. Jenny is, or was, James. James Edward Norman Yeo."

"J.E.N.Y.," Ogilvy said. "Yes. Frank liked James. I suppose the letters must have been a dotty way of being with him. And now he's gone and joined him, or so he thinks."

"I never heard such twaddle in all my life. Never mind. It's done now. Got your speech ready, padre? Let's go and tuck him away."

A dozen hurricane lamps lit the grave, reminding Paxton of the Chinese lanterns on the terrace. The entire squadron was there. As often happened, the wind had dropped when the sun went down and the churchyard was silent apart from the endless drumroll of the distant barrage. Paxton, standing in a corner of the crowd, looked around at the lamplit faces, washed empty by fatigue and a little grief, and he didn't realise that he was searching for O'Neill until he found him. O'Neill saw him looking, and simply looked back. No nod, no shrug, no half-smile. No need.

"Frank Foster wasn't a bad sort," the padre said. "He paid his debts, told a few good jokes, and took five wickets for 39 in the Harrow match. I'm not sure I can add a lot to that, but I'll try." He tried, but he couldn't add anything that he thought Foster would have approved of, except perhaps at the end, when he quoted a verse from Proverbs, chapter 25: "Yet a little sleep, a little slumber, a little folding of the hands to sleep".

Chapter 21

Fidler came in with mugs of tea at 4 a.m. and got cursed for his stupidity. "Don't blame me, sir," he told O'Neill, "blame Mr. Haig. He's decided to have a battle."

'A' Flight ate boiled eggs for breakfast and took off at twenty to five. The dawn came up, glowing with goodwill to all men, and German archie spattered the sky like slum kids throwing mud at someone's washing. The four FEs separated and went looking for troop movements behind the German lines, as briefed, but there was thick mist everywhere. Away to the east, enemy planes could be seen rising from their airfields like hatching flies. 'A' Flight landed at ten to six, with little to report to Brazier. "Our guns are still hammering away fifteen to the dozen," Paxton said. "But of course you can hear that."

He was hungry for real breakfast: eggs and bacon, fried tomatoes and devilled kidneys, toast and Cooper's Oxford marmalade. The mess was full, including a couple of new faces. Private Collins poured coffee for Paxton and O'Neill. They clinked mugs in a toast. "Fuck you," O'Neill said. "And fuck you too," Paxton said. The newcomers stared.

Cleve-Cutler was scribbling with chalk on a blackboard, consulting bits of paper, changing, adding. At length he dragged the easel around so that everyone could see the board. The buzz of conversation got knocked on the head. Chair-legs scraped as men turned to look.

"The balloon goes up in an hour," Cleve-Cutler said.

"Seven-thirty prompt. Unpteen officers will blow umpteen whistles and over the top will go the poor bloody infantry. Now I've written here a very large figure given to me in strict confidence by a very drunken gunner. One million, five hundred thousand. That, he assured me, is the total number of shells fired at the Hun Front Line during the past week. Can a drunken gunner be trusted? Of course not. He was guessing. But a drunken gunner's guess is as good as anyone's and my guess is he's not far out. That means that each area of the German Front Line approximately the size of Paxton's tennis courts has received about twenty shells. And who knows? Several may have exploded. So much for my simple arithmetic. Next . . ."

The steady thunder of the barrage expanded to a degree of savagery that was far greater than anything they had heard before. "My goodness," Cleve-Cutler said. He had to pitch his voice to cut through the noise. "You see what happens when you poke fun at the artillery. No sense of humour at all."

Everyone laughed. It was time for a joke. Might as well laugh now while you still could.

"I've made some changes," Cleve-Cutler said. "Frank O'Neill is the new flight commander. He takes over 'C' Flight."

Paxton stared at O'Neill. "Jesus Christ," he said before he could stop himself.

"No, I couldn't get him," Cleve-Cutler said. "He hasn't won his wings yet." More laughter. "And I've reshuffled a few people, as you can see." He went through the changes, ticking them on the board, until he suddenly stopped. The next names were *Goss/Stubbs*. "How did they get there?" He wet a finger and rubbed them out. "Nothing personal, Dougie," he muttered.

After the briefing there were ten minutes to spare before the squadron began taking off at seven. The sun was starting to melt the mist. It would be a hot day. 'C' Flight gathered outside the pilots' hut.

"I suppose you'll be twice as bloody obnoxious now," Paxton said.

"Stand to attention when you snivel at me," O'Neill said. "I like to watch the drool running down your chest."

Ogilvy belched, resonantly. "That's better," he said. "I really shouldn't have had those tomatoes, they're death to my tubes."

"I knew a chap at Cambridge who swallowed tomatoes whole," Essex said. "Party trick. He said they did him good."

"Did they?"

"Dunno. He copped it at Mons."

"Everyone copped it at Mons," Ogilvy said. "That's where I learned to run backwards. Very educational show, Mons was."

"Today's going to be different," Paxton stated. "Today's going to be a walkover."

"Today's going to be a balls-up," O'Neill said.

"Piss off, Bunny."

"Today's going to be a balls-up, because every battle is a balls-up. The generals always cock everything up, and they'll cock this up today. You watch."

"Bet you."

"How much?"

"Fiver."

"Done." They shook hands.

The mist was still thick enough to hide the flash of the guns when 'C' Flight crossed the Lines, but its surface was disturbed by the thousands of shellbursts beneath it. It reminded Paxton of a time when he had seen a big shoal of fish create ripples in the sea. *Must remember that,* he thought. *Judy will be interested in that.* The enemy balloons were up already. Seemed pretty pointless, in all this mist, but Master Fritz knew best. In fact Paxton found it hard to believe that anything special was about to happen down below, it all looked so bland. Then, to the north, there was a massive flash that printed itself on his eyes. A hill of earth climbed through the mist, and kept climbing until it was as high as the aeroplane, and higher. The first mine had been exploded. Cleve-Cutler had told them to expect large mines to go off under the German trenches, and to keep clear of those spots. Paxton had expected a big bang but this was volcanic in its violence. When its noise reached them it was a clang as if the sky had split and its halves had collided. It tossed the FE on its ear. The column of earth seemed to hang, indifferent to gravity.

304

And it was only the first mine: eight more followed. Paxton was enormously impressed. Nobody could have survived *that*.

'C' Flight's orders were to go trench-strafing in support of the attack, but the mist would have to clear first. O'Neill hung about until the archie became a pest. It was curious how they could see him up here when he couldn't see them down there. He changed height and course, and flew near some British Nieuports having a scrap with some Fokkers. It was none of his business until a Nieuport dropped out, looking unhappy: one wing down, dirty smoke pumping from the exhausts. It was heading west at no great speed and being overhauled by one of the Fokkers.

O'Neill flew an interception course and arrived in time to make a nuisance of himself. Paxton fired a drum at long range, the Fokker got distracted, the Nieuport limped across the Lines. O'Neill was ready to leave it at that but the Fokker was determined to fight someone. It wanted to make a flank attack while O'Neill preferred a head-on attack, so they had a head-on attack. Paxton welcomed it. The Lewis clattered cheerfully, the enemy blossomed in his sights, tracer drifted towards the Hun as if it were being hauled in by hand. The enemy tracer flicked harmlessly past, as it always did. Someone stuck a red-hot poker through his right arm, ripped his hand off the Lewis and flung him back in his seat. Then the sun went in.

It came out again, but the sky was not blue. It was a milky white. O'Neill's fixed Lewis was banging away. The Fokker was twisting and dodging. Paxton reached out to grab his own Lewis and discovered a right hand and arm covered in blood. There was so much blood he couldn't work the trigger. There was so much blood, the slipstream blew it along his sleeve. The funny thing was, his arm didn't hurt. He used his other arm to feel it. *That* hurt. Oh Christ, did that hurt! The sun went in again. Night fell early.

The really funny thing, the thing Paxton tried to tell everyone at the Casualty Clearing Station, was the way getting shot in the arm turned other people deaf. It was really very funny. He could clearly remember O'Neill and someone else lifting

305

him out of the cockpit and O'Neill asking something, or at least his mouth kept opening and shutting but no sounds came out. Same with Dando, when Paxton was lying on a stretcher. Much mouth-action, no sound. Which meant they had all gone deaf, and that was very funny, you must agree. Paxton tried to tell everyone. Some smiled, some didn't. They were all deaf, too. In the end he gave up. It was awfully tiring, talking to deaf people. He fell asleep.

Paxton went to a hospital in Paris. He arrived there before noon; few casualties were coming back from the battlefront, so the army had ambulances to spare. This hospital had a very good arm man, and the doctors at the CCS wanted him to scout about inside Paxton's forearm to see if they had missed any fragments of bullet. While he was at it he would check on the quality of their embroidery. Especially the hemstitching.

In fact it wasn't a bad wound. Paxton woke up next day with a thudding headache and a taste like glue. His arm felt as if it had been slammed in a barn door but he could move his fingers, and the phenomenon of universal deafness had disappeared. What pained him most of all was the discovery that he was in Paris, out of the battle, out of the fun. Why had he fainted, if he'd only been pipped in the arm? It was feeble. Pitiful. A thoroughly dud show. He complained bitterly to the first doctor he saw.

Later in the day, after a couple of meals, one of the doctors drew him a little picture. The bullet had entered just above his wrist, made its way up his forearm, disintegrating as it went, and emerged near the elbow. It had scraped the bone but missed the artery and the major veins. He showed Paxton the fragments of metal they had collected. Paxton fingered them, and in his imagination he tried to assemble them into a 7.92 mm bullet fired from a Spandau through the prop of a Fokker. They failed to take shape. "Why did I pass out?" he asked. "Shock, and loss of blood," the doctor said. "By all reports you were wading in the stuff when you landed."

The next day he got up. They tried to stop him but he wouldn't be stopped, and when he didn't fall on his face they let him stay up. He ate, and ate. When a man came to collect the plates, Paxton asked him if he knew how the battle was going. "I haven't had much chance to look at the papers, sir," he said, "but I saw a headline yesterday I think it was, said something about an advance on the whole front, twenty-five miles I think it said but I'm not much of a one for figures, sir."

"We advanced twenty-five miles? But that's wonderful! Did you hear that?" Paxton called to a passing nurse. "Twenty-five miles! How's that for progress?"

"You won't make any progress if you go on waving that arm like that," she said.

He lay on his bed, feeling pleased and a little drowsy. He woke up six hours later when a doctor checked his condition. "What's the best thing to take for loss of blood?" he asked.

"Salt water. Fruit juice. Guinness if you can get it."

"Fetch me a crate of Guinness," Paxton told the nurse.

He ate a meal and drank a pint of salt water.

If that report of a British advance had been in yesterday's paper, he thought, then the news was three days old, at least. Tremendous things could have happened since then. "I say!" he said to a nurse. "Where can I get some newspapers?"

"I don't know. Why don't you go and talk to the captain in the next room? The poor man's got double vision, so he has."

Captain Kerr suffered more than double vision. He had led his company of infantry over the top and halfway across No-Man's-Land until a shell blew him up and broke various bones. He had crawled back to the trenches, often hiding behind the bodies of his men. Now he welcomed both images of Paxton.

"Sit down, old chap," he said, "make yourself comfortable. Got pipped in the arm, did you? Lucky blighter. I got crumped, you know, well and truly crumped, I remember one second I was thinking 'Shall I ask my sergeant about that Jerry wire?' and the next second I was twenty feet up in the air, never heard the bang, came down one hell of a wallop, long way to fall, twenty feet. Just as well I didn't ask the sergeant, because he wasn't there any more, was he?" Captain Kerr began to laugh and hurt his chest, so he stopped. "He got even more thoroughly crumped than I did," Kerr said. "He got completely dismantled. His constituent parts were laid out for inspection. Or perhaps not. Hard to tell.

There were large numbers of constituent parts all over the place, including a few of mine." He held up his left hand. It had no fingers.

Paxton looked away from the bandaged stump. "I hear we've advanced twenty-five miles," he said.

"Load of balls. Who told you that?"

"Chap who works here. He said there's been an advance along the whole Front. Twenty-five miles was his figure. Mind you, he wasn't very bright."

Using his right hand, Kerr picked at a small scab on his forehead. "That's the *length* of the attack," he said.

"Ah. Yes, of course it is." Paxton slumped in his chair. "It's still jolly good, though, isn't it?"

"No, it's still a load of balls. My mob didn't get anywhere and we weren't the only ones. Absolute shambles, it was."

"Excuse me," Paxton said. "I have to get my dressing changed."

"Good idea," Kerr said. "Get them both changed while you're at it."

Paxton ate and slept, ate and slept. He slept fitfully. Sometimes the pain in his arm made him clench his teeth until his face was wet with tears and sweat; when it stopped, sleep took over immediately and completely.

Next morning he wandered about the ward, growing more and more bored and restless, until he went to see if Captain Kerr was awake. He was. "I don't want to be a nuisance," Paxton said. "I just wanted to ask about the wire."

"Too late, old chap. Far too late. Somebody should have asked about the wire before we went over the top . . . Do me a favour, will you? Get these bloody wasps out of the room. They're driving me potty." Kerr flailed at the empty air with his right hand.

"All right," Paxton said. "I'll open a window. They'll soon buzz off." He made a fuss of opening the window.

The effort had exhausted Kerr. He lay with his arm across his eyes, and so he did not see a middle-aged woman in a blue coat and hat walk into the room. She was bright-eyed and smiling. She had an up-tilted nose and rosy cheeks and a cheerful expression. Everything about her was bright, especially her voice, which was light and brisk, the voice of someone who has spent her life being a good mother. "Good morning!" she said. "I am Mrs. Cruikshank, and I've come to read the newspaper to Captain Kerr."

Paxton liked her as soon as he saw her. "Allow me," he said and brought her a chair. "You're very kind," she said. "I'm sure you'd like me to start with the big news." Kerr let his arm slip from his eyes. "Oh Christ," he mumbled.

"Are we all ready?" She gave the newspaper a shake. "*Allies Still Advance. Desperate Battle Fought. German Losses Very Heavy.* Then there's a bit from a special correspondent. He says: 'I was particularly struck by the general air of complete satisfaction with the way in which operations had gone in this length of the front. More than was really expected had in places actually been done.' Isn't that good?" She smiled brightly at them. "I think that's very good, don't you?"

"Anything about my lot?" Kerr asked. His head kept twitching. "Anything about the Manchesters?"

"Shall we see what we can find?" She turned the pages. "Ah-ha! Now *here's* something. It's all about the Somersets." Kerr groaned and shut his eyes. "I think you'll find this very interesting." Her voice had developed a rhythmic, musical rise and fall. "Shall we read all about the Somersets?"

"Manchesters," Kerr said.

"*West Countrymen in Big Advance*," she read, "*A Sprint With The Gordons. Wounded Sergeant's Stirring Narrative.* Doesn't that sound exciting?"

Paxton nodded. He had identified her swooping, perky voice: it was that of a good mother telling a bedtime story to a dull child and squeezing the juice out of it. "Jolly thrilling," he said.

"*Suddenly,*" she read aloud, "*suddenly the order came to mount the parapet of our trenches, and you never saw anything equal to the sprint between the Gordons and the Somersets.*"

"Sprint . . ." Kerr was shaking his head, or maybe it was twitching more strongly. "What sprint? Nobody ran."

"*Helter skelter we peltered across the ground which was intervening and as we drew up to the German defences—*"

"The wounded sergeant said all this?" Kerr asked. "Helter pelter?"

309

"Not helter pelter," she said, sweetly correcting him. *"Helter skelter we peltered across—"*

"Rubbish. I never knew a sergeant who talked like that."

Paxton asked her: "What happened when they reached the German defences?"

"Let me see . . . *We met a hellish machine-gun fire.*" She shivered deliciously. *"Bullets whizzed in all directions. One after another I saw my pals fall . . . The Manchesters on our left suffered very badly.*" She glanced at the rest of the story. "What a shame. That's all there is about the Manchesters."

"That's all there would be," Kerr said. "There wasn't any more."

She folded up the newspaper. "I don't suppose you're interested in the Eastern Front, are you?" she said. "No. Well, I'll be back tomorrow."

"This is an awful chore for you," Paxton said. "Why not just let me have the paper and I'll—"

"Heavens, no! It's my little war-effort. I enjoy it." She went out, brightly.

"Awfully sorry about the Manchesters," Paxton said. Kerr said nothing. He had his arm over his eyes again. Paxton left him.

He asked the nurses about Mrs. Cruikshank and was told that she was the wife of a surgeon. They had five children. She regularly read the lesson at services in the hospital chapel. She put lots of expression into it.

Paxton slept a bit better that night; he had learned how not to lie on his arm. But during the spells when pain came back and shook him awake, time dragged by and he felt like a prisoner in the gloom.

Next morning he made sure he was in Kerr's room when Mrs. Cruikshank arrived.

"Have you both been jolly good lads and done what you were told?" Her eyes twinkled. "Because if you have, I've got *such* a reward for you here!" Already her voice was swooping and peaking like a roller-coaster.

"It's all bunkum," Kerr whispered, but if she heard him she didn't show it.

"Here's the best medicine for you," she said; and for one terrible moment Paxton thought she was going to ruffle Kerr's hair; but instead she sat on the side of his bed. "The big headline says *Good Day For Allies!*" she announced, "and the little one says *Success on All Fronts, British Gaining Ground.* That means," she explained, "we're doing jolly, jolly well."

"I don't suppose there's anything about the Flying Corps," Paxton said.

"I've found a topping story on one of the inside pages. It's called *Tales of Bravery. What our men faced. The deadly machine-gun.*" She made her shoulders shiver. "They got it from a wounded major when he reached London."

"Not our major," Kerr said. "Our major won't see London again."

"Are you ready? He says *the Hun kept up a slow machine-gun fire during the last half-hour of our intense bombardment preceding the assault.*"

"What?" Paxton was appalled. "That can't be right, can it?"

"The Boche knew," Kerr said. "Or guessed. Same difference."

Mrs. Cruikshank rattled the pages. "Then there's a heading that says *Cheering Into a Bath of Lead.*"

"I don't remember any cheering," Kerr said.

Mrs. Cruikshank sighed, a dramatic in-and-out of breath. "Honestly, what a pair of fusspots! This major remembers it, and he ought to know. He says: *Never in my life have I seen anything finer than the way our successive waves of men marched, singing and cheering, into that bath of lead. The more casualties they saw in front of them the louder they cheered and sang, the harder they pressed forward into it.*" She paused because Kerr was blowing his nose, not an easy thing to do when his head twitched so violently.

"Perhaps that's enough for today," Paxton suggested.

"Oh, but you must hear this bit. It's from a young lieutenant who went over the top. He told a reporter, *Excepting a few, the fellows who'd been hit came on with the others, shouting just as loud and running nearly as hard, too!*"

"Poor bastards," Kerr whispered.

Paxton shook his head. "It's not possible," he said. "How can it be possible?"

"It's perfectly clear," she said. "He saw it happen. *Some bowled over like boys doing Catherine Wheels when they were*

311

hit, and rushed straight on with hardly a check . . . Let go. Let go!"

Kerr had grabbed a corner of the newspaper and was trying to drag the rest of it out of her hands. It tore, slowly and raggedly. Kerr was swearing, an endless, hoarse, stammering stream of obscenities.

Paxton went and found a nurse.

Later, when his dressings were being changed, he asked the doctor how much longer he would have to stay. "I'd very much like to rejoin my squadron," he said.

"We'll see about that in due course."

"This place is getting very full. You could give my bed to someone who really needs it."

"We'll see about that."

"Hornet Squadron's got a damn good MO. He could do this."

"We'll see."

In the afternoon he had a visitor: Kellaway. Paxton was delighted and wanted to hear all his news from Pepriac, but Kellaway had banged his head yet again in another forced landing, and his memory was patchy. He was in Paris to have his skull X-rayed. "Spud Ogilvy went west, I do know that," he said. "Collided with a Hun. I know Spud went west because he owed me forty francs . . . It's been very busy since you left, lots of changes. O'Neill asked me to give you this."

It was a tinted postcard showing a very jolly-looking naked lady. On the reverse side O'Neill had written: *You owe me a fiver.* "I don't remember borrowing a fiver from Bunny," Paxton said.

"Beats me, old chap. I don't remember eating breakfast."

"I'm fed up with this hospital," Paxton said. "I've asked them to send me back to Pepriac. They keep saying they'll see about it, but they never do. I'm fed up with doctors, and their bloody silly wives."

"Come with me. I'm going back tomorrow, in a car."

Paxton was startled by the simplicity of the idea. People were walking in and out of the hospital all the time. "All right," he said. "All right. Yes. All right, I'll do it."

Paxton slept, woke, ate, drank salt water, and was chatting to a gunner captain who had only one foot when a nurse stopped to say that Captain Kerr was asking for him. Paxton collected the newspapers and went to see him.

"I'd like to apologise," Kerr said. "Unforgivable way to behave." He looked grey and tired. His twitch was worse.

"Not a bit of it, old fellow. I quite understand."

"To tell the truth, I don't remember very much. All a bit hazy."

There was a newspaper clipping on his bed. "Is that about the Manchesters?" Paxton asked.

"One of the nurses gave it to me. I haven't read it, of course."

Paxton read it, silently. There was nothing there that he could tell Kerr, so he gave him the clipping and said: "Everyone agrees the Manchesters were very brave." It didn't seem enough, so he added: "And all the papers say we've nearly won."

"Nearly won." The clipping shook in Kerr's hand like a paper flag being waved. "Nearly won."

The problem next morning was finding something to wear, something better than hospital-blue pyjamas. He wandered about the corridors, pretending to read a newspaper, and came across a huge wicker laundry-basket, open. He pretended to be resting against it. Nobody even glanced at him. The hospital was very busy now; everyone had too much to do. He fished out a pair of white trousers and a white jacket, both spattered with blood, and a white coat. If he wore the coat loosely, over his shoulders, it would hide the fact that his arm was in a sling.

Kellaway's car was waiting outside the hospital at the agreed time. Two other RFC officers were in it, but they made room for him. Nobody wanted to talk about the war. Before they had left the suburbs he was asleep.

When he awoke they were bouncing and jolting along a rutted lane and his arm didn't like it. This went on for a very long time, as they delivered one pilot to his aerodrome, and then the other. There was no sun. The roads were clogged with troops and transport. Everyone was in khaki, everyone was moving eastward, nobody was smiling. "I bet the Hun's feeling jolly sick," Paxton said.

"Oh?" Kellaway yawned. "Why's that?"

"Well, he must be retreating like mad."

"Don't ask me, old chap. I can't remember what I had for breakfast." They trundled through a crowded village where military police directed traffic. "Did I tell you Charlie Essex went west?" Kellaway asked.

"No. You said Spud Ogilvy."

"Really? Are you sure?" Kellaway worried about it for a mile or so. "The thing is, Spud owes me forty francs." He chewed a thumbnail and looked at it with distaste. "I could use forty francs," he said. "What would you do, if you were me?"

"I'd forget it." Paxton was feeling very weary. "There are more important things going on, you know."

"Mmm." Kellaway chewed the other thumbnail and didn't like it either. "Eggs!" he said suddenly. "Just remembered what I had for breakfast. Eggs." He smiled and looked out of the window. They passed yet another column of troops. "Or maybe that was yesterday," he said.

Paxton was asleep when they reached Pepriac. Kellaway poked him in the ribs and then helped him out of the car. It was late afternoon, cloudy, and a gusty wind was making a bloody nuisance of itself with dust and scraps of paper. The place was very active. FEs kept coming and going. Paxton watched one land, its wings wobbling in the gusts. It bounced twice. He felt at home. Doing a bunk from that hospital was absolutely right.

"You look like a second-class cricket umpire," Kellaway said.

Paxton looked down at the stained whites and felt foolish. "I'll get changed. Then I'll go and see the old man."

The billet was empty. Paxton sat on his bed. He felt as if he had just walked a thousand miles but it was worth it. Kellaway said he would go and get Fidler. Paxton nodded. "I'll get changed," he said, "then I'll go and see the old man."

Aero engines roared and throbbed, subsided, settled down to a steady growl. Paxton looked at the wooden hut, the three beds, the stove, table, chairs, and he liked what he saw. A stranger came in and nodded to him. He was about Paxton's age but slim. His hair was black and sleeked-down until it

314

looked polished. He had a long straight nose and a very small mouth. He was in his shirt sleeves and he carried a towel and sponge-bag. He dropped them on O'Neill's bed and said as he put on his tunic: "Have you come to give the place a coat of paint?"

"Who the shit are you?" Paxton asked. Fidler and Kellaway came in. "Shame about Mr. O'Neill, sir, isn't it?" Fidler said. "This is Mr. Lucas, sir."

Paxton stopped breathing, and for a moment all sound drained away. When his lungs went into action they swelled and stretched his ribcage; and the sounds of the world flooded back. Lucas was apologising, saying that he mistook Paxton for a workman, awfully sorry. Paxton could only look at O'Neill's bed. He felt frozen inside. O'Neill hadn't gone, not O'Neill, Fidler had got it wrong. It was all impossible, it was a blunder, it made him angry, very angry, furious. He got up fast and ripped the towel off O'Neill's bed, picked up the sponge-bag and hurled it at Lucas. He heard himself shouting disgusting things at Lucas and they were all true. The bed got overturned, blankets and pillows torn off. He must have done that too. He must have used his damaged arm because pain rushed into it like a wild animal. O'Neill wasn't in his bed. It was all a filthy swindle and Paxton told them so as loudly as he could. Lucas was to blame, so he hit Lucas. Fidler tried to stop him and grabbed his damaged arm. Fidler wasn't to know. The light went out.

Paxton woke up for a few seconds. He was in bed, his own bed, and Dando was poking a needle in his other arm. "I want O'Neill," he told Dando. Dando simply shook his head. Paxton tried to explain but the words wouldn't fit together. Soon, that day ended.

Chapter 22

Dando knew that he couldn't keep Paxton in bed, not while machines were taking off and landing all day. Dando let him get up after lunch on the following afternoon, provided he didn't go berserk and chuck beds at people. Paxton promised to behave himself. He was restless but he was also tired.

He let Fidler shave him and then went and sat in a deckchair. The dog Brutus found him and made a great fuss, before settling down on the grass. Private Collins brought a glass of lemonade. There was always an FE warming up, or coming back, or circling.

From time to time pilots or observers waved to him, or paused to chat. Paxton hadn't much to say and they didn't stay long. He watched an FE hurry over the grass, raise its tail and come unstuck. It droned away. He dozed, and woke up when Cleve-Cutler sat beside him and said, "Nobody told you to come back here. You're guilty of indiscipline, dereliction of duty, gross neglect and deserting your post in the face of the medical profession, just because they wanted to saw your arm off at the shoulder. I should have you court-martialled."

"I wasn't doing any good in that hospital, sir," Paxton said. It was a struggle to wake up.

"They don't like losing patients. Not like that, anyway. It spoils their record-keeping. You've no idea how bad-tempered they've been, and Christ knows I've got enough complaints descending on me from a great height already."

"Sorry to hear that, sir." There was a rough edge to the

CO's voice that worried Paxton.

"You're a pretty bloody depressing sight to have lying about the place, aren't you? Just what the new boys like to see, I don't think."

"Dando says it's healing up nicely," Paxton lied.

"Give me one good reason why I shouldn't give you a boot up the backside and send you back to the quacks toot sweet."

Paxton thought desperately hard and could offer only one bad reason, so bad it was worse than nothing. But he had to say something. "If you send me back I'll do another bunk tomorrow," he said. "*What?*" Cleve-Cutler shouted. "This is mutiny!" He got up laughing, and walked away laughing. It was as if he had heard the first real joke for a week. He picked up one deckchair and threw it over another. "Go and see the adj," he said. "Tell him to find you something to do." He headed for his office.

Brazier was dictating summaries of combat reports to Corporal Lacey. Paxton sat in a corner and chewed his lip. Leaning against the wall was a blackboard with the flight commanders and their crews chalked on it. He studied the names. When Lacey went out, he said: "No Piggott."

"Tim got a bit burnt. He's in Blighty, at some special hospital. I must say you don't look too wonderful. I've seen plates of porridge that had more colour than you."

"I'm fine. The CO says you're to find me a job, until I can fly."

"Oh. That's what you're here for, is it? I thought it was this." Brazier opened a desk drawer and took out an envelope. Paxton took it and tore it open and then stopped. "It's not from O'Neill, is it?" If it was from O'Neill he didn't want to see it. Not yet; perhaps not ever. Brazier shook his head. Paxton pulled out a pair of photographs.

"Colonel Bliss said you might as well have them. He said they're a bit grisly for his taste."

Paxton grunted, and shoved the pictures into a tunic pocket.

For a long moment they sat and looked at each other.

"So you've had a taste of war," Brazier said. "Does it suit your palate?"

"It's a bit salty," Paxton said. "Actually I don't mind the

taste so much as the noise. Don't those bloody guns ever stop?"

Brazier found an empty pipe and used the stem to scratch an eyebrow. "I can remember a time when you were quite proud of our guns," he said. "You quite enjoyed them, in fact."

"I can remember a time when the poor bloody infantry were going to walk across No-Man's-Land and capture the Boche front line. Nice quiet stroll after breakfast, so everyone said."

"We've just captured their front line, so the papers say. Not all of it, but quite a lot. Took rather longer than we thought."

"Because of the machine-guns."

"Because of the dugouts. Fritz is a wily bird. He'd dug a great number of very deep dugouts, twenty feet down in the chalk. Thirty feet, some of them. Very, very strong."

"And that's where he kept his machine-guns."

"So I'm told." Brazier stuffed tobacco into his pipe. "You live and learn, you live and learn."

Paxton shifted his arm in its sling. The damage was beginning to throb and burn. "But why on earth are we going on with the battle? The stupid plan failed, so why . . ."

"Because," Brazier said. "Because Tweedledum, said Tweedledee, had broke his nice new rattle. It was time to have a battle, therefore a battle we must have." He gazed at Paxton, who was looking disgruntled. "Not good enough," Brazier said.

"It's a load of fucking bollocks, adj."

"I don't know, Pax. Nothing seems to please you today. You don't like being shot, you don't approve of cock-ups in battle, you didn't even seem to enjoy looking at your own souvenir snapshots."

Paxton sniffed, and looked away. "That was just a kill," he said. "Two poor sods in a flamer, that's all." He stood up. "Have you got anything for me to do?"

"I don't suppose you feel like inspecting the men's latrines."

"No."

"No. Well then, get your strength back and see me tomorrow."

Paxton went out and closed the door. Lacey looked up from his work. "How was the hospital?" he asked.

"Full of blokes with bits missing from them."

Lacey nodded. "I understand that since the war began the artificial limb industry has made great strides."

Paxton rubbed his left eye with this left hand and stared bleakly at Lacey.

"Sorry," Lacey said. "It wasn't meant to be a joke."

"Joke?" Paxton said. "What's a joke? I wouldn't recognise a joke if it bit me in the backside." He walked to the door and leaned against its frame.

"Is there anything I can provide?" Lacey asked.

"No." Paxton looked up and watched an FE climbing in a wide, easy spiral until it bored him. "Yes. Yes, there is. Can you get me a car? I can't ride a motorbike, you see. Car and driver."

Lacey said it might take a little while, an hour or so. Paxton told him there was no hurry, he would probably be in the mess.

He walked to the mess, slowly because the afternoon was hot and still, and ordered lemonade. Plug Gerrish was reading a newspaper. "Same old tosh," he said.

"Same old tosh," Paxton agreed.

After a while Spud Ogilvy came in, his flying boots folded below the knee, and carrying his sheepskin coat. "Stinking hot," he said. "D'you mind?" He took a long drink of Paxton's lemonade.

"Kellaway said you'd gone west."

"Kellaway's a bloody idiot, isn't he?" Ogilvy threw his coat onto a chair and flopped down on a sofa. "God, I'd give a fiver for a nice cool swim."

Paxton waited for someone to say the obvious thing but nobody did, so he said it himself. "What's wrong with the pool?"

"Out of order," Gerrish grunted, and took his cap and went out. Paxton looked at Ogilvy, but Ogilvy seemed to be asleep; at least there was a newspaper over his face. Paxton decided to go and see for himself.

Flies followed him across the aerodrome, and through the gate into the next field. It was a nuisance having only one hand to flap at them. They were obstinate, constantly touching his ears and eyebrows and lips, until he tied two corners of a handkerchief together and wore it like a mask.

There was a Casualty Clearing Station in the field: a cluster of khaki tents, some the size of marquees. From time to time they quivered in the heat-haze. Ambulances came over a distant rise, rolled down to the CCS, unloaded and went away by a different route. From the back of the CCS a tender drove along a chalk-white track to where the swimming pool had been. Paxton stood in the shade of a tree and watched all this for perhaps ten minutes. He didn't want to go and see what had happened to the pool. He knew what had happened to the pool. On the other hand he didn't like to think he wasn't brave enough to go and look. And so he went, and the flies went with him. They knew the way. All their friends were there already.

The existence of the pool had saved the CCS a lot of time and effort. All they had to do was divert the little stream back to its original course and the pool drained dry in no time. When Paxton reached it, the hole was about half-full and four soldiers wearing rubber gloves and sterilised face-masks were carefully stacking bodies on top of the neat rows of bodies already in place. They were working carefully, not out of any sense of respect for the dead, but because it made best use of the space and the last thing they wanted was to have to dig another fucking great hole like this one.

Paxton watched them work. The stench of decay was just tolerable as long as he breathed through his mouth. The soldiers ignored him. The flies had a gala day.

He strolled around the hole and went across and took a look inside the tender. There was one body that he recognised at once, even though it was lying face-down. It was young and small, and the cords of the neck were undeveloped, like a boy's. That body was unmistakable. He climbed inside and turned it over.

Wrong face. Wrong body.

He walked back to camp, trailing a few diehard flies behind him.

*

When the old man shuffled out of the lodge to open the gates, Paxton got out and told the driver he would walk up to the house. The day was cooler, and trees cast long shadows over the grass. The car drove on. Now that the old man was closer he could see that Paxton's right sleeve was empty. He ducked his head and gave a shaky salute. "*Merci, m'sieur*," Paxton said, seriously. They shook hands, Paxton using his left hand. The old man's skin was as smooth and hard as a Sam Browne.

He had dozed in the car and now he felt fresh if not strong. The grounds were empty and very quiet. A heron took off from the lake and steered away from him, wings beating slow, and lost itself behind the island.

Someone had seen him: a maid was waiting at the door. She led him upstairs and along a corridor he hadn't been along before. A door opened onto a balcony. The balcony overlooked the little ballroom. Ballet music was playing and down below Judy Kent Haffner, in a black leotard, was putting her elastic body through the same old astonishing routine.

"To drink?" the maid asked.

"Whisky-soda."

Judy danced, a different maid changed the record, she danced again. The light had faded; she was a pattering shadow, a picture in a fairy story. Paxton drank his whisky-soda and gave himself up to the show. He had the odd and very pleasant sensation he always got when he came to this house: that everything was arranged, that there was no need to think or to decide about anything, and certainly no need to worry. Just relax and make the most of life. Everything would work out fine.

When the music and the dancing finally ended she stood in the middle of the floor, hands on hips. It was too dim to see her face; he could hear faint gasps for breath. She pointed up at him, so he pointed down at her. She walked to the door.

The same maid led him through unfamiliar parts of the house and indicated that he should wait in a long, handsome room. He guessed he must be on the top floor. There was a view of the last of the sunset that made the British bombardment look like children's fireworks. He relaxed and made the most of it.

"I could murder that composer," she said. "He makes you do things God never meant you to do . . . Hell's bells, David, where've you *been*? Oh!" She saw the empty sleeve. "What a stupid question." They kissed, awkwardly because of his sling.

"Hospital. I stopped a bullet."

"But that's *terrible*." She didn't look as if it was terrible. Her forehead creased and her voice stretched the word thin, but her mouth and eyes smiled happily. They might have been talking about a black eye from playing rugby. Paxton didn't mind; he didn't think it was so very terrible; in fact he didn't give it much thought at all. What he thought was she looked lovelier than ever. She was wearing Turkish-style pyjamas, deep red and silky. They didn't button at the front, they just hung loosely. Whenever she moved they swung apart slightly and then came together again. He noticed, and she noticed that he noticed, so she deliberately swayed to tease him. "I like to be cool," she said. "Don't you?" He got a glimpse of something pink that might perhaps have been a nipple, and turned to look at the dying sunset. His heart was pounding at a rate that couldn't possibly be doing it any good, and his arm had started to throb. "I shouldn't be here, really," he said. "If the MO knew about it he'd raise the roof."

"I won't tell him, if you won't." She linked their little fingers and took him into the next room. It was the biggest bedroom he had ever seen, with the biggest bed. "Tell me about your great big beautiful war." They sat on the bed. "Mr Kent Haffner is in Paris, polishing his little apples." She kissed his ear, gently, and tickled it with her tongue. He stretched his neck and grinned at the sheer luxury of it all. "Are you an ace yet?" she asked.

"Nearly."

"Tell me. I want to know all about your kills."

"Well . . . there was the Aviatik we scrapped with . . . It was a lovely sunny morning, I remember, and the Hun looked so pretty, all purple and green, and we were miles high, so everything was blue sky . . ." Judy Kent Haffner was taking his tunic off, easing it away from the arm in a sling. "He dived on us and I waited until I couldn't miss and he simply blew up. Nothing left but a wisp of smoke."

"That must have been such a thrill." She was undoing his

tie, and he saw a flicker of envy in her smile. It made him feel stronger, more confident. He knew how to please her.

"The Halberstadt wasn't so easy. Two-seater, with a hell of a good gunner . . ." His tie was off and she kissed his forehead. "There were twenty-three bullet-holes in the bus when we landed, not counting the wings." She was untying his shoes, "*Twenty-three!*" she said. "That's incredible."

Paxton leaned back and rested on one elbow. He wasn't sure about the Halberstadt. Maybe that had been the Fokker. The kills got all mixed up in his mind. Who cared? It didn't matter. She unbuttoned his shirt and said, "Tell me again about the flamer. The one like a flower."

"Oh, that . . ." The right side of the shirt had been slit so that it came away easily. "I think I got a fuel tank with an incendiary bullet. It was so sudden. One second the Hun was all there, the latest style in aeroplanes, the next second he'd turned into an enormous ball of flame, all red and yellow. Rather like a dahlia."

"Dahlia." She pushed him back on the bed and propped herself above him. Now the pyjamas swung open and stayed open. She kissed him generously on the mouth and his chest tensed at the startling touch of her breasts. "Dahlia," she murmured.

"Yes, dahlia." Paxton frowned. He realised he wasn't at all sure what a dahlia looked like.

"It must be so beautiful. So wonderful." They stood up. She undid the top of his trousers but he said: "I can do this better." His voice was flat and empty. He turned his back on her as he stepped out of his trousers. "To tell the truth," he said, "it might have looked more like a geranium." He turned. "What does a geranium look like?"

She had lost her pyjamas. "Not like *that*," she said. "So who cares?"

They got into bed and, as she had done when they lay on the boulder on the island, she sat astride his legs. At first he was worried about hurting his arm, but the act of sex turned out to be astonishingly easy. She did most of it; he just lay back and helped. It had a beginning, a middle and an end. The end felt like the way the sunset had looked. He was sorry when it was over.

That feeling of sorrow gradually intensified. He closed his

eyes. She was humming to herself, contentedly, as she moved about the room, and he resented her contentment because a sense of dejection and regret was beginning to grip him. "You really are an ace," she said. "You know that?" He said nothing. He wasn't an ace, and he took no pride in the stories he had told her. His kills were none of her damn business.

"How did you get shot?" she asked.

He levered himself up on the pillows. She was sitting at the bottom of the bed, still naked, brushing her hair. "Listen," he said. "You don't want to hear about all that stuff."

"Oh, but I do. Dahlias, geraniums, the lot."

"Most of it's fairly . . ." For some reason he thought of O'Neill's face the day O'Neill had said to him *It only takes one bullet*. Grief sank its tiny claws. "It's a fairly bloody business."

"I'm tough, I can take it. Want a sandwich?" There was a tray of food and a bottle of wine on a bedside table.

Paxton took a sandwich and bit into it. It tasted of nothing. He didn't want to eat her fucking food. He put it back. "This is the closest you ever get to war, I suppose," he said.

She glanced at him sideways. "I'd get closer if I could."

Paxton watched her doing things to her hair. He looked down and fiddled with bits of loose bandage poking out of the sling.

"Now what are you brooding about?" she said.

That angered him. "D'you really want to know? All right, I'll tell you." Anger swelled, and he didn't try to hide it. "I'm brooding about a man called Foster. He shot himself. Duncan got his head cut off. Milne flew slap-bang into an enemy machine. Ogilvy got badly burnt. He might be dead, he might not. Is that enough for you?"

Silence, while she looked at herself in a hand mirror.

"It's no reason to sulk," she said.

"You don't know what you're talking about." He swung his legs over the side of the bed, reached out, grabbed the hand mirror from her and threw it across the room. The glass broke. "Here comes your bad luck. Go and look in my left-hand tunic pocket. There's a couple of photographs. Group photographs. You'll recognise one of the group."

She got up and found the pictures and carried them to the light. "There's no group here," she said. "What's the joke?"

"It's no joke. Look harder."

She looked again, searching the prints. Paxton heard her grunt with shock.

"German crew," he said. "Now you know what a flamer looks like after it's stopped flaming."

She coughed, and swallowed repeatedly.

"No point in being sick in here," he said. "Not when you've got two dozen bathrooms."

"I'm not going to be sick."

"Perhaps you should." He went and took the pictures from her. "What else would you like to know? There's lots I can tell you. Mind you, I may be sick in the middle. I'm not as tough as you."

She put on a dressing gown. "I think you'd better leave," she said. Her face was full of disappointment and disapproval.

"Yes, I'll leave," he said. "I wouldn't want to bleed on your patriotism." He wasn't sure what that meant. The words just came out.

The car was waiting for him when he got downstairs. "Wonderful intelligence system you've got here," he said to the maid. She didn't understand and she didn't want to understand. She simply handed him his hat and opened the door. "Perfect," he said. "But then you've done it before, I expect."

A squadron party was roaring at the top of its voice in the mess when he got back.

He went to his billet and lay on his bed and watched a couple of moths having a scrap with the naked lightbulb. It was a gallant battle, fought against overwhelming odds, a splendid example of heroism and devotion to duty, but in the end they made the supreme sacrifice. Sometimes the racket from the mess drowned the rumble and boom of the guns. Usually it didn't.

He got up and walked across the room and lay on the other bed, the bed that had been O'Neill's.

At midnight Kellaway came in with the new man, Lucas,

both of them bedraggled and drunk. "Hullo!" Lucas said. "You're on my bed, old chap."

"O'Neill's bed. I'll fight you for it."

Kellaway found that very funny. Lucas did not. He said: "Now look here, old man—"

"O'Neill went west," Paxton said, and scratched his crotch. "You'd have liked O'Neill. He wouldn't have liked you, though."

Lucas stared. He stared so long that he swayed and stumbled. "This fellow's a pig," he told Kellaway. "An absolute pig."

"It's a dirty job," Paxton said, "but somebody's got to do it."

Author's Note

War Story is fiction built on a framework of fact. The reader has a right to know which is which.

All the technical aspects of the air war in the summer of 1916 – in particular the design and performance of the BE2c, FE2b and FE2d – are as accurate as I could make them. (For instance, the observer in the FE2d did in fact stand on his seat to fire a gun to the rear over the top wing and the tail.) Lieutenant Paxton's age and standard of training when he went to France were quite usual; some new pilots were even younger and had logged even fewer flying hours. The fact that his journey took five days, and that three other pilots crashed on the way, may not have been common but it was certainly far from rare. (In 1917 Lieutenant A. S. G. Lee and five other pilots ferried six Quirks from St. Omer to Candas, a flight of about fifty miles. Lee arrived safely but three planes crashed on landing, one crashed *en route*, and one went missing. "I felt rather a cad not crashing too," Lee wrote to his wife, "because everyone is glad to see death-traps like Quirks written off, especially new ones.")

Other details – such as the dropping of message-bags by enemy aeroplanes, the use of canvas 'coffins', the attack by a French pilot on a British machine – are authentic. And RFC pilots did return from patrols to play cricket or tennis, or to go swimming. Indeed, the contrast between life in a squadron and life in the trenches was startling. The latter was cramped and dirty, often wet, usually lousy. The airmen flew home to good meals and warm beds, to games, music and parties in the mess. Not that the average front-line soldier wanted to change places with an airman: he watched too many pilots and observers fall to their death.

Which brings me to parachutes. Apart from balloon crews, nobody in the RFC wore a parachute. (The same was true of the German air force until the very end of the war.) The official reasons against the development of parachutes were many and varied. It was claimed that parachutes were too heavy; that in an emergency pilots would have no time to use them; that having a parachute would "impair a pilot's nerve when in difficulties" (i.e. he would quit the fight); that there was no real call for parachutes; and so on. Those were the views of members of the Air Board, who were not in France and who did not fly. Pilots and observers in the RFC saw things differently. They knew how easily a machine could break up, even without enemy attack. Sudden death was one thing, but they dreaded being trapped in a falling plane. Nevertheless, in the first half of the war there was surprisingly little demand for parachutes. The existing models were bulky, and cockpits were small; they were heavy, and engines were not powerful. Pilots were reluctant to sacrifice performance for safety. Yet the horror of being unable to escape from a doomed plane – especially one that was on fire – disturbed many a pilot's sleep. Nightmares were commonplace in RFC squadrons.

I have tried to get my facts right concerning the war on the ground. The preparations for the battle were lengthy and they included the kind of dress-rehearsal watched by generals (with white tapes to indicate the German trenches) described in chapter 11. Some troops were assured by their officers that the advance would be quite literally a walkover: they would stroll across No-Man's-Land and occupy the German trenches without firing a shot. However, the army took the precaution of preparing mass graves, dug by civilian Chinese labour.

There is ample evidence that Captain Brazier's actions in compelling troops to fight by shooting one or two of them was not unique. The regiments and units that I have named did in fact take part in the battle of the Somme (although the cavalry found little to do). Pals' Battalions were a feature of that army and they suffered very heavy casualties. The length, pattern and scale of the British bombardment took place as described.

Then there is the account of the celebration of the Fourth of June by Old Etonians, in chapter 4.

Maurice Baring, himself an Old Etonian, was private secretary to the commander of the RFC. In his book 'Flying Corps Headquarters 1914–1918' he quotes a friend's letter, dated June 5th, 1917:

'Last night there was an Old Etonian dinner at the Lord Roberts Memorial Hall. There were three hundred Old Etonians present. I knew about five by sight. All my contemporaries were Lieutenant-Generals. They sang, accompanied by the Coldstream Band. and after dinner everything in the room was broken; all the plates. all the glass, all the tables, the chandeliers, the windows. the doors. the people. A bomb raid was nothing to it. Lord Cavan presided, and made a very good speech in Latin.'

I took the liberty of shifting that event from England to France, and from 1917 to 1916, but I tried to keep intact the spirit of the occasion, which seems to me to suggest an upper-class appetite for violence and an educated taste for devastation that is often forgotten nowadays. Perhaps it goes some way towards explaining why that war went on so long.

The verses quoted in chapter 18 ('A year ago, at Henley') were written during the war; I do not know the author's name.

Finally, I should make it clear that the newspaper items which Paxton quotes in chapter 21 are not invented. All the reports appeared, word for word, in English newspapers in the days after the battle began. By a curious twist of events, the men at the Front often relied on those papers for news of the battle as a whole, but the papers could report only what the War Office told them. Thus the soldiers read of victories while they witnessed disasters.

We know now that the first day on the Somme took place almost exactly in the middle of the war. It certainly formed a watershed: it was the worst day ever for the British Army. with nearly sixty thousand casualties, of whom twenty thousand were dead, most of them in the first hour of the attack. The men of the Royal Flying Corps, living just a few miles behind the trenches, were not to know about that. Only they could see the entire battlefield, but even they could not see the tragedy.